IMAGES
*of Rail*

# Railroad Depots of Central Ohio

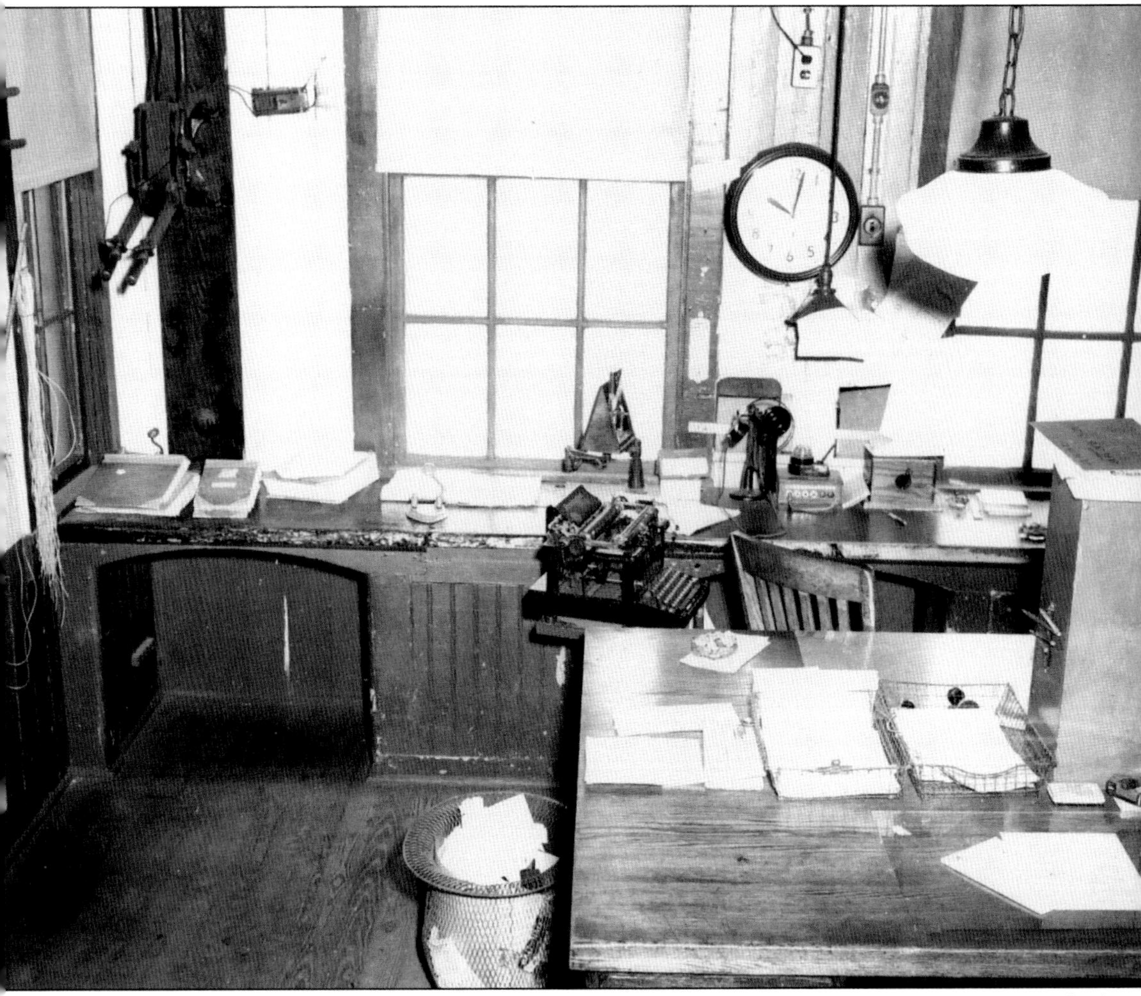

The agent's office at the Toledo and Ohio Central Railroad depot in Johnstown is typical of many a small-town depot. To the left in this 1961 photograph are the levers to adjust the outside order board, which signals the train crew as to whether they have passengers or important messages to pick up at the station stop. On the left wall is a Y-shaped order hoop used by the depot staff to pass messages or orders to a passing train crew without the need of a train stop. The ever-present sounder box, telegraph key, scissors phone, typewriter, station clock, and ledger sheets complete the scene. (Photograph by Bernard Kern.)

*On the cover*: The agent and his helpers pose for the postcard photographer on the platform of the Cleveland, Cincinnati, Chicago and St. Louis Railroad (Big Four) depot at Ostrander around 1915. This combination depot was typical of many built across central Ohio in the late 1800s. (Author's collection.)

IMAGES
*of Rail*

# Railroad Depots of Central Ohio

Mark J. Camp

ARCADIA
PUBLISHING

ISBN 978-0-7385-6174-5

Published by Arcadia Publishing
Charleston, South Carolina

Printed in the United States of America

Library of Congress Catalog Card Number: 2008929824

For all general information contact Arcadia Publishing at:
Telephone 843-853-2070
Fax 843-853-0044
E-mail sales@arcadiapublishing.com
For customer service and orders:
Toll-Free 1-888-313-2665

Visit us on the Internet at www.arcadiapublishing.com

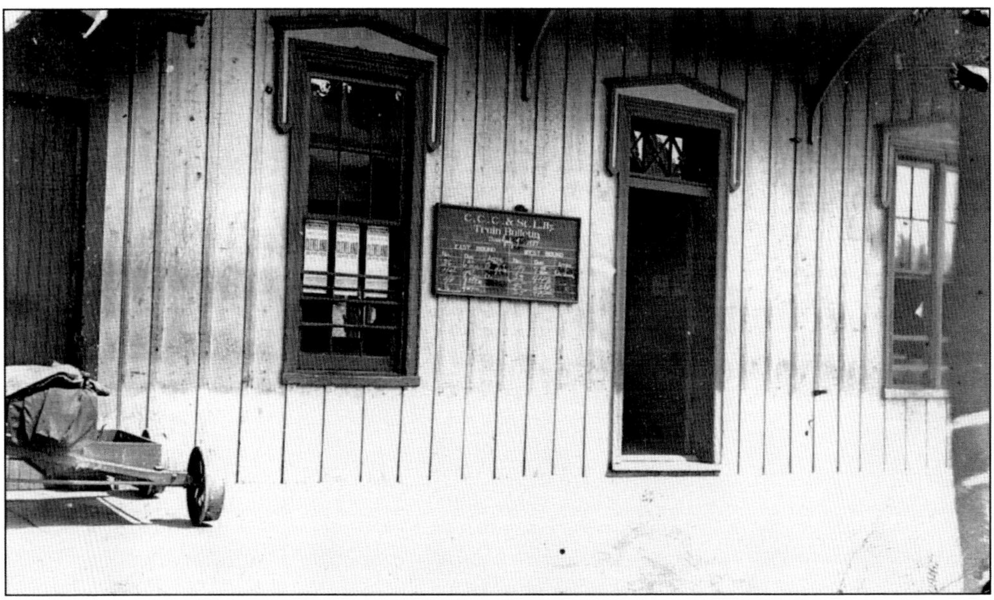


It is July 9, 1921, sometime before the arrival of the late afternoon westbound No. 23, at Shelby Junction just northeast of downtown Shelby. Two morning Big Four trains were on time; only the eastbound 6:20 a.m. train rolled in late. The posters advertise an excursion scheduled for the next day. This depot sat at the junction of the Baltimore and Ohio Railroad (B&O) and Big Four. The B&O trains used the opposite side of the depot. (Author's collection.)

# Contents

# ACKNOWLEDGMENTS

An undertaking of this scope requires the assistance and cooperation of many organizations and individuals. Without the help of the following organizations over the years this project would be far less complete. Thanks are extended to the Allen County Historical Society, Bremen Historical Society, Columbus Historical Society, Columbus Metropolitan Library, Delaware County Historical Society, Fairfield County Fairgrounds, Fairfield County Historical Society, Franklin County Fairgrounds, Grandview Heights Public Library, John McIntire Library (Zanesville), Licking County Historical Society, Marvin Memorial Library (Shelby), Norfolk Southern Railway, Ohio Historical Society, Ohio Railway Museum, Ohio Room of the Delaware Public Library, Ohio State University Library, Pickaway County District Public Library, Public Utilities Commission of Ohio, Shelby Chapter of Ohio Genealogy Society, Sherman Room of the Mansfield/Richland County Public Library, Sunbury Public Library, Toledo Lucas County Public Library, University of Toledo Carlson Library, and all the libraries and historical associations of central Ohio. Among the individuals that have contributed in one way or another to this book are Charles Bates, Chris Burchett, Bob Carter, Bob Chilcote, Jeff Darbee, Paul Dunn, Michael Frazier, Charles Garvin, H. Roger Grant, Herb H. Harwood, Jim Henry, John Keller, Bernard Kern, Bob Lorenz, Tim Brian McKee, Ed Miller, Max Miller, Eldon Neff, David P. Oroszi, Ed Pool, Gary D. Rolih, Jeff Spencer, Scott D. Trotsel, Ed Weber, Dan West, and Carl T. Winegardner. Some contributed photographs, others have written on the railroad history of this region, and still others have served as an inspiration through the years. As usual, I also thank Kevin Capurso for his help in scanning the photographs.

Among the books and references that aided in this study are the *Reports of the Ohio Railroad Commission*, *Annual Reports of the Public Utilities Commission of Ohio*, *Poors Manuals*, *Railroad Gazette*, *Railway Age*, and other trade journals. County histories, centennial/sesquicentennial publications, newspaper articles, and various railroad and historical Web sites have also been perused. Reference has also been made to George H. Burgess and Miles C. Kennedy's *Centennial History of the Pennsylvania Railroad Company*; Jeffrey T. Darbee's *Taking the Cars: A History of Columbus Union Station*; Edward H. Miller's *The Hocking Valley Railway*; John A. Rehor's *The Nickel Plate Story*; Scott D. Trostel's *The Detroit, Toledo and Ironton Railroad*; and Carl T. Winegardner's two volume set *A Historical Account B&O Rail Lines 1830–1989*.

# INTRODUCTION

The initial growth and prosperity of many small communities in central Ohio was dependent on the railroads built through this region in the mid- to late 1800s. Shelby welcomed its first passenger train in 1846 along the Monroeville and Sandusky City Railroad; by 1851, trains of the Cleveland, Columbus and Cincinnati Railroad were stopping at Shelby Junction. The first lines to enter Columbus were the Columbus and Xenia Railroad in 1850, the Cleveland, Columbus and Cincinnati Railroad in 1851, and the Central Ohio and Columbus, Piqua and Indiana Railroads in 1853. The Springfield, Delaware and Mount Vernon Railroad served Delaware and Marysville by 1854. Mansfield and Newark were connected by the Columbus and Lake Erie Railroad in 1852. By 1857, the Cincinnati, Wilmington and Zanesville Railroad reached Bremen. These lines eventually came under control of the Baltimore and Ohio, New York Central, and Pennsylvania lines and were joined in the later 1800s by predecessors of the Chesapeake and Ohio Railway; Detroit, Toledo and Ironton Railroad; Norfolk and Western Railway; and more New York Central and Pennsylvania Railroad precursors.

The railroads were responsible for the platting of a number of towns including Brice and Summit Station. At each town, a depot was eventually erected to handle passenger and freight business. Depots were also necessary at railroad junctions to provide a means of interchange. It is estimated that during the heyday of railroad travel, some 265 depots dotted the central counties of Ohio.

The first depots were often small utilitarian structures, sometimes a mere roof over a wood or gravel platform. Others rather looked like barns through which the trains ran, for example the 1862 Columbus union station. If a community already existed, a hotel or inn might have served as the initial depot. As railroad travel became the fashion, depots evolved into a standard three-room structure with space for the agent and staff, a passenger waiting room, and a freight room. Beginning in the late 1800s, railroad construction crews modified some depots by lengthening the freight and or passenger ends to fit the local needs. In larger towns and cities, for example Delaware and Mount Vernon, separate passenger, baggage, and freight depots were erected; while in smaller communities like Pickerington and Ostrander, combination passenger-freight depots were the rule. As towns grew in population and importance to the railroad, the original combination depot may have been converted to freight use and a new passenger depot constructed; such was the case at Delaware on the Cleveland, Cincinnati, Chicago and St. Louis Railroad (Big Four) line. A union depot or station was a design serving two or more railroads, often constructed at junction points, for example Lancaster and Mansfield, or in major rail hubs, like Columbus.

The town depot rapidly became the gathering place for the local populace. Before the common use of radios and telephones, the depot was the communication center to the outside world. News arrived daily over the telegraph and from passengers and trainmen. The depot was commonly open 24 hours with varying numbers of local, express, and mail trains arriving at scheduled intervals. Near train-time, the depot became a beehive of activity. Inside, the waiting room was often jammed with travelers and well-wishers, either sitting on the robust hardwood benches or milling about, scanning the colorful advertisements and travel posters plastered on the walls. A line of travelers stretched into the center of the room from the little wrought iron grid of the ticket window behind which a uniformed clerk and agent hurriedly filled requests. The distant blast of the familiar whistle acted as a magnet, drawing people out onto the platform. Here a baggage clerk busily readied wagons piled high with luggage and mail. A newsboy hawked papers, as the train hissed into the station with bell ringing, handing them to passengers on the train through open coach windows. Greetings were exchanged as friends and relatives returned home and others debarked on their journeys. Horse-drawn buggies from local hotels awaited visitors in search of a place to stay. After a few routine maintenance checks the train was on its way again. In the depot office, the telegrapher was sending word to the next station that the train had left on time.

The arrival of the automobile spelled doom for railroad passenger service, and by the end of World War II, many trains had been discontinued and depots abandoned. Many were demolished, burned, or allowed to decay to the point that they collapsed, some were relocated and used in various ways, and others were used for storage or maintenance operations by the railroad. With the continued decline of passenger service in the 1950s and 1960s, only a few depots remained open to passengers, namely those in major towns. Many were demoted to strictly freight use; many lost their agent. Amtrak brought renewed life to a select few of the still-existing depots in 1971. But the service was short-lived, and once again, central Ohio was without passenger trains.

Following is a compilation of photographs, many taken from early postcards—an attempt to present the wide variety of structures once present and to emphasize their importance to their respective communities in 17 central Ohio counties. The boundaries of this study are roughly Richland, Morrow, and Delaware Counties to the north; Union, Madison, and Fayette to the west; Pickaway, Fairfield, and Perry to the south; and Muskingum, Licking, and Knox Counties to the east. The compilation is far from complete and the author welcomes additions and comments sent to him through the Railroad Station Historical Society Web site (www.rrshs.org) or the University of Toledo Web site (www.utoledo.edu).

# One

# Baltimore and Ohio Lines

In 1846, construction crews opened a deep cut near Plymouth that allowed trains of the then Mansfield and Sandusky City Railroad to travel from Lake Erie to Mansfield. In 1850, the Columbus and Lake Erie Railroad began construction of a line south from Mansfield through Butler and Mount Vernon to Newark. Within two years, the line reached Newark. The two lines north and south of Mansfield merged in November 1853 and took the name of the Sandusky, Mansfield and Newark Railroad (SM&N). The SM&N was taken under the wing of the Baltimore and Ohio Railroad (B&O) through a leasing by the Central Ohio Railroad in 1869.

The year 1847 marked the incorporation of the Central Ohio Railroad at Zanesville to build a line between a point to be determined on the Ohio River and Columbus. Delays followed and the road was not opened to Columbus until 1853. During a period of receivership, a share in the track between Columbus and Newark was sold to the Steubenville and Indiana Railroad, a Pennsylvania Railroad predecessor. The Central Ohio line became associated with the B&O in 1866.

Another eventual B&O line, the Newark, Somerset and Straitsville Railroad, incorporated in 1867 to lay track from Newark to Shawnee, was leased by the SM&N in 1872. This line allowed the B&O to directly tap the important coal and clay deposits of Perry County and made it a rather straight shot to the port of Sandusky.

The final predecessor line to the B&O in central Ohio was the Columbus and Cincinnati Midland Railroad, which linked Columbus to Midland City in 1884. This line fell under the lease of the Central Ohio Railroad in 1890. All these lines lost their original identities when the B&O formally merged them into its system in 1896. This line became known as the B&O Southwestern Railroad. Today the survivors are part of CSX.

Due to the early construction of many of these lines, depots still standing in the later 1900s were generally at least second-generation structures. The B&O conducted a depot replacement program from around 1900 to 1910, using a standardized plan that could be either lengthened or shortened depending on the local passenger and freight traffic.

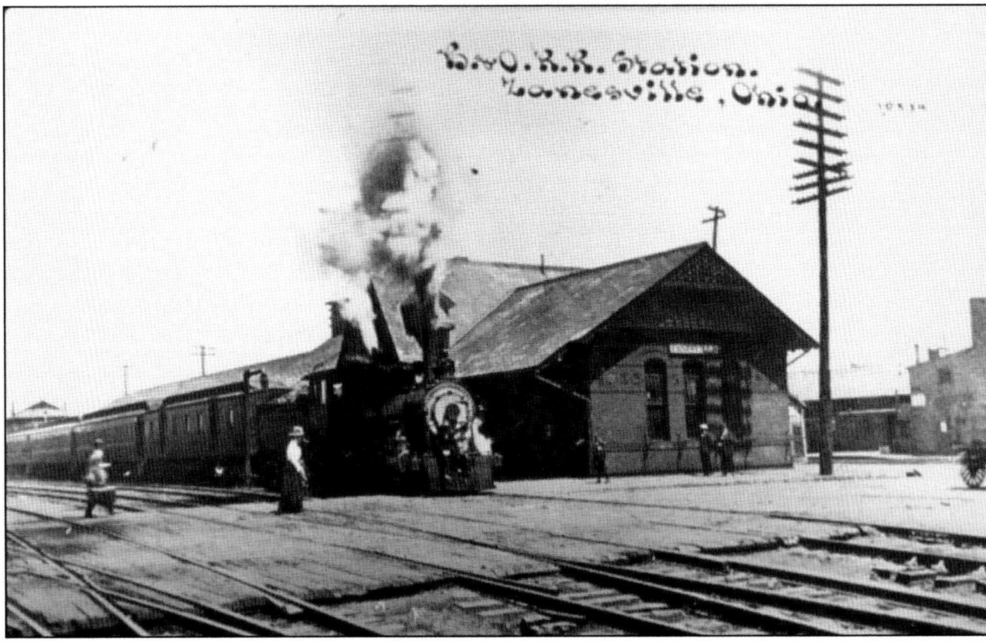


The Central Ohio Railroad opened service between West Zanesville and Newark in 1852. The first depot was on the west bank of the Muskingum River. The river was bridged in 1853 and Beckets River Hotel became a temporary waiting room for east side passengers. After the B&O gained control of the Central Ohio this substantial brick passenger depot was built in 1873 at what is now Second and Market Streets. Nearby was a New York Central (NYC) freight house and the passenger depot of the Cincinnati and Muskingum Valley Railroad. The Ohio River and Western Railroad also used this depot until the 1920s. The depot was built on the floodplain of the Muskingum River and subject to flooding. The view below shows one of the greater inundations—the 1913 flood. The depot was again stranded by the 1937 flood. (Author's collection.)

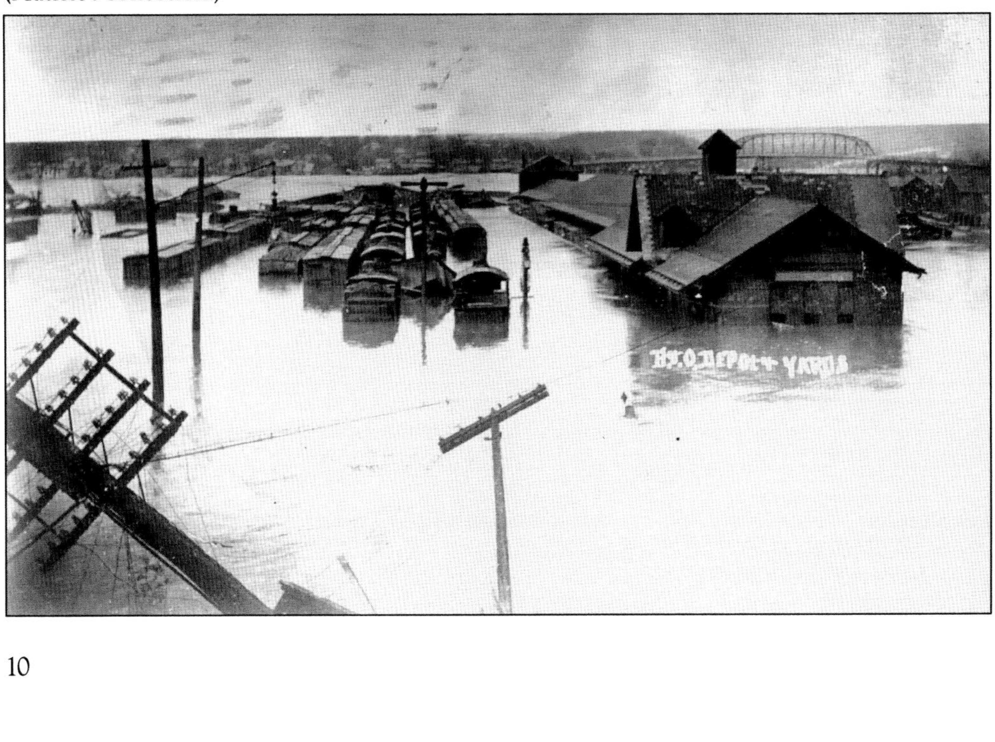

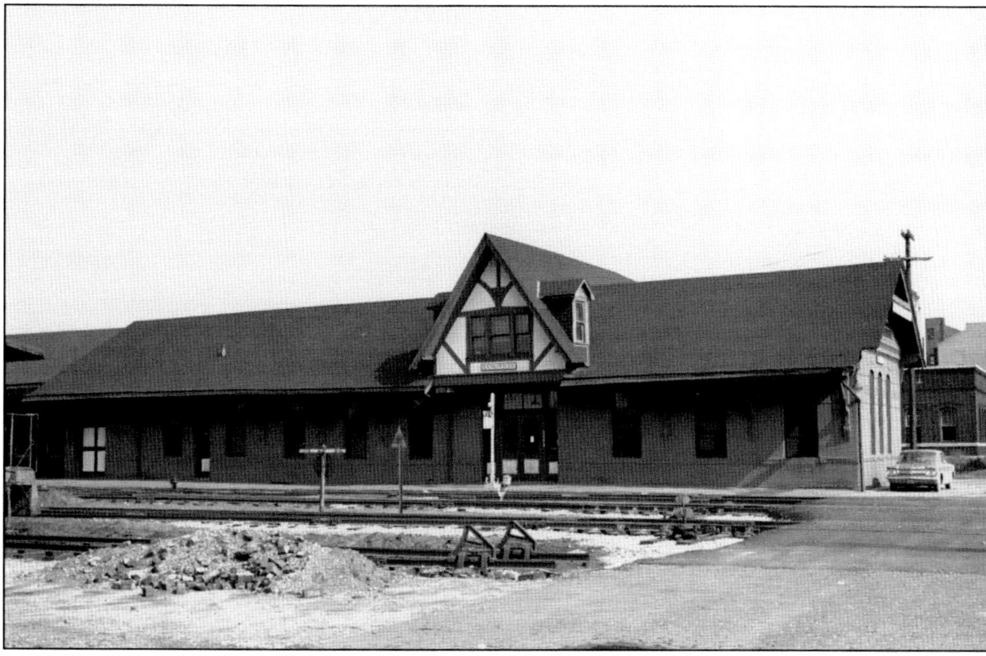

In 1967, the B&O still used the Zanesville depot. Behind it can be seen a portion of the NYC freight house, which still stands. The 1873 B&O depot, however, was demolished in the spring of 1999. (Photograph by Charles Garvin.)

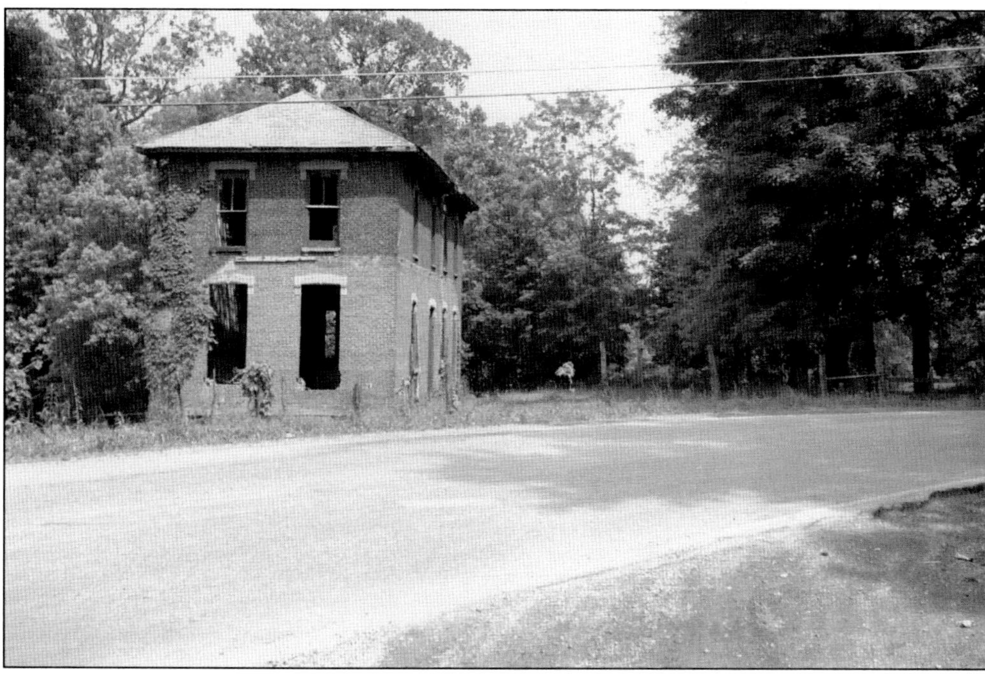

The B&O facilities at Toboso consisted of a small frame combination depot dating to the late 1800s. The depot closed in 1957. West of Toboso, this abandoned brick building reportedly had a ticket office and served as the depot for the small community of Clay Lick. By the 1920s, the B&O had discontinued services at this station, seen here in 1975. (Photograph by the author.)

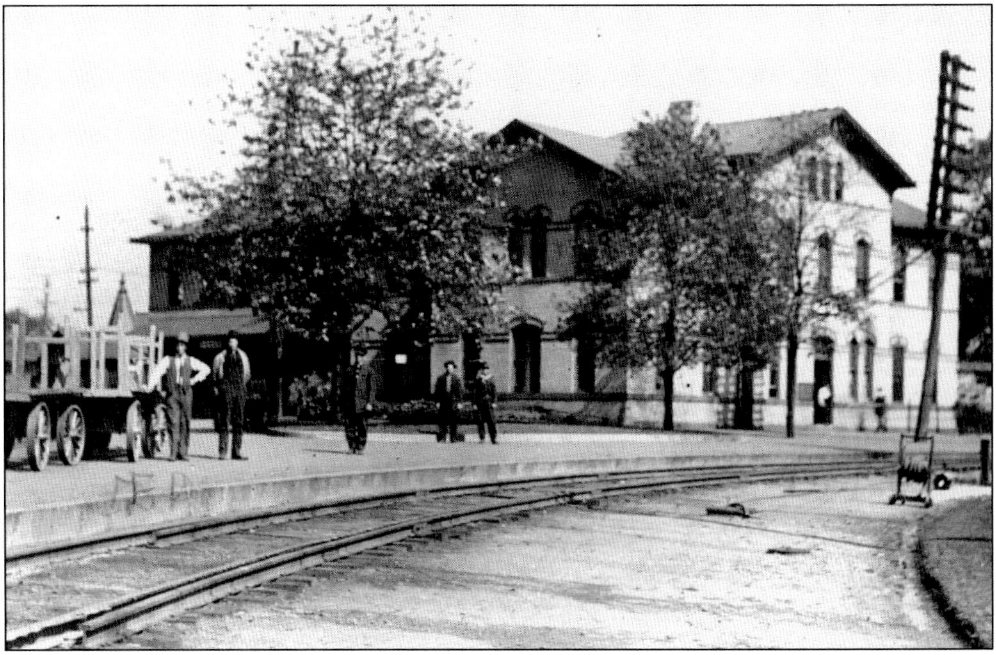

The first stretch of the Central Ohio Railroad to be put in service was between Zanesville and Newark. This two-and-a-half-story passenger depot/hotel was erected in 1878. Before the days of dining cars, passengers detrained for meals at the depot restaurant. East of town, the B&O maintained an engine terminal—a major employer into the mid-1900s. It is seen below in 1967. This once-grand structure was unceremoniously destroyed in a fire department training exercise in 1989. (Above, author's collection; below, photograph by Charles Garvin.)

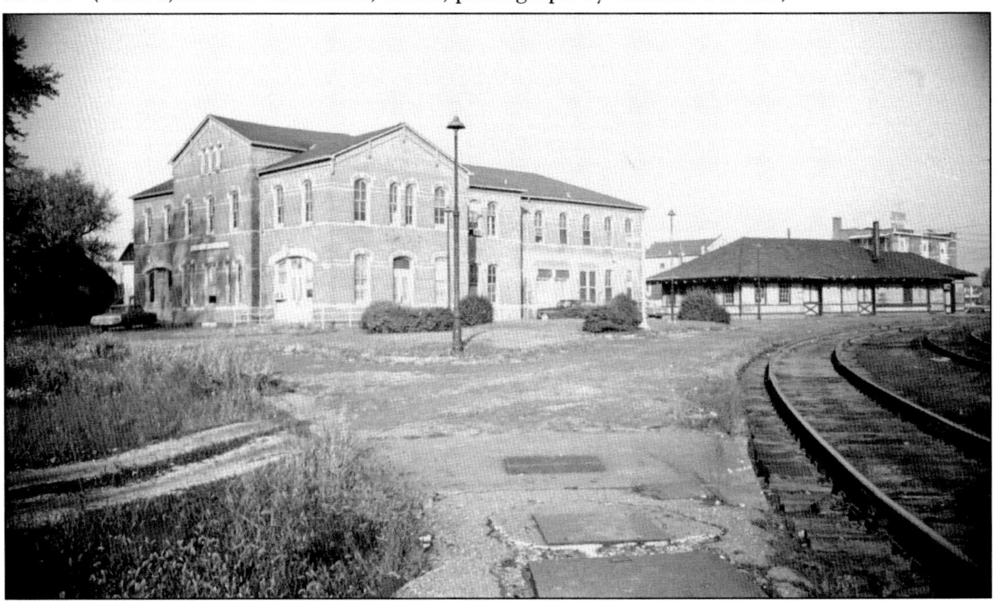

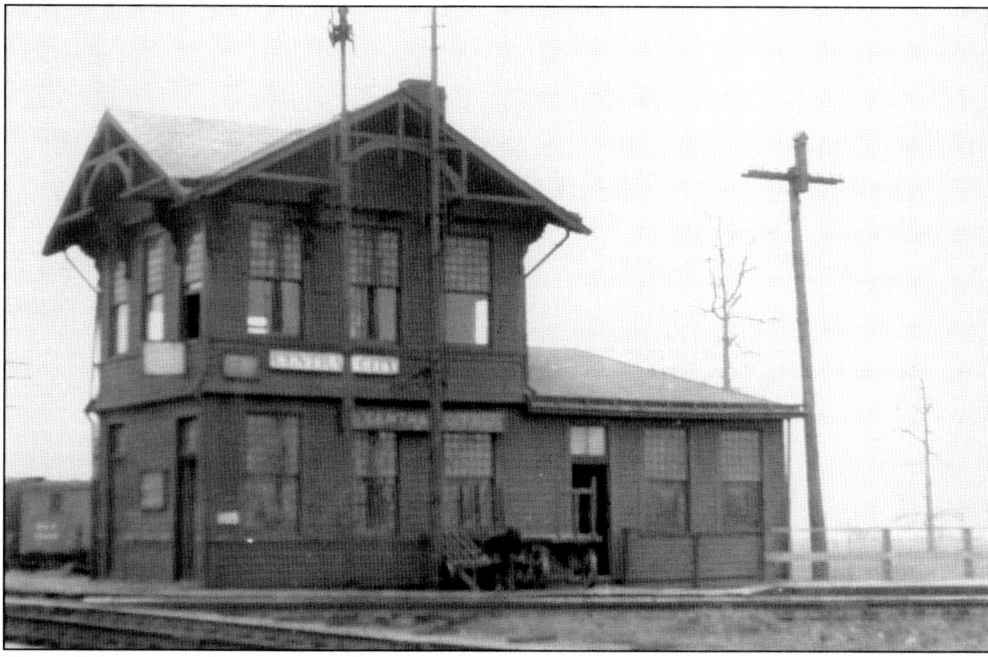

Central City was a lonely railroad junction in 1919. The depot became necessary around 1882 when the Ohio Central Railroad opened its line from Toledo to the Ohio River. The second story allowed for a good view down the tracks for the operator who controlled the semaphores that governed the passage of trains through the junction. Below, by the 1930s, this depot had been reduced to one story and a brick interlocking tower had been built across the tracks. The station was renamed Heath after a large refinery was built here in the late 1940s. The photograph below was taken in 1970. (Above, Toledo and Ohio Central Railroad photograph, Allen County [Ohio] Historical Society Collection; below, photograph by the author.)

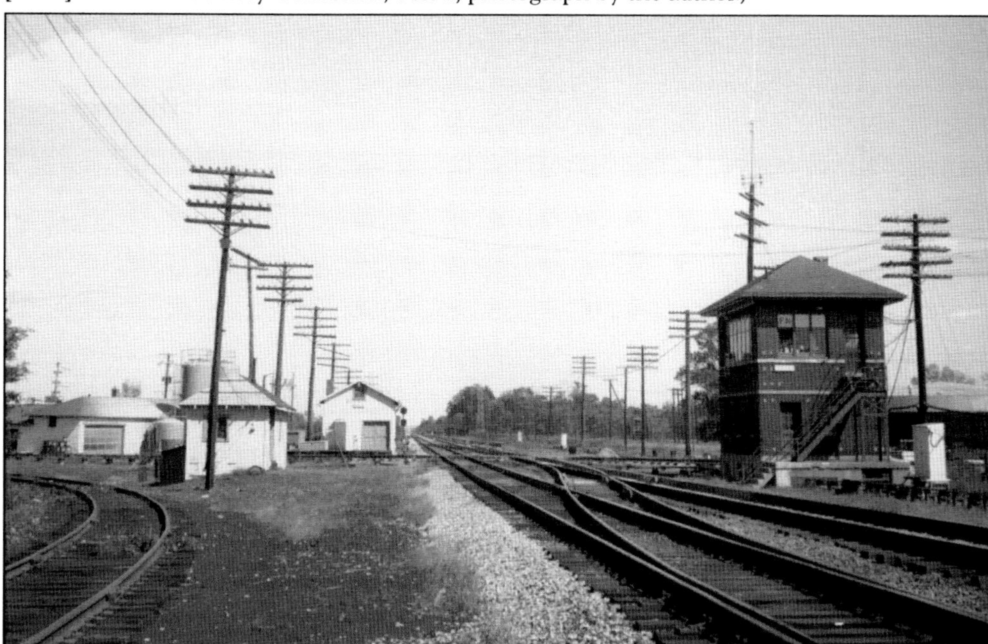

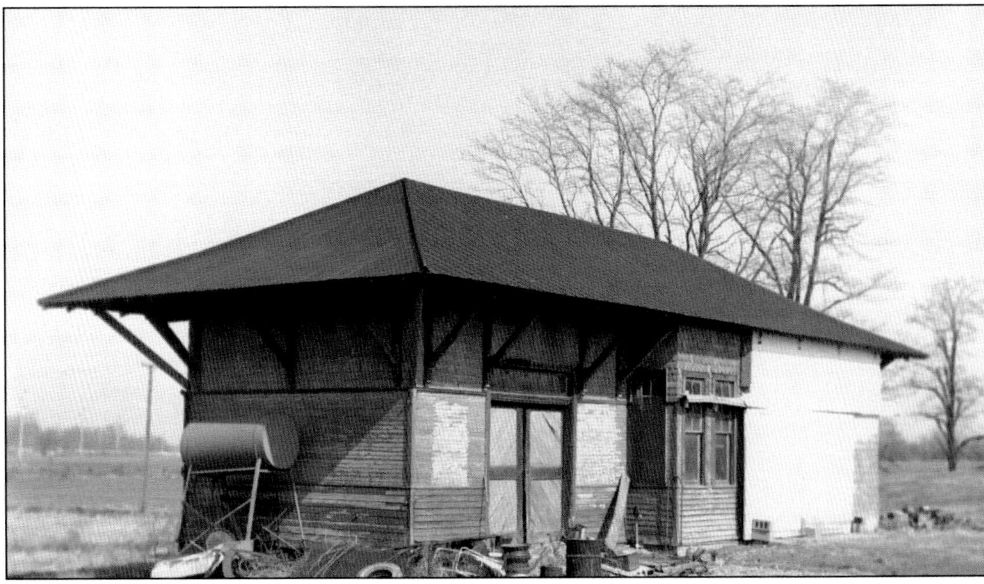

The B&O had a standard frame combination depot and adjacent standard design telegraph and switch tower at Outville. The Pennsylvania Railroad (PRR), which jointly used the depot, converted it to a freight-only agency in 1950. The tower disappeared early, but the depot was moved off-site in 1963. After serving as a storage building as shown in the above 1974 view, it was restored around 2000 by the community. Below, a similar tower was just a few miles west at Pataskala where there was a switchover. Most towers had a letter designation, in this case KO, to aid train personnel and telegraphers in identification. The semaphore was a signal to train crews to allow safe passage past this watering station and the depot in the distance. The small building in the right foreground is the pump house. (Above, photograph by the author; below, author's collection.)

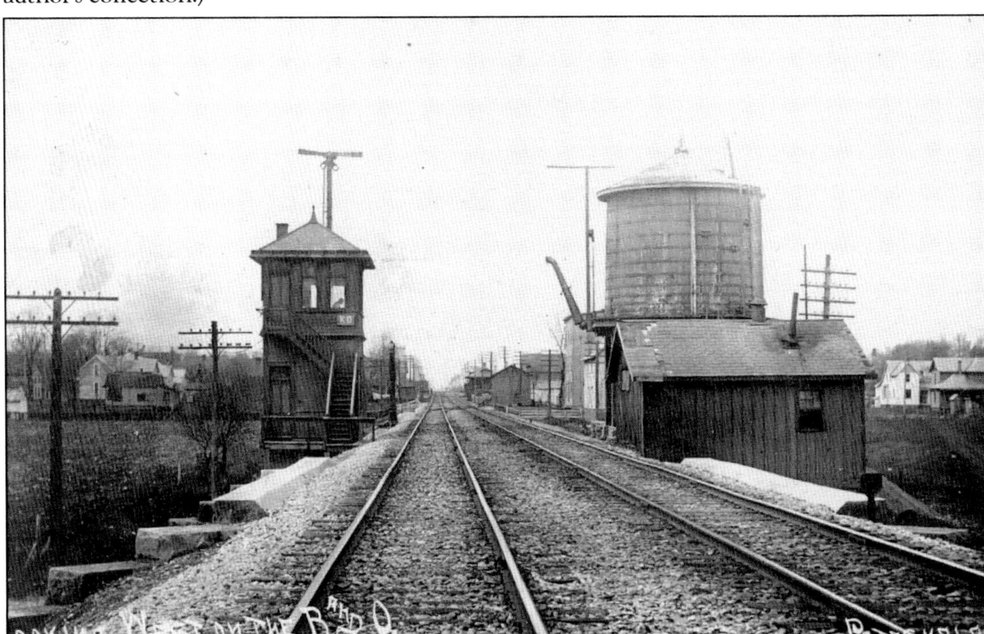

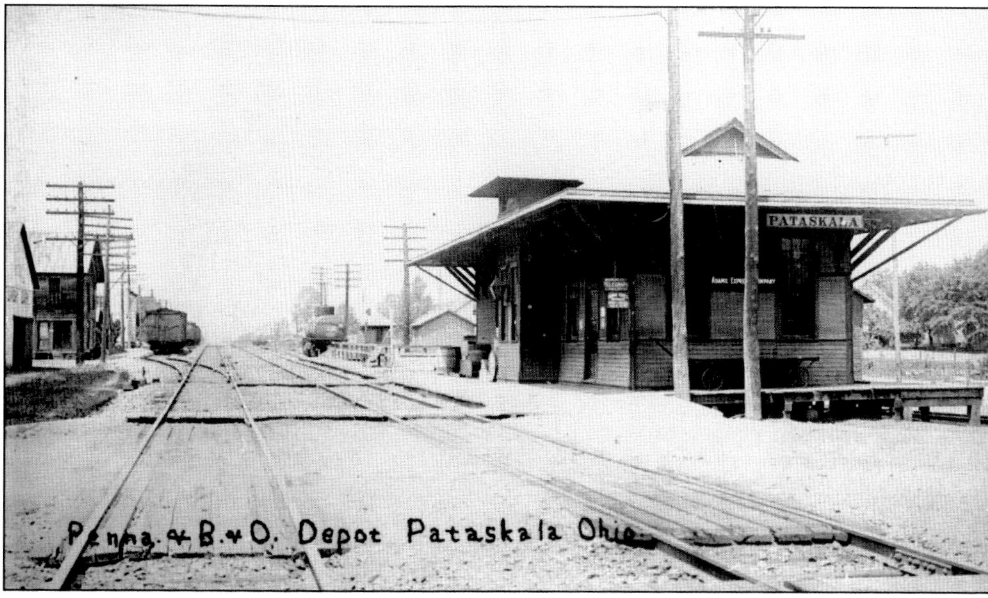


The Pataskala depot served both the B&O and PRR. Passenger service on the PRR ended here in 1953, and the PRR closed its agency here in 1963. In later years, the wide overhang of the depot was removed, producing the rather odd-looking structure shown below in 1974. Unfortunately the depot has been removed. (Above, author's collection; below, photograph by the author.)

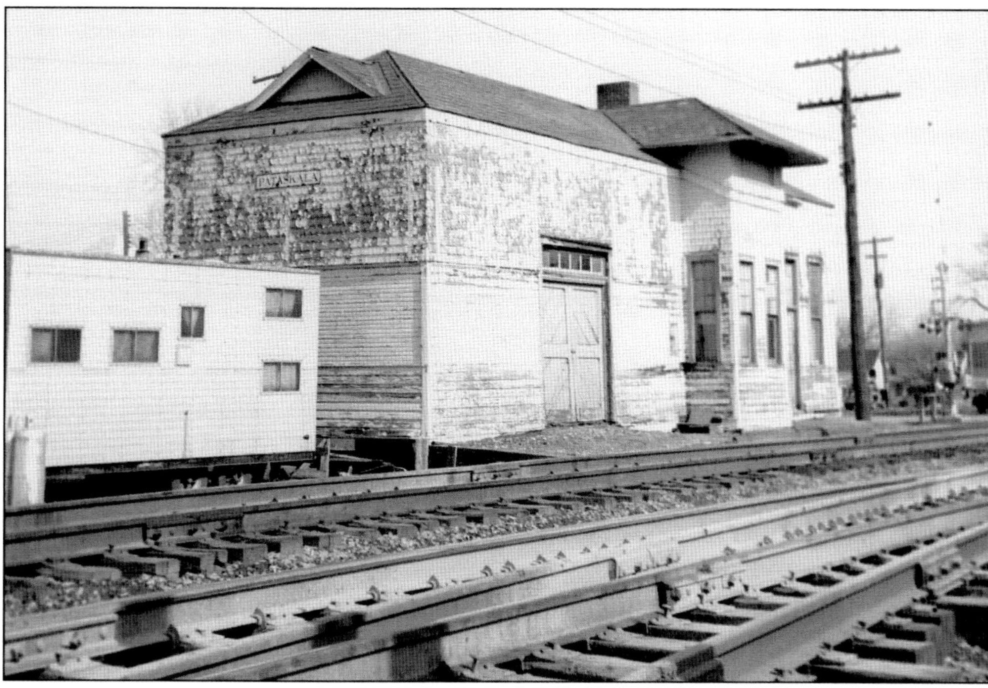

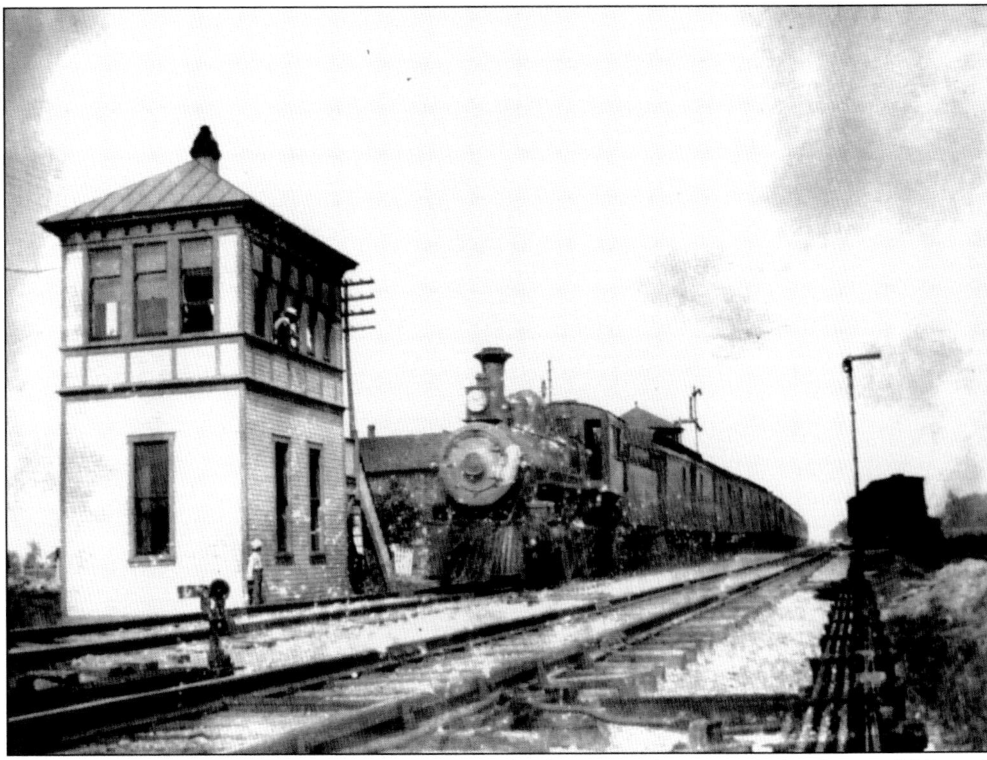

Another depot and tower were located at the highest spot between Columbus and Newark originally called Columbia, but later renamed Summit. The tower, shown in the above undated photograph, changed very little over the years; in 1971, it was known as SI tower. Summit's combination depot was of standard design. PRR removed its agency in 1950. Unfortunately the depot burned down on May 6, 1974, just about three years from the date of the photograph below. (Above, author's collection; below, photograph by the author.)

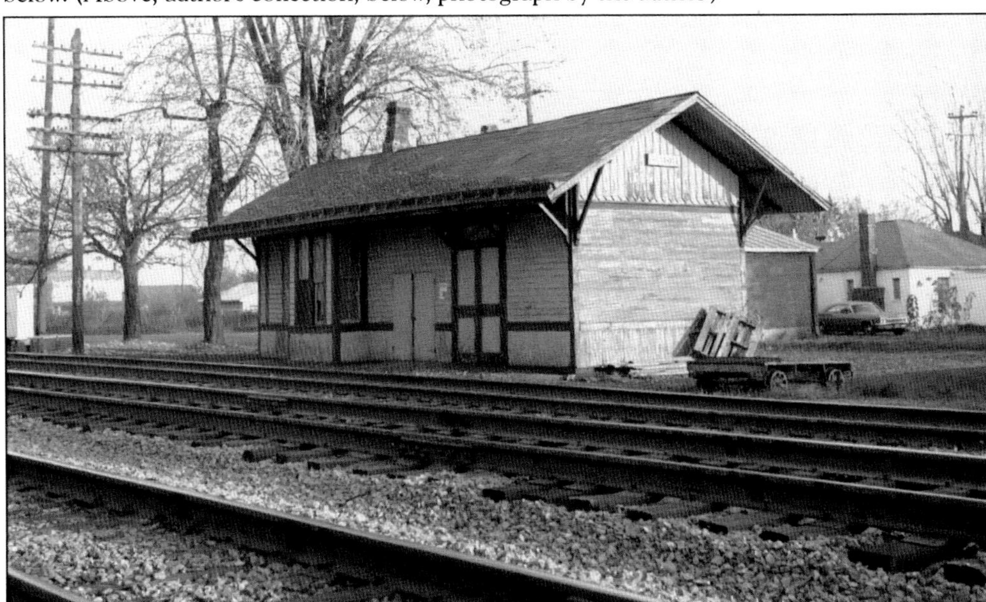

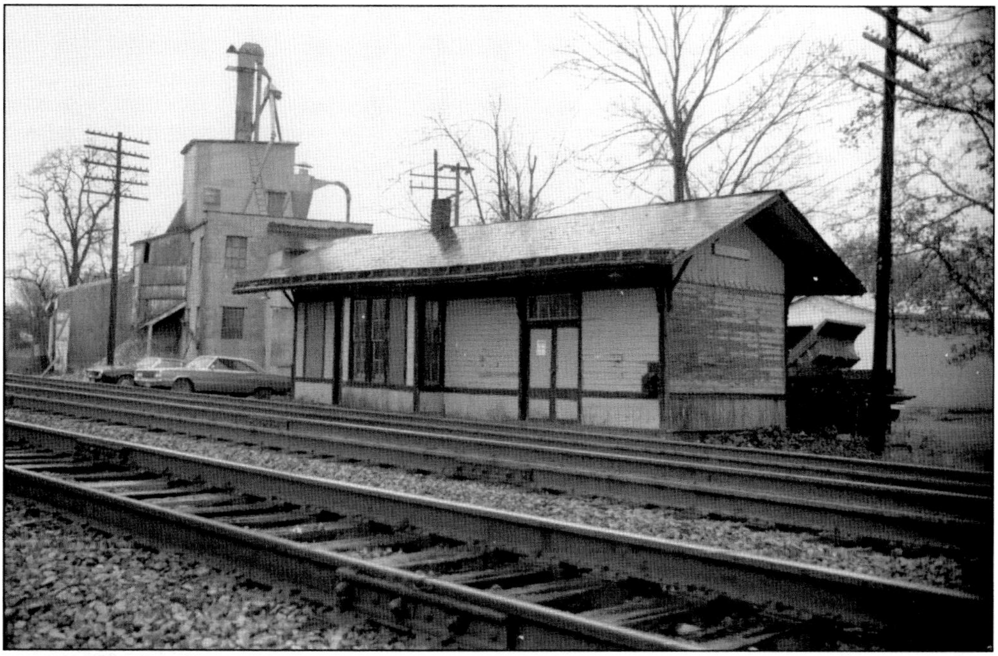

In 1969, Black Lick's combination depot was just used for storage by the railroad. Note that it is of similar design to Summit. The PRR closed its agency here in 1963; the B&O, in 1971. The B&O maintained a similar depot at Taylor, which was kept in business by a large nearby brick and tile plant. (Photograph by Charles Garvin.)

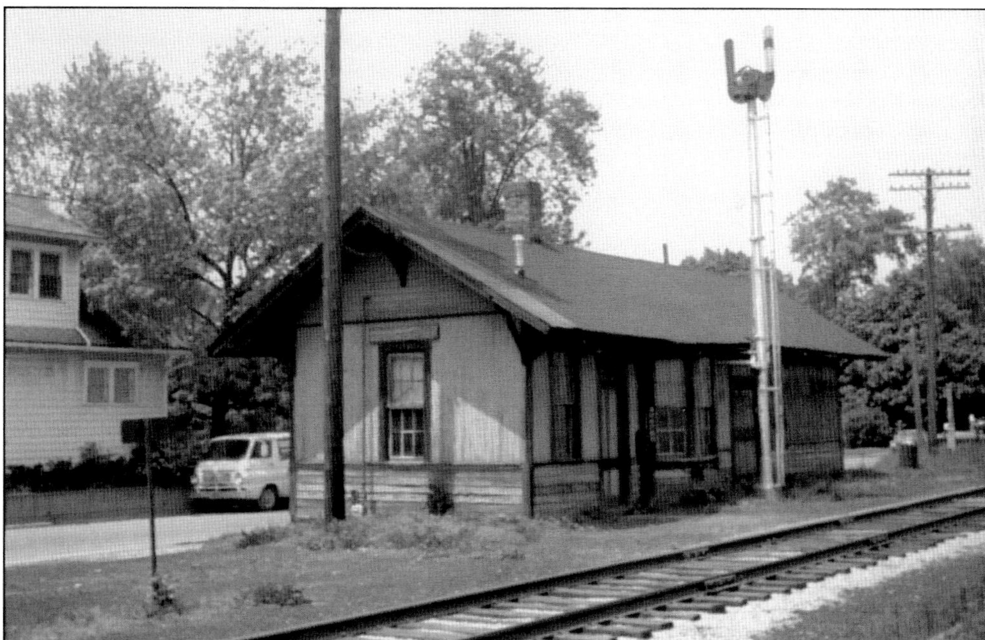

The depots on the B&O line from Columbus to Midland City, the old Columbus and Cincinnati Midland, date to the 1880s and are all variations on the Grove City plan. The Grove City depot closed as a passenger agency in 1955. The depot remained in railroad use, but now is the home of the local historical society. It is seen here in 1971. (Photograph by the author.)

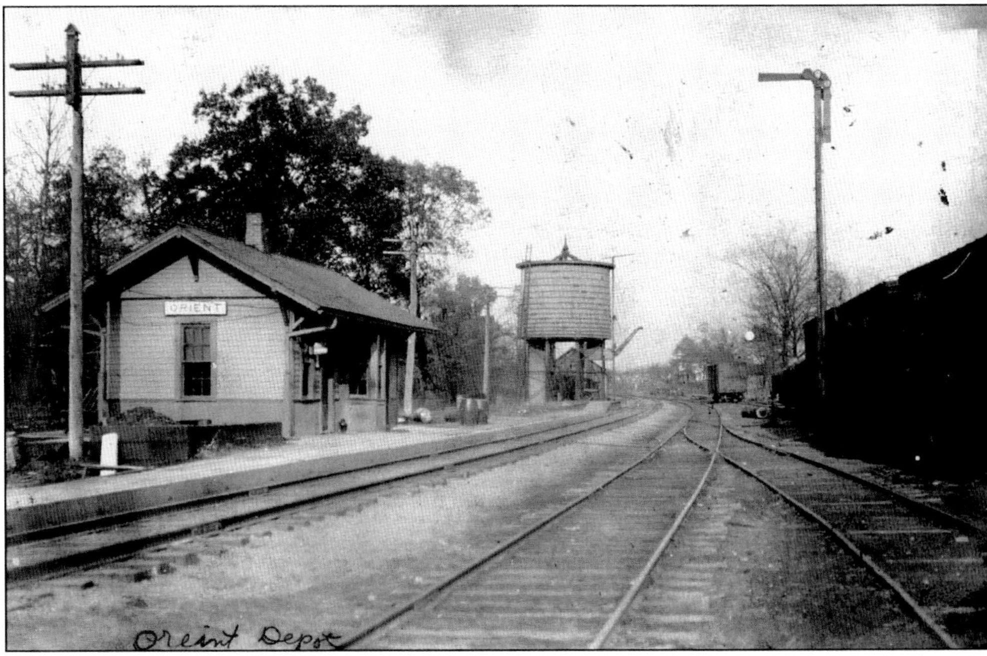


It is quiet time between trains at Orient's combination depot, above, but the arrival of a train brought a flurry of activity to Derby's nearly identical depot, the next station stop south. Orient was the home of Morgan's State Farm, later the Orient Institute, and thus saw considerable passenger traffic for such a rural location. Both agencies closed in the 1950s and the depots have been gone for many years. (Author's collection.)

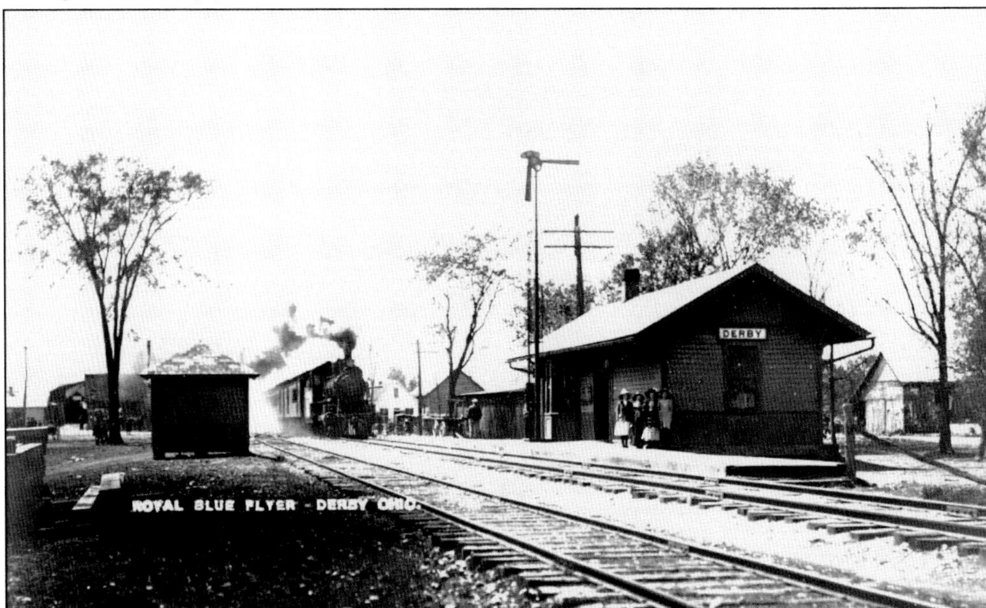

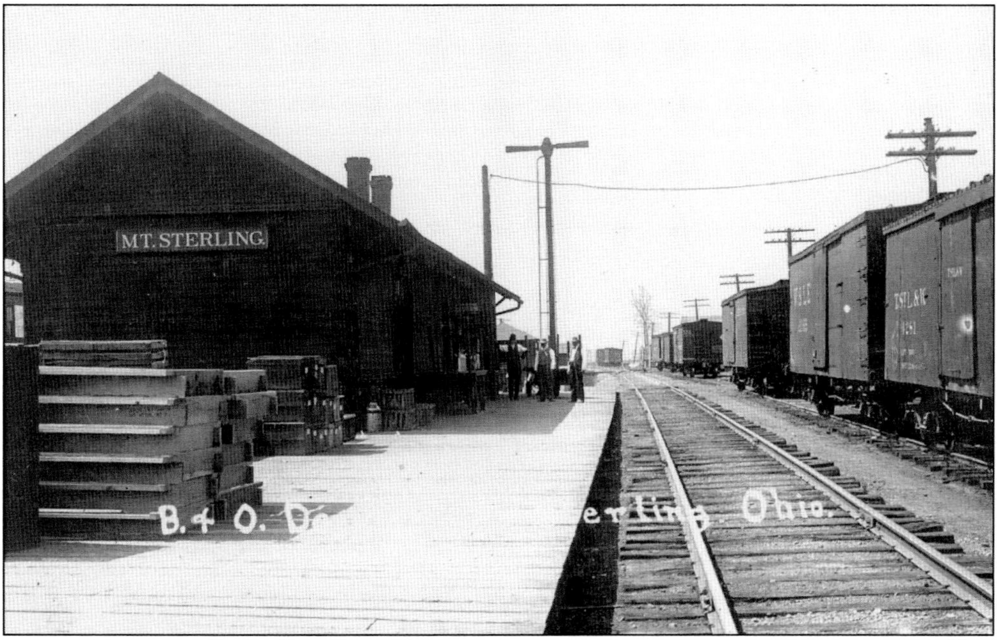


The next station south of Derby was Era. A small combination depot of similar design served this community. Mount Sterling's depot, shown above in 1907, has remained in railroad service, although closed as an agency for some time. The agent and his staff await the next train with a load of local products stacked on the plank platform. CSX uses it as a maintenance facility. Madison Mills, below, was a much smaller community but its depot was of equal importance to the surrounding farms. (Above, author's collection; below, Gary D. Rolih collection.)

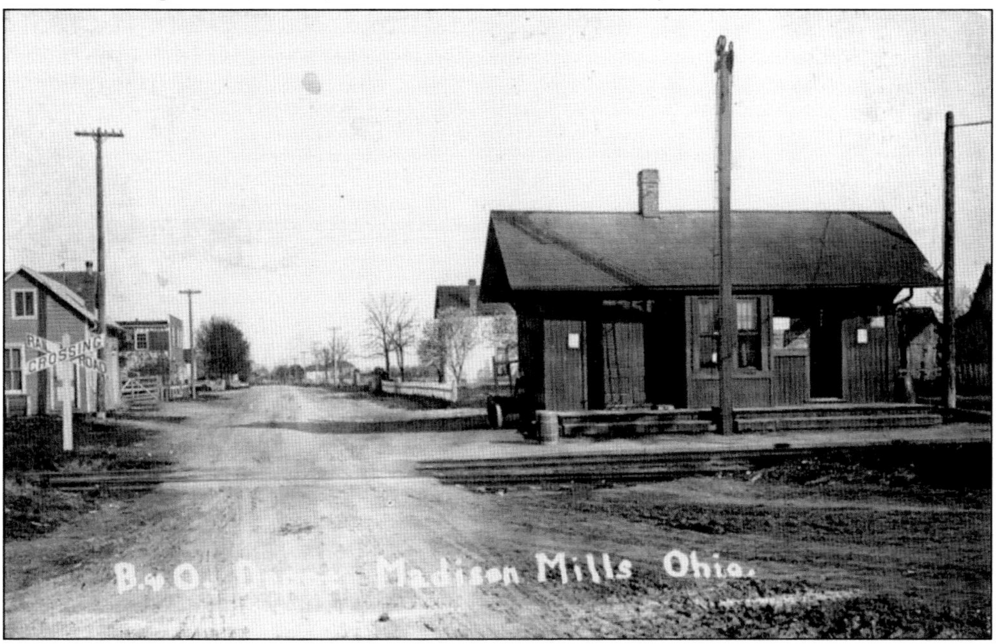

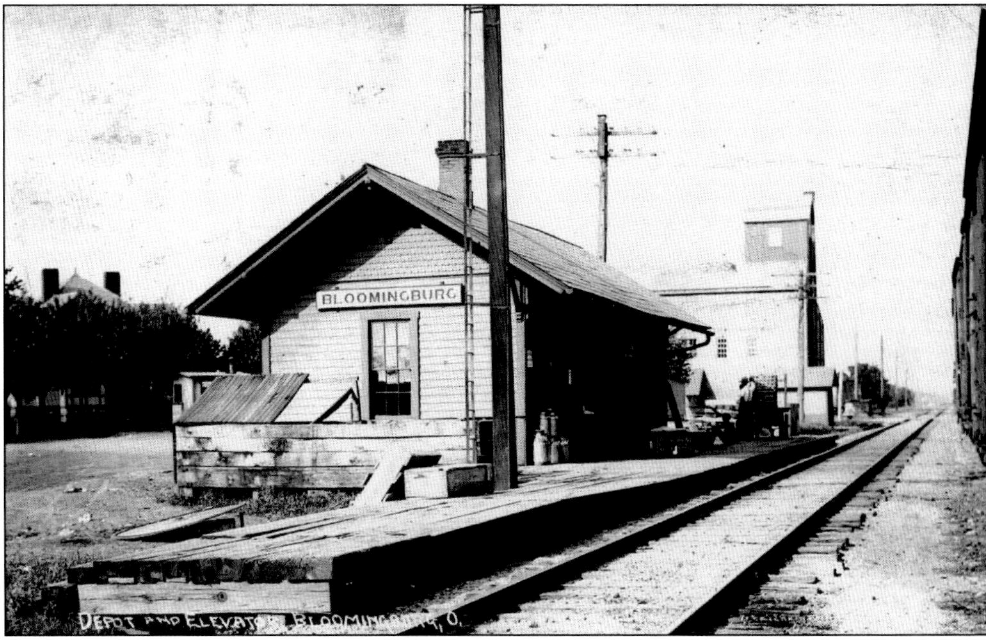


Bloomingburg was another typical farming community; note the grain elevator down the track. Another depot of similar design served this community. The depot was removed around 1970. (Author's collection.)

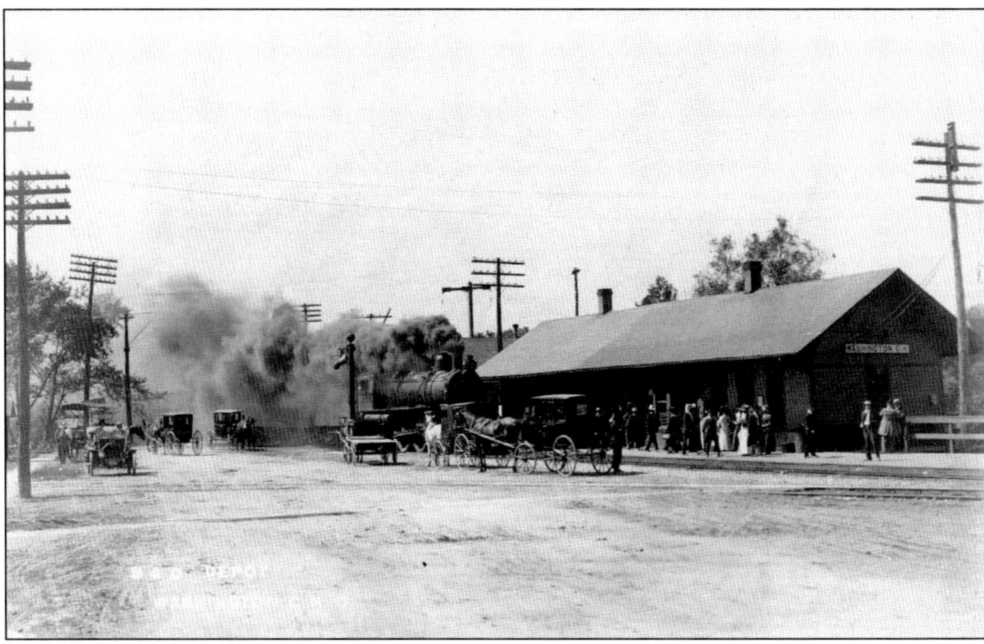

The county seat of Fayette County, Washington Courthouse, had an extended version of the typical depot design. It is train time in 1911, and the depot is alive with activity. Horse-drawn hacks await passengers needing transportation to hotels or other places around town. A newfangled automobile seemed harmless back then but obviously lead to a change in lifestyle within 10 years. By 1970, the B&O had replaced this depot with a metal prefab. (Author's collection.)

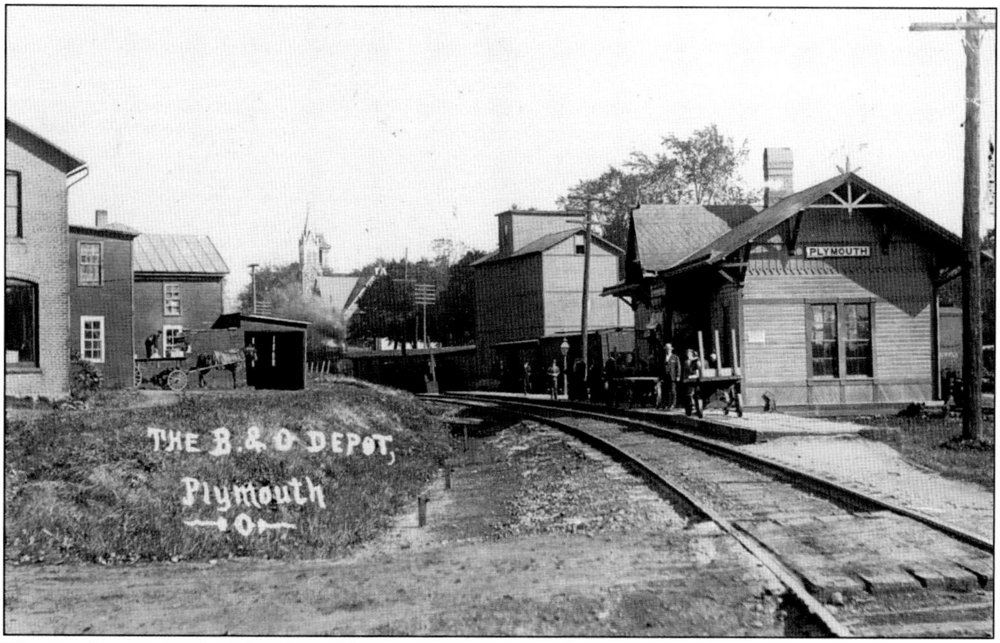


Plymouth was reached by the old SM&N in 1846. The town was about the last point on the line to be finished since the thick glacial deposits necessitated a deep cut. This depot was a second-generation structure probably built in the 1870s–1880s, replacing an earlier SM&N building. Above, around 1915, passengers wait for the approaching southbound train. Note the awnings over the operators windows to shade the afternoon sun and the ornamental finials. Around 1886, an interlocking tower was built at the crossing with the Pittsburg, Akron and Western Railroad. The view below was taken about a year after the agency closed in 1967. The depot was then converted to business use. Unfortunately the structure is again vacated and deteriorating. (Above, author's collection; below, photograph by the author.)

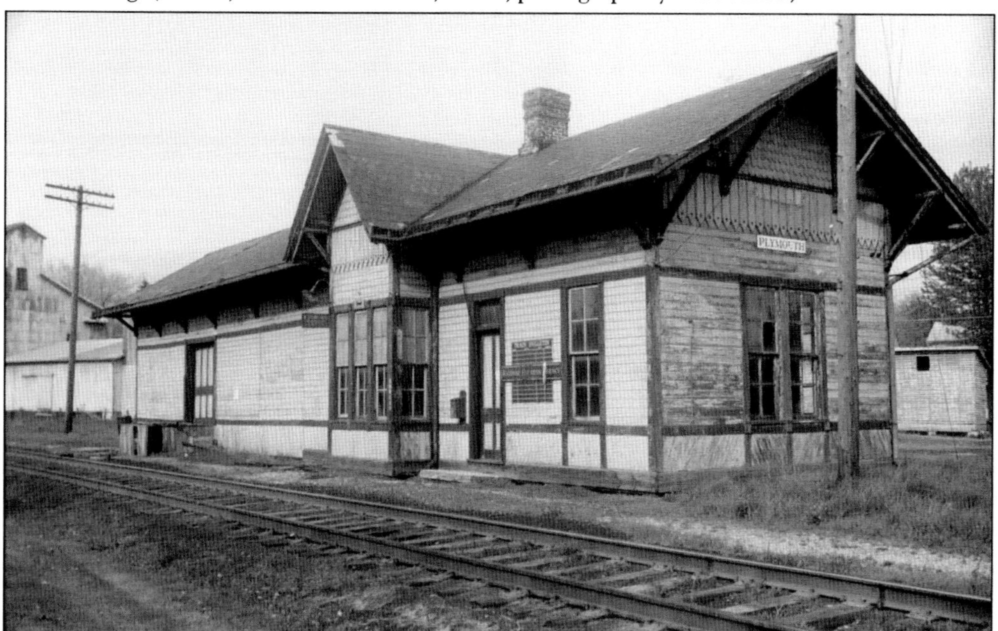

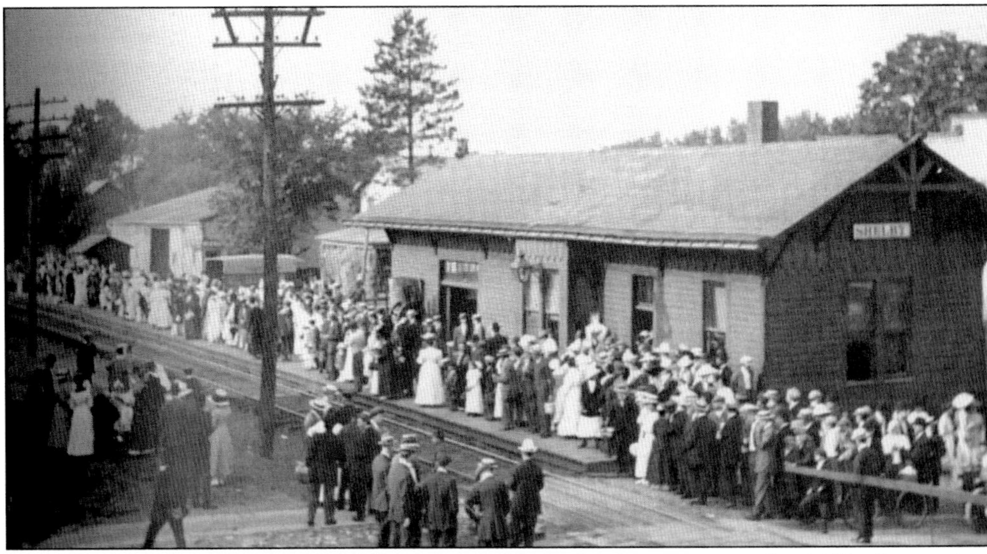


Shelby was connected to Mansfield by an SM&N construction crew in the 1840s. Later when the B&O took over the line, this combination depot was built. The above view shows the crowd at the depot awaiting the Shelby Tube Works excursion to Cedar Point in the early 1900s. This depot stood into the 1960s, but was torn down and replaced by a metal prefab building, which still stands. (Above, Marvin Memorial Library, Shelby collection; below, photograph by Max Miller.)

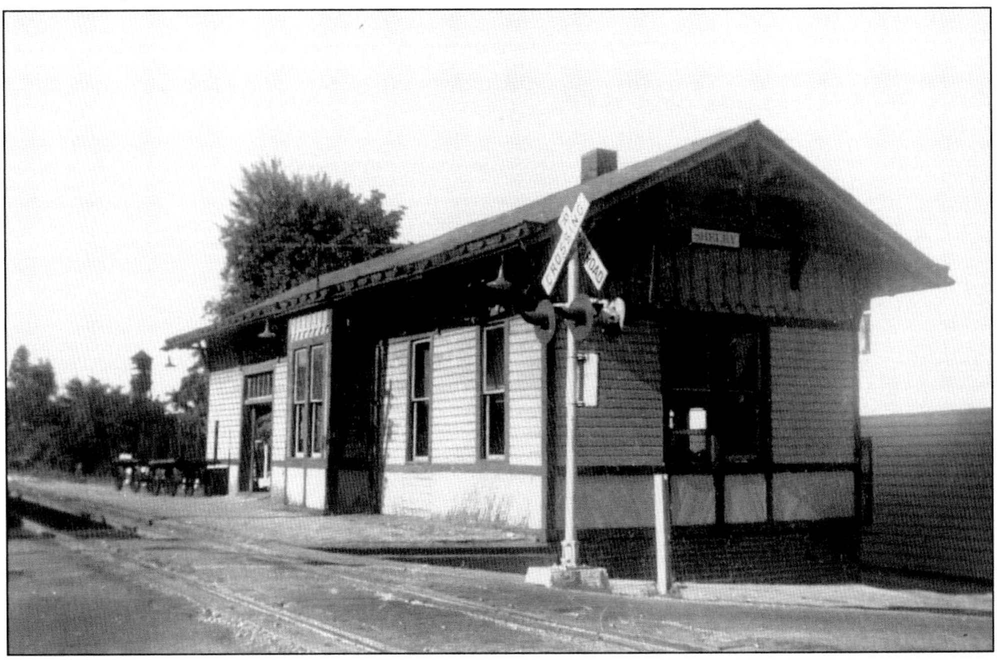

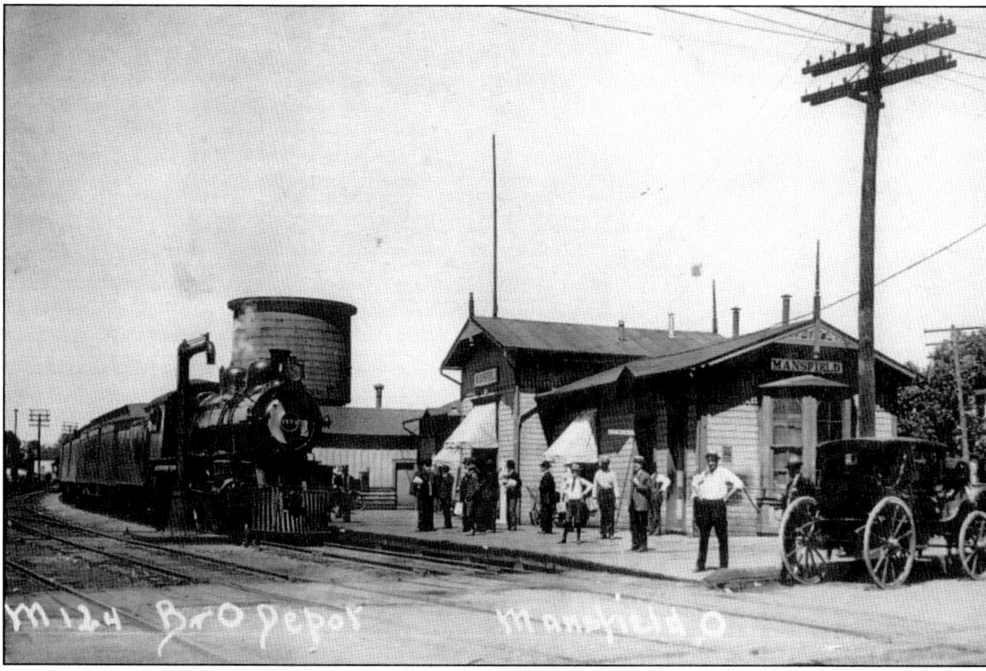


Mansfield's B&O depot was located on North Mulberry Street. This wooden depot is of SM&N design or early B&O design; a passenger facility with a separate freight house located nearby. Locomotive No. 1474 is about to take on water in the *c.* 1910 view above. The depot was heated by several potbellied stoves as indicated by the numerous roof stacks. Below, soldiers of Company M of the Ohio National Guard troop await transport to the southwest in 1916 after Pancho Villa raided Columbus, New Mexico. (Sherman Room Photograph Collection, Mansfield Richland County Public Library.)

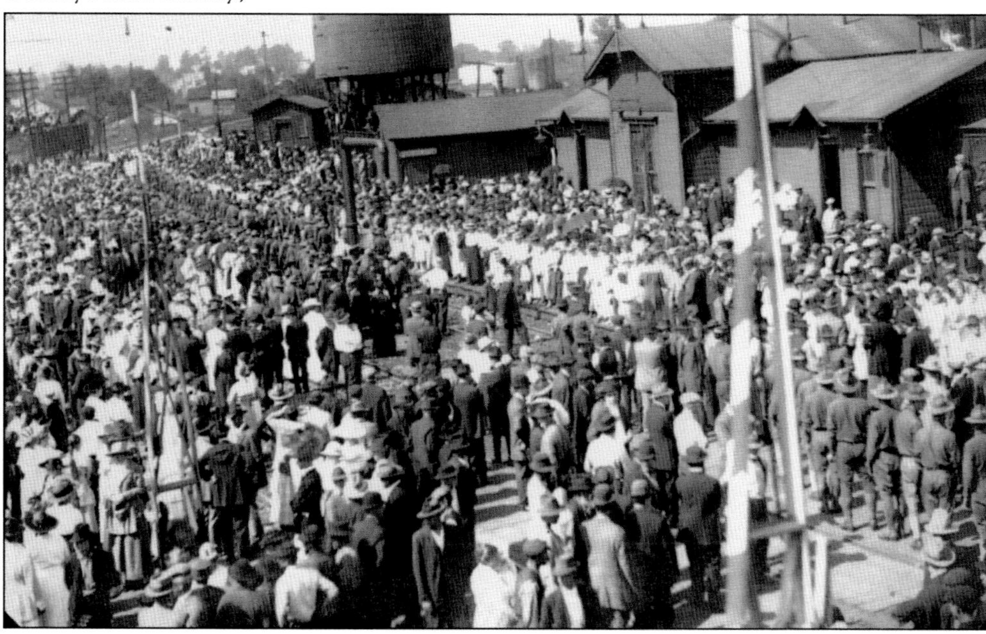

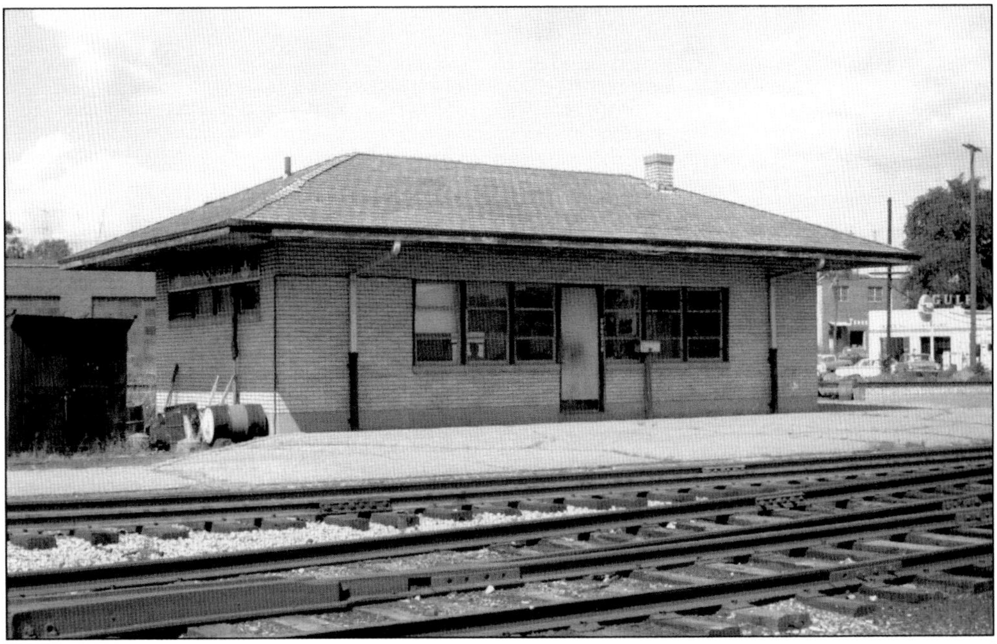

The B&O replaced the older frame passenger depot with this brick structure that served Mansfield until passenger service was discontinued on the Sandusky branch. Although a nearby freight station has been torn down this "modern" passenger depot remains the only railroad depot still standing in Mansfield. (Photograph by Charles Garvin.)

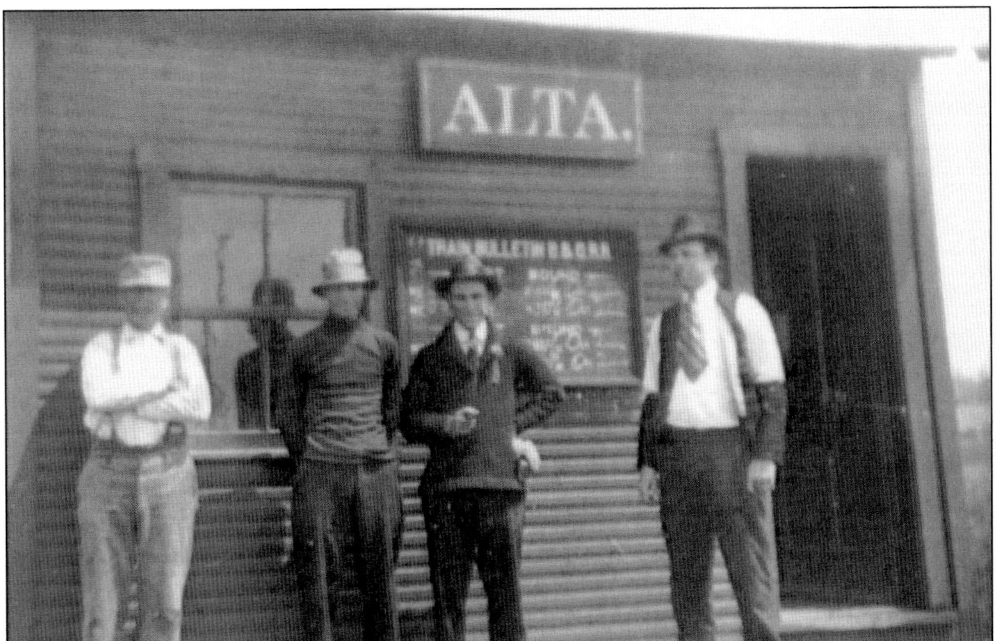


A few miles south of Mansfield was this frame telegraph office called Alta. It has been gone since the mid-1900s and the location has been surrounded by the city. (Sherman Room Photograph Collection, Mansfield Richland County Public Library.)

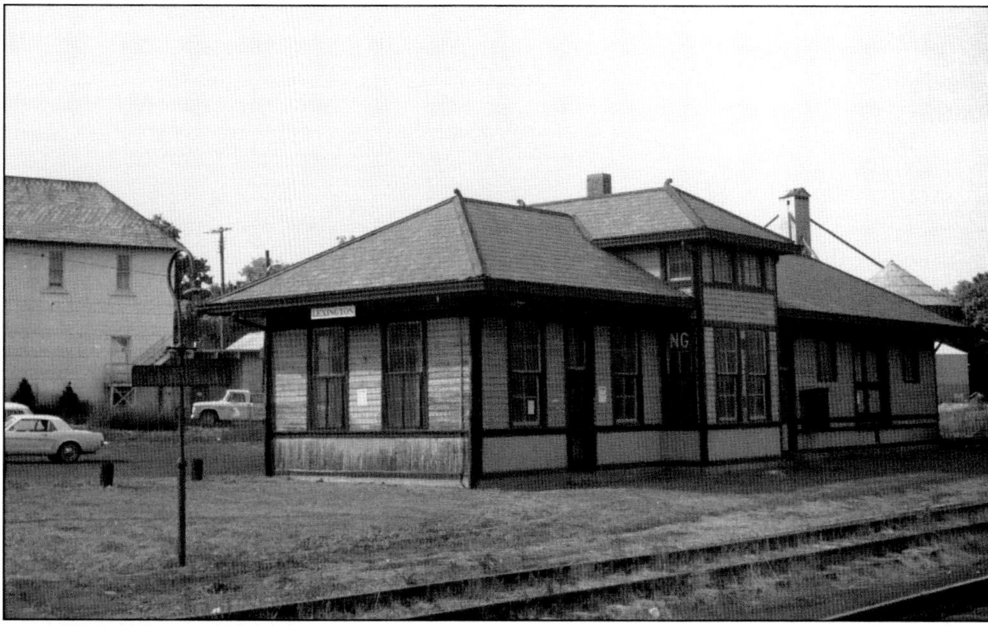


The SM&N Lexington depot burned down and was replaced with this 1906 B&O standard design combination depot in 1914. The depot, shown in 1968, was a modified version of the standard plan including a built-in tower. The letters *NG* are the call letters for this tower. The depot was purchased in 1989 and eventually incorporated into the Lexington Senior Civic Center. (Photograph by the author.)

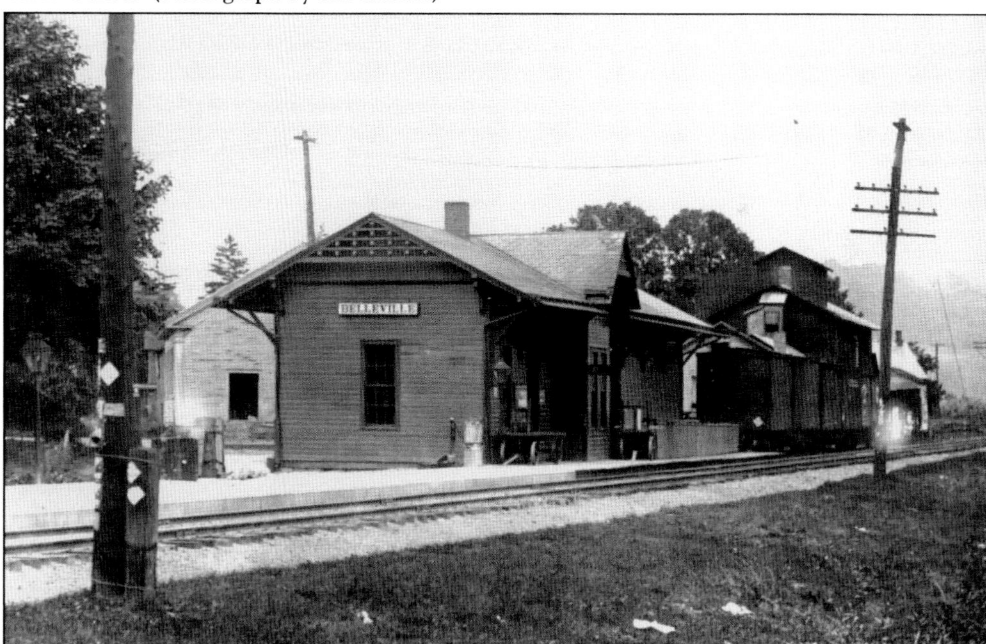


The first SM&N depot at Belleville reportedly was destroyed in a train wreck. This is the second depot at the site, probably dating to about 1895. The neatly-kept platform is ready for the next train in this *c.* 1907 view. The combination depot was torn down around 1963. The track was officially abandoned in 1987. (David P. Oroszi collection.)

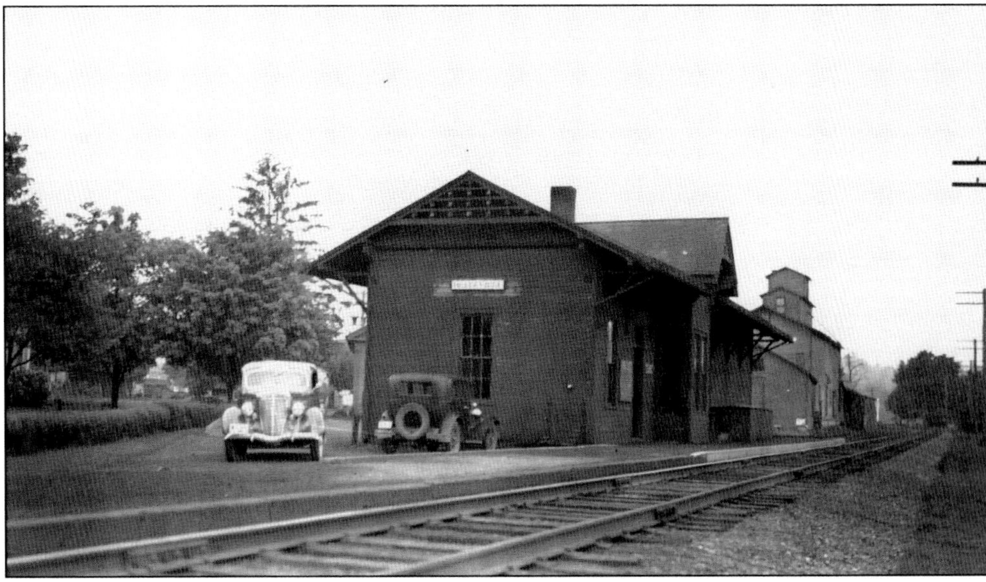

Little had changed at Belleville by the 1930s, except for the prevalence of automobiles. Later the roadbed became the Richland B&O bike trail and a depot replica now shelters cyclists. (Author's collection.)

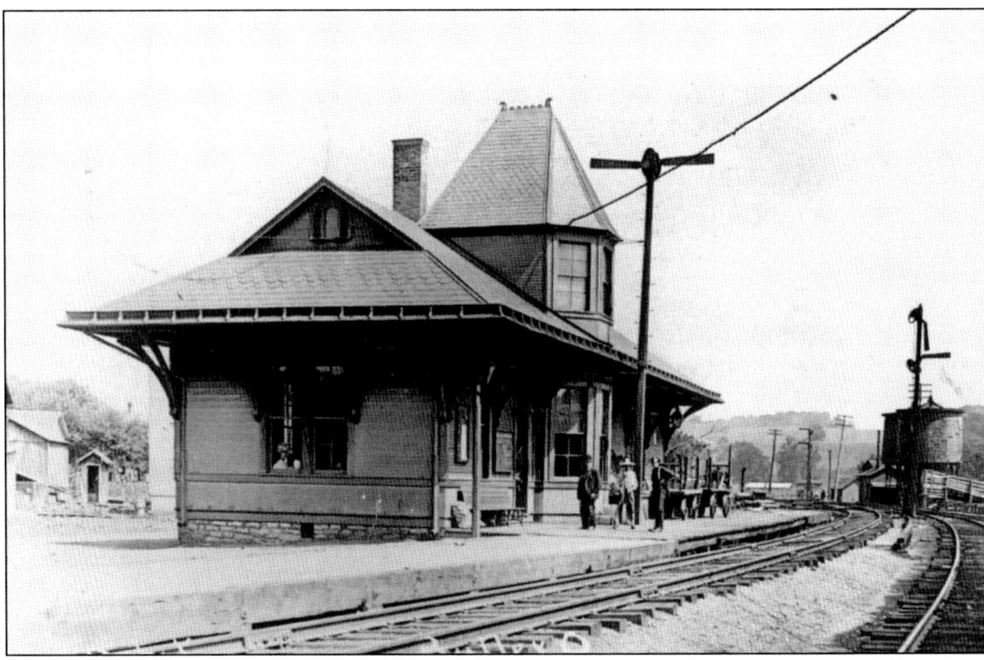

The B&O replacement depots between Mansfield and Newark were of similar architecture, some containing a tower for the telegraph operator like this combination structure at Butler. Down the track are double water tanks and a number of accessory buildings. Out of view in the opposite direction was a railroad hotel. The earlier SM&N frame depot was moved back from the tracks and became a restaurant with completion of the new depot around 1900. (Author's collection.)

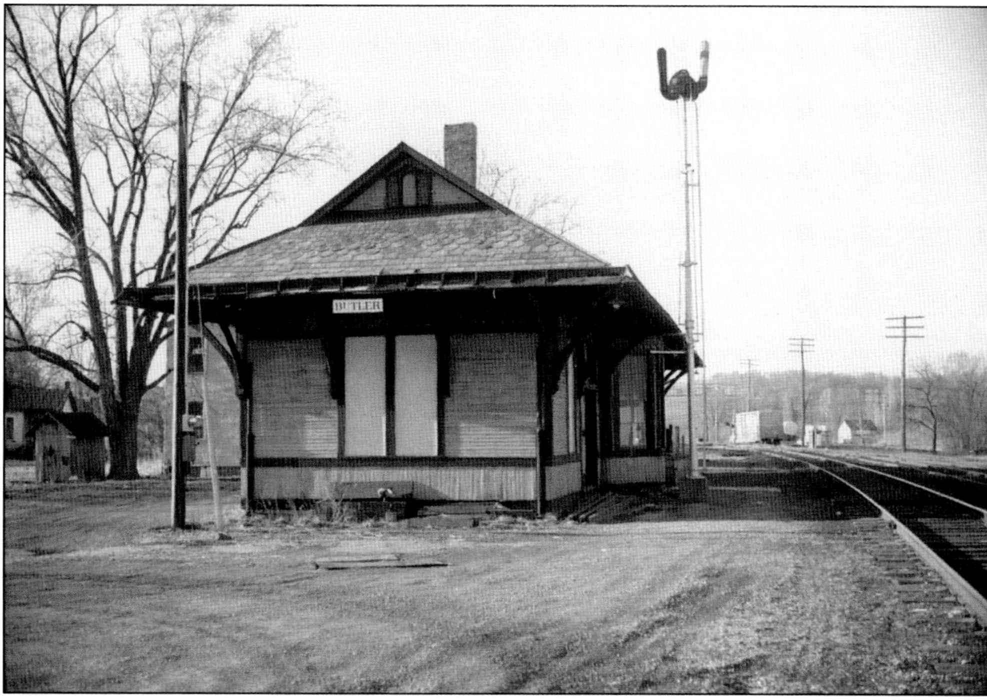


The tower was removed sometime after the 1920s, probably during a B&O modernization program. Photographed here in 1967, there was hope that the Butler depot would be preserved and used along the local rail trail but the building was unfortunately torn down. (Photograph by Charles Garvin.)

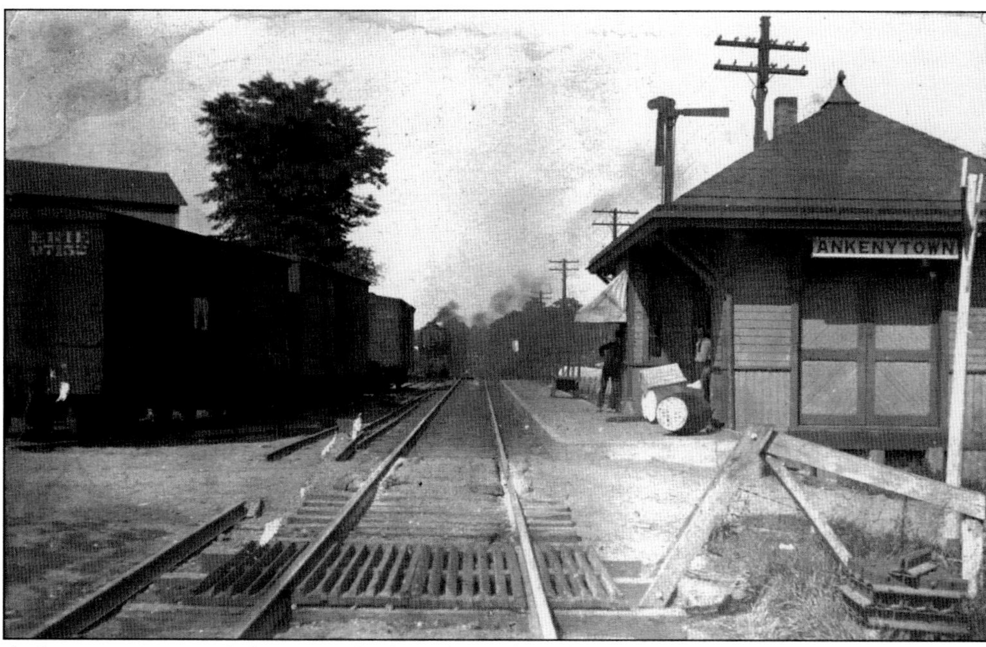


Ankenytown's second depot was built without the telegraph tower following a 1906 standard plan. The combination depot disappeared long ago. (Author's collection.)

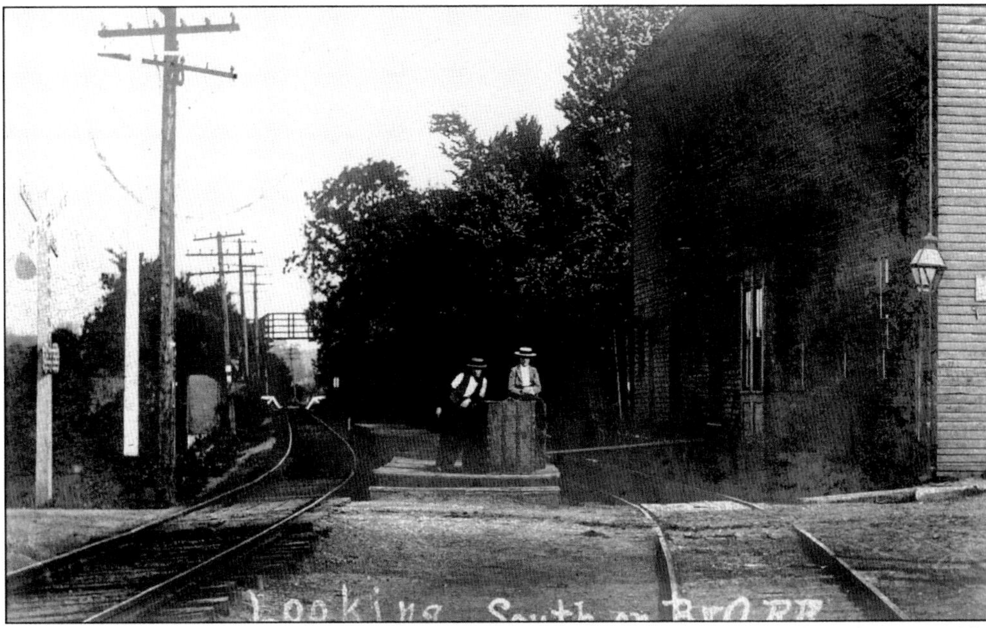

The above view shows the earlier SM&N depot at Fredericktown, a rather plain storelike building. Below is its 1895 B&O replacement. Except for the lack of the tower it is identical to Butler. The second Fredericktown depot was disassembled in the early 1970s and rebuilt near West Lafayette as part of a gourmet food and gift complex. (Author's collection.)

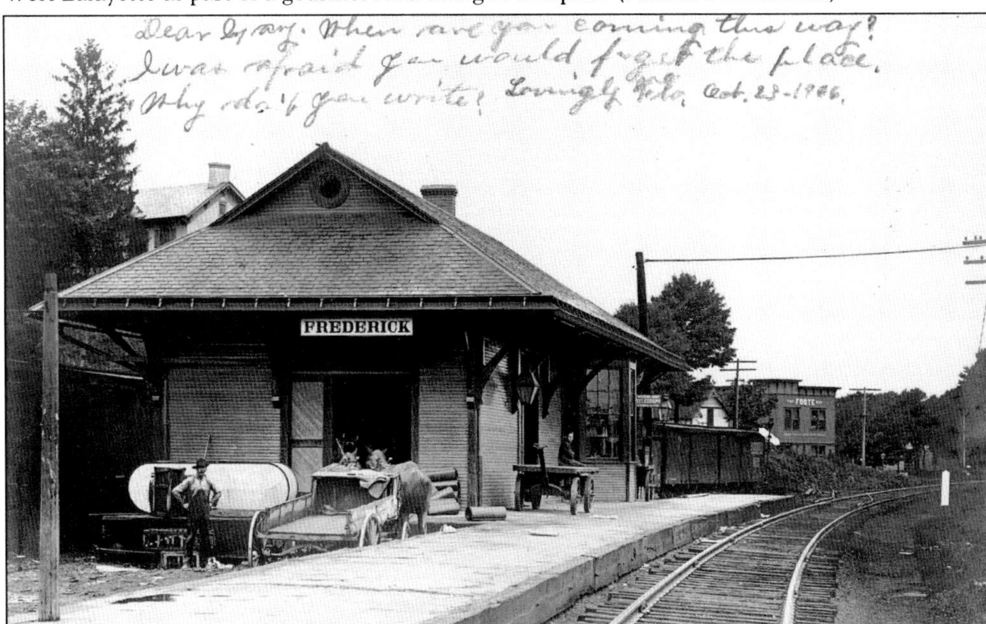

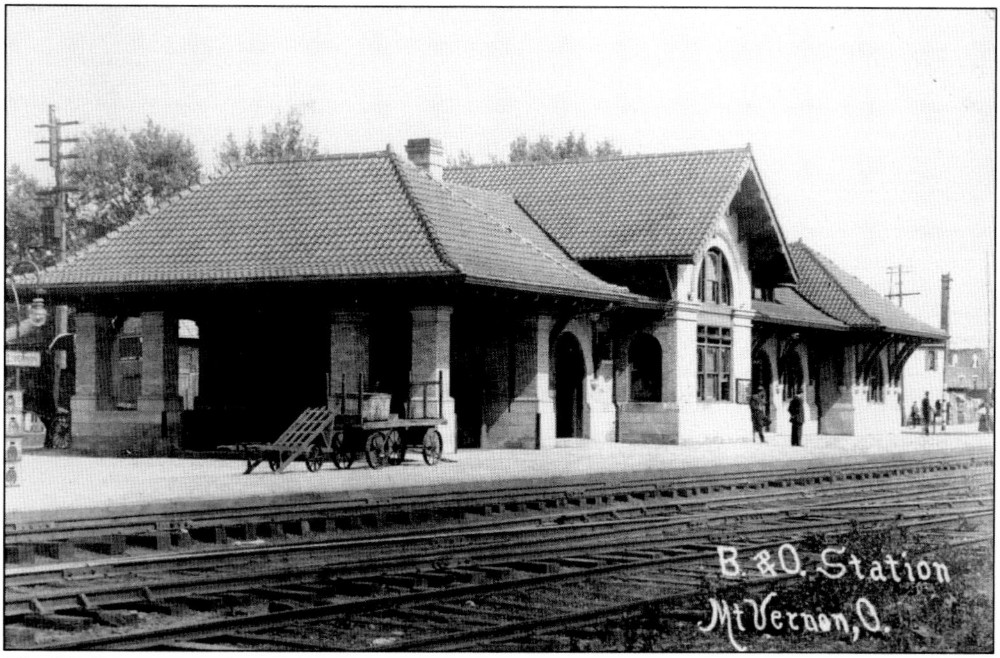


The B&O passenger depot on West High Street in Mount Vernon opened in 1907 after a series of construction delays beginning in the fall of 1906. The first train, headed north, pulled into the handsome depot November 25, 1907. The above view depicts the depot around 1908. After passenger service ended in the early 1960s, the building continued in railroad use. Below is the depot in 1967. The city purchased the building in 2002 and began plans for a grand restoration. A grand reopening took place in October 2007, and the depot opened for community use the next month. (Above, author's collection; below, photograph by Charles Garvin.)

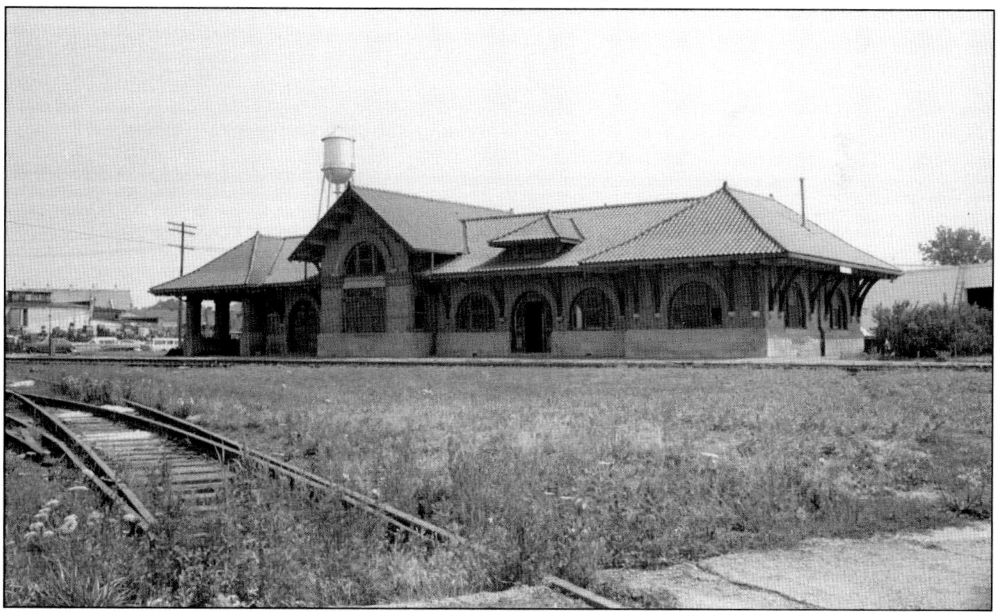

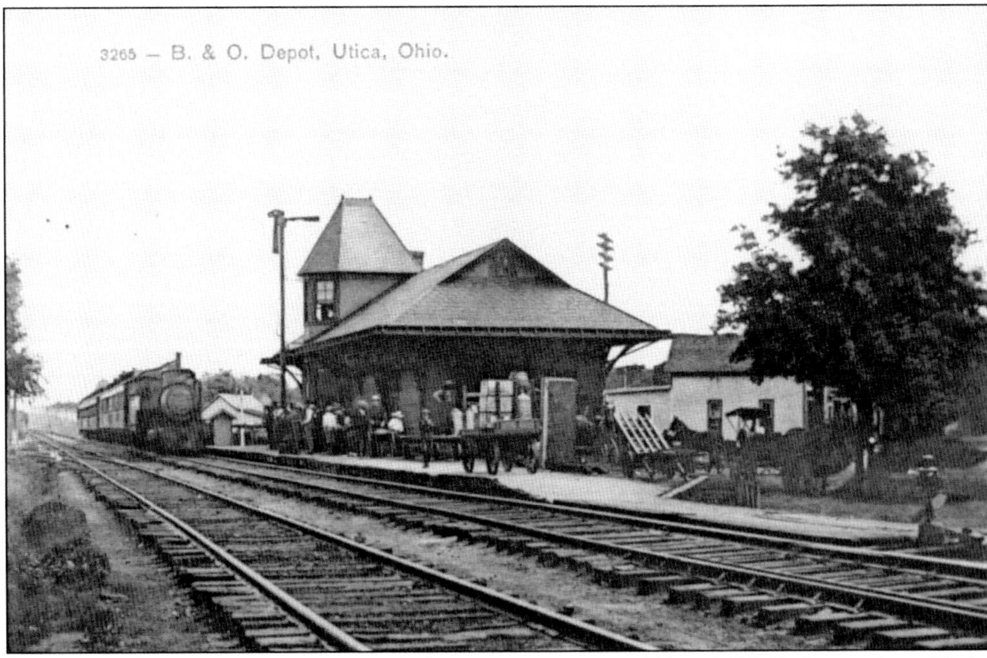


Compare the above, about 1908, and below, 1967, versions of Utica's B&O depot. As at Butler the original operator's tower was removed during a modernization program. The depot, although slightly modified, remains in community use. (Above, author's collection; below, photograph by Charles Garvin.)

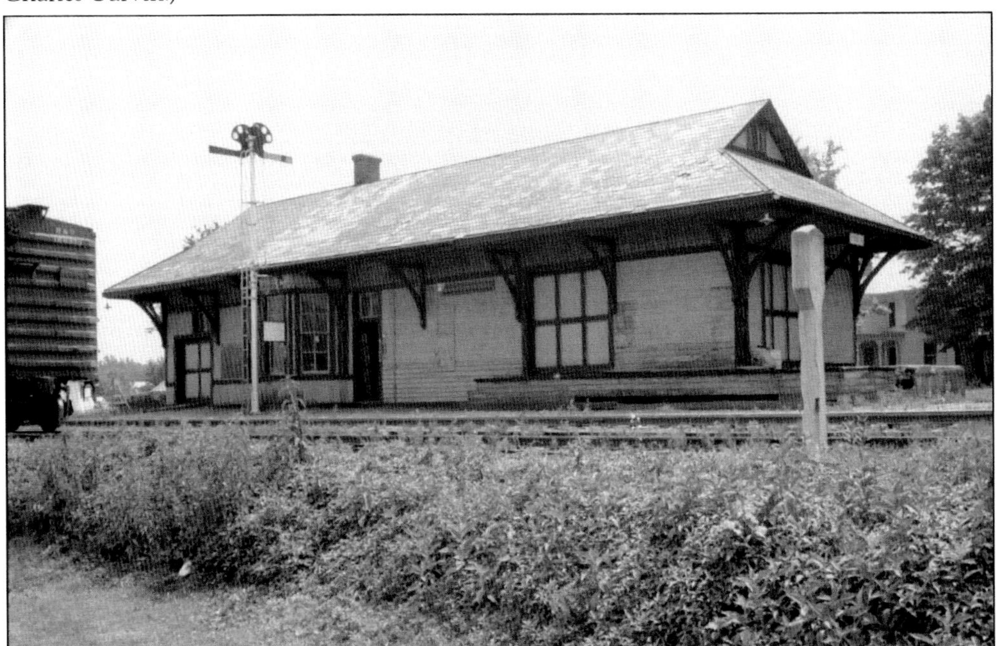

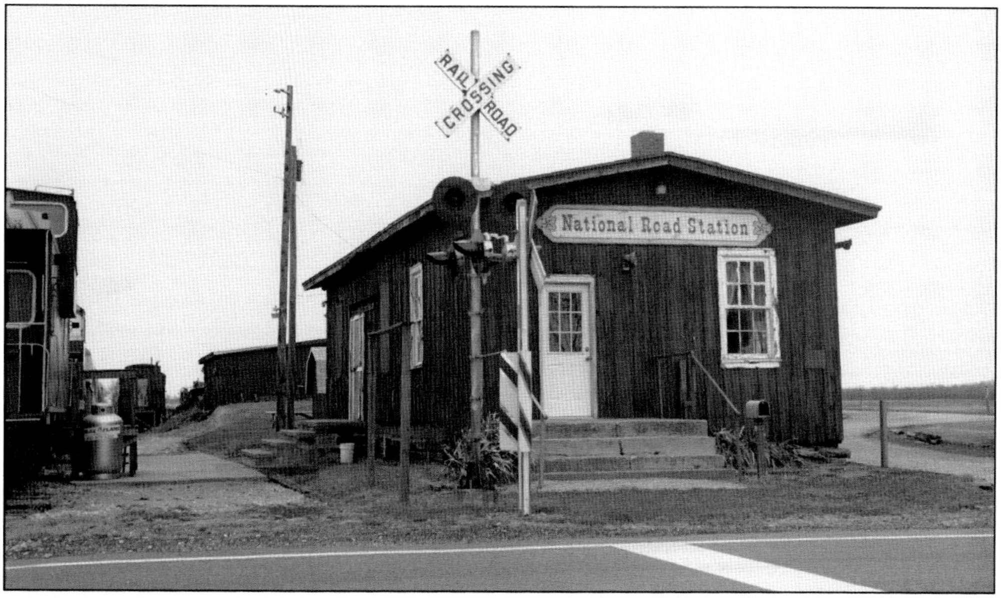


The Newark, Somerset and Straitsville Railroad (NS&S) erected this depot at the National Road crossing around 1872–1874 after completion of the line between Newark and Shawnee, seen here in 2001. This line became part of the B&O and was eventually abandoned in 1971. It served as a ticket office on the Buckeye Central Scenic Railroad until the line was forced to disband in 2007. (Photograph by the author.)

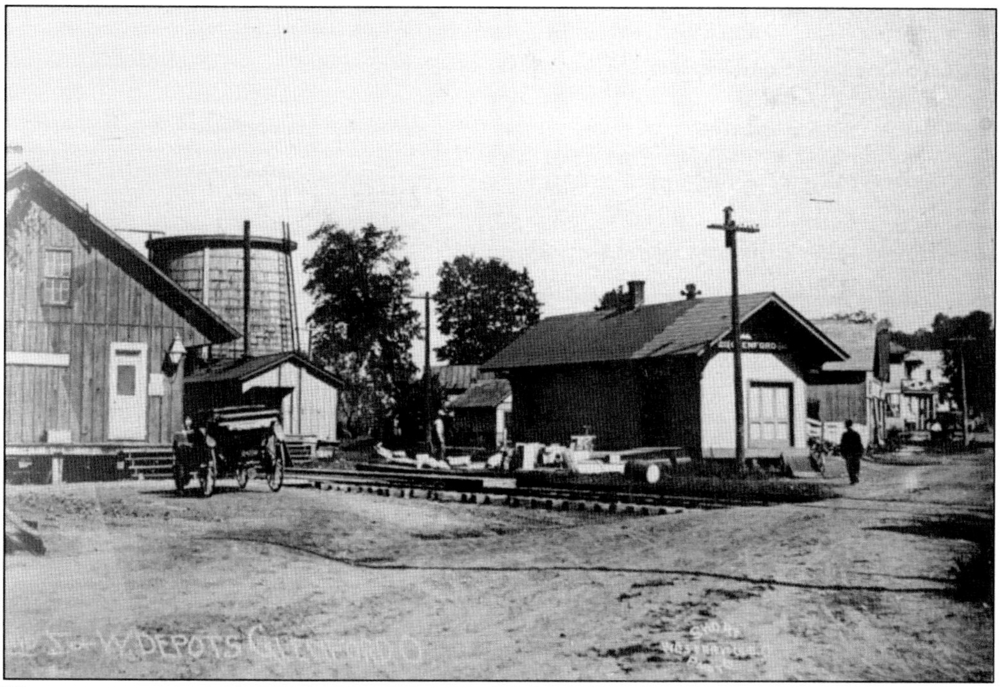

The next station south on the NS&S was Avondale, later Bruno. The Avondale Hotel sold tickets. Above is a view of the NS&S depot at Glenford, where the NS&S was adjacent to the Zanesville and Western Railroad (Z&W). The Z&W depot is to the right. All are long gone. (Author's collection.)

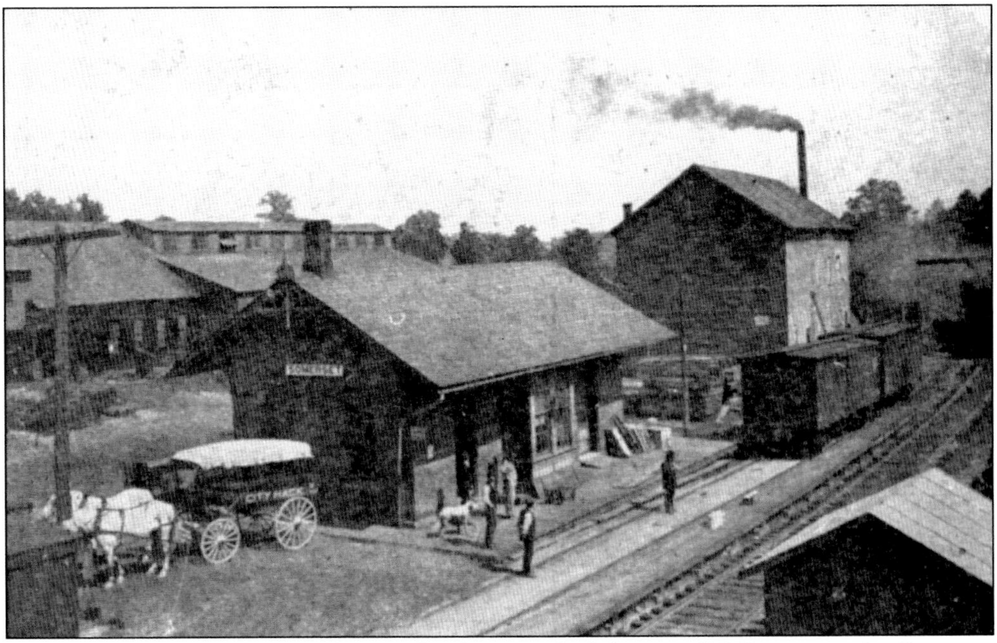


The City Hack's horses patiently wait for the arrival of the next B&O train at the Somerset depot around 1910. The combination depot was removed many years ago. The B&O depot at Junction City appears on pages 73 and 94. (Author's collection.)

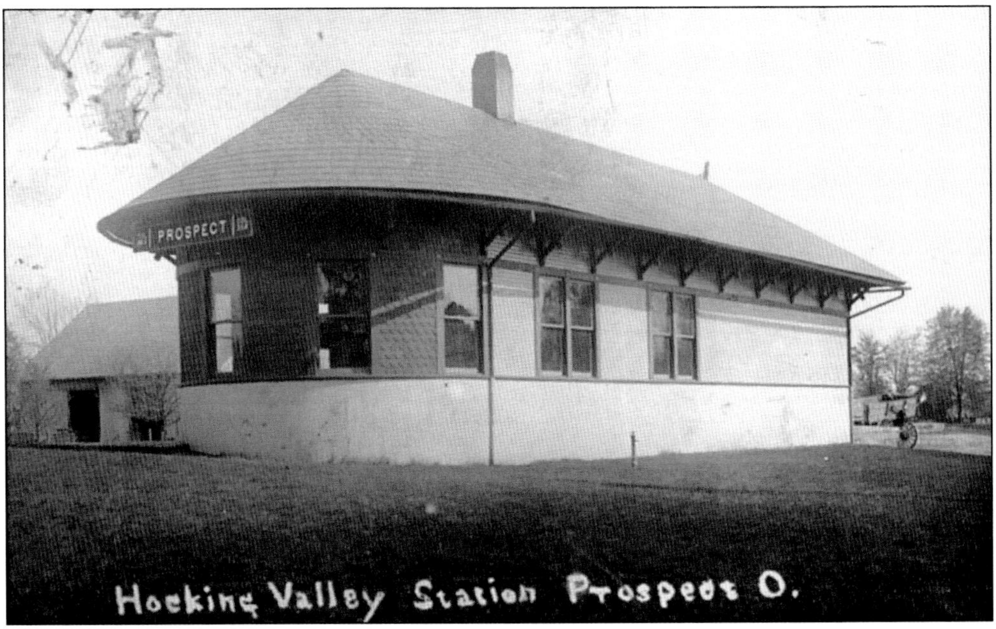


The Columbus and Toledo Railroad erected a standard design combination depot at Prospect in 1876. This depot continued to serve the Columbus, Hocking Valley and Toledo Railroad until the opening of this standard design Hocking Valley Railway combination depot across the tracks from the original depot in 1901. It is shown here in about 1907. (David P. Oroszi collection.)

# *Two*

# Chesapeake and Ohio Lines

The mineral resources of the Hocking River valley and southeastern hills were tapped by the Cincinnati and Muskingum Valley Railroad; NS&S; Scioto and Hocking Valley; and Toledo and Ohio Central Railroad, but perhaps no line was more associated with the region than the Hocking Valley Railway. The beginning of this coal hauler extends to the incorporation of the Mineral Railroad in 1864, a line intended to connect Athens with Columbus. Before any track was spiked down, the line underwent a name change, becoming the Columbus and Hocking Valley Railroad (C&HV) in 1865. Construction began on the south side of Columbus in November 1867 and proceeded southeastward. Lands for depot and yard facilities were donated around what became Mound Street. The C&HV connected with the Columbus, Chicago and Indiana Central tracks to allow the use of Columbus Union Station across town. The line reached Lancaster in September 1868, Logan and Nelsonville in 1869, and finally Athens in 1870. After a number of attempts to connect Gallipolis with the C&HV at Logan the line was finally opened in 1881. While the troublesome Ohio River route, lastly known as the Ohio and West Virginia Railway, was under construction, the Columbus and Toledo Railroad (C&T) was incorporated and construction began on this link between Walbridge, near Toledo, and the capital city in 1875. The C&T line opened between Columbus and Marion in November 1876; two months later the entire line was open. August 1881 brought the merger of the C&HV, C&T, and Ohio and West Virginia lines into the Columbus, Hocking Valley and Toledo Railway (CHV&T); this in turn became the Hocking Valley Railway in 1899. The Chesapeake and Ohio Railway (C&O) gained control in 1910 and began operating it as part of their system in March. Today remaining portions of the line are part of CSX.

The earliest depots on the C&HV were simple utilitarian frame combination structures, certainly adequate for the passenger traffic of this region at that time. With the formation of the CHV&T and then the Hocking Valley Railway, new sets of depot plans were drafted and many depots were replaced with an attractive half-hipped roof design, built in town after town from the Ohio River to Walbridge.

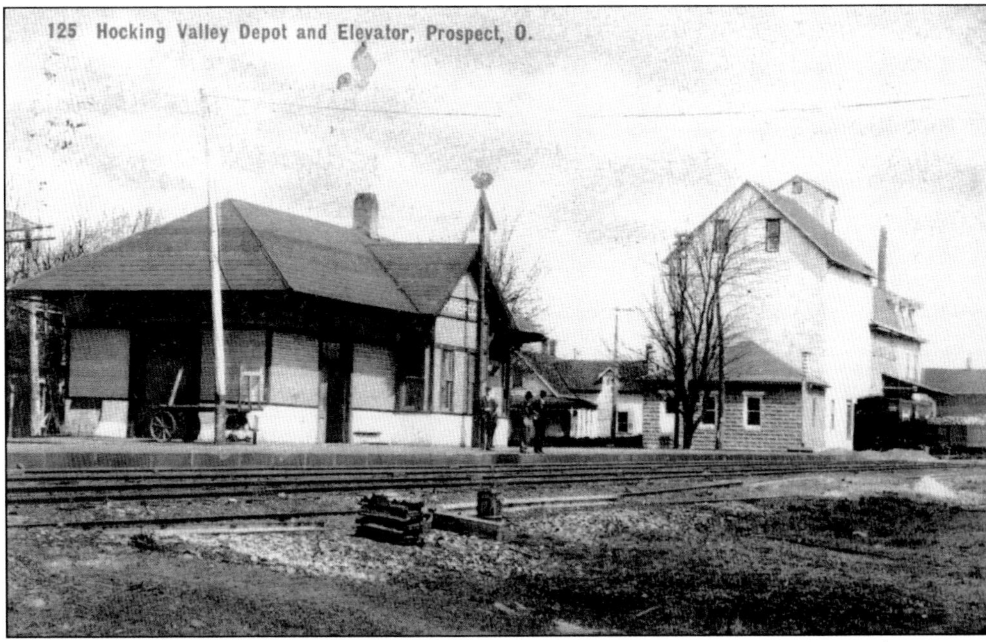


Prospect was one of two depots built by the Hocking Valley Railway that featured a waiting room with a rounded end. A nearly identical depot was at Sugar Grove, south of Lancaster. The last local passenger service ended in January 1952. The last C&O passenger train, the *Sportsman* was May 1, 1971. Prospect's depot and grounds were well maintained by the last agent up until its closing March 10, 1975. The depot has since been moved several blocks and has been home to two restaurants with railroad decor. (Above, author's collection; below, photograph by Charles Garvin.)

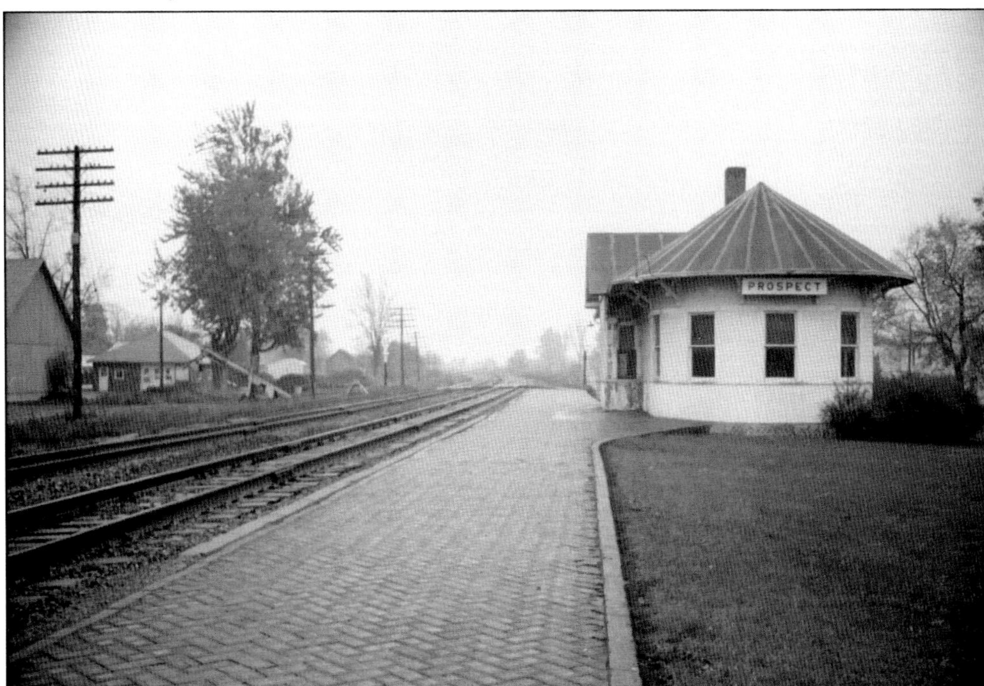

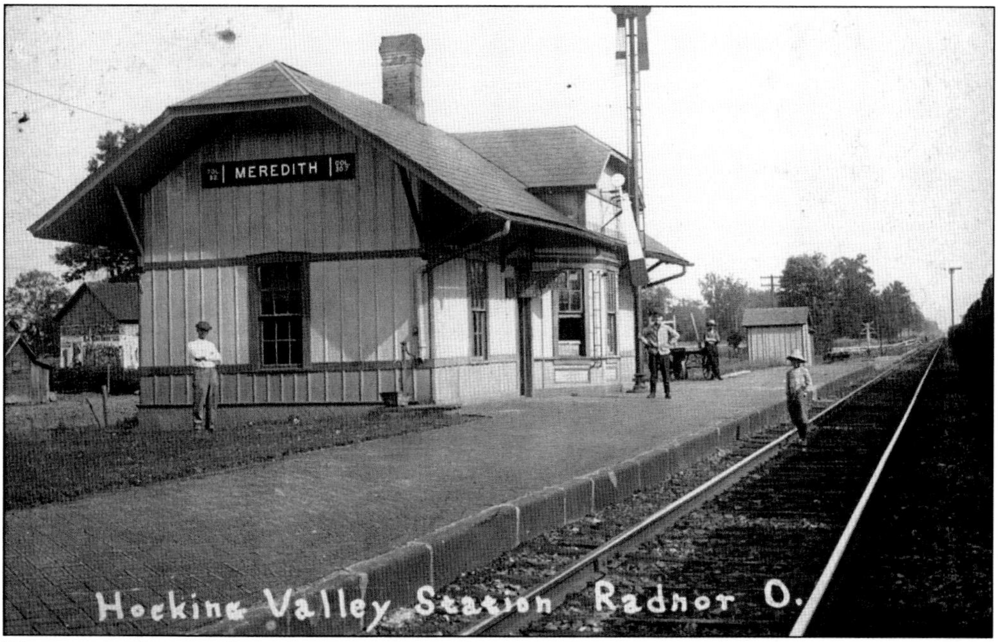


These *c.* 1907 views show the CHV&T combination depot at Meredith, just east of the village of Radnor. The depot's building date is thought to be around 1890. This hipped-roof design was repeated many times along the Hocking Valley; individual depots varied in length, floor plan, and door and window placement. The Meredith building was closed in 1955 and retired by the C&O in December 1956. (Author's collection.)

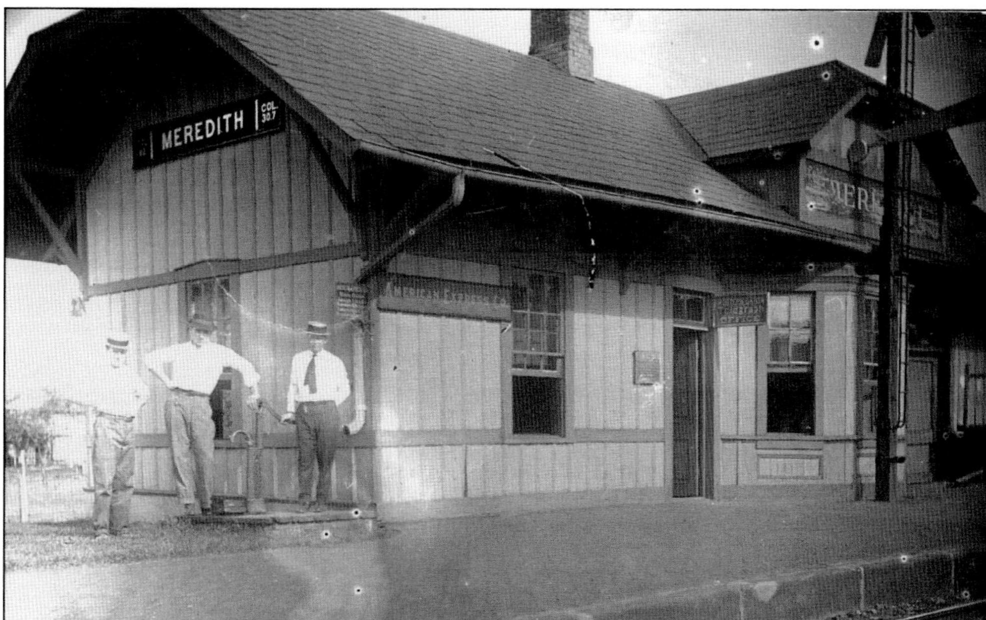

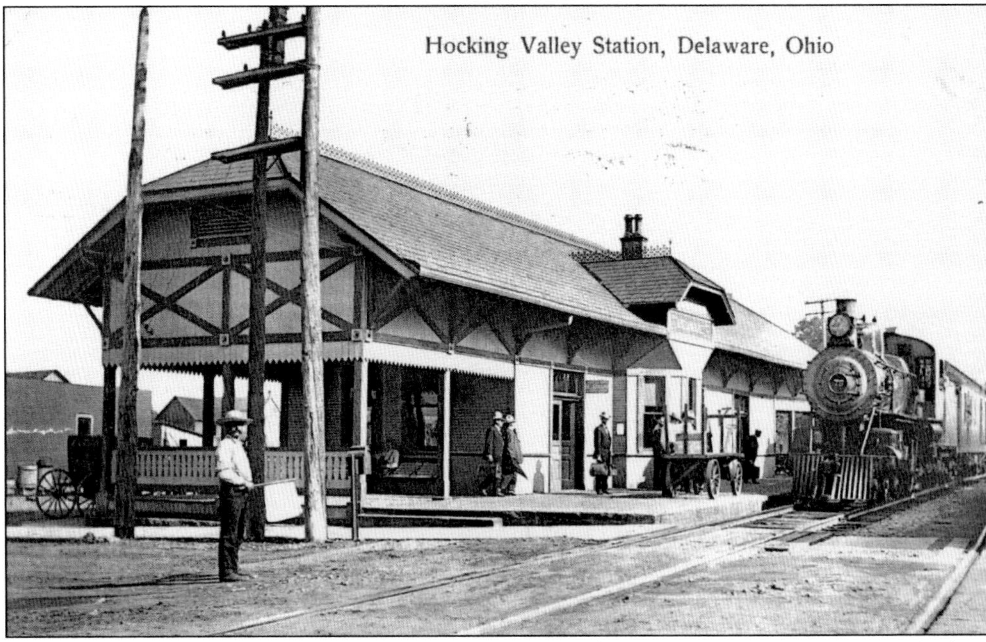


The C&T built both passenger and freight depots in Delaware in 1876. In 1887 or 1890, these were replaced by depots of CHV&T design. A feature in common with a number of other CHV&T depots was the covered outside waiting area with the ornamental scalloping seen in the above *c.* 1910 view. Note the crossing watchman on West William Street. During its heyday, this depot served around 12 passenger trains daily. South of here was WA tower, which guarded the crossing with the Big Four until 1953. Nearby was a frame freight house. The passenger depot, shown below in 1965, was closed in the summer of 1970 and demolished in late October 1987. The freight house stood until 1994. (Above, David P. Oroszi collection; below, photograph by Charles Garvin.)

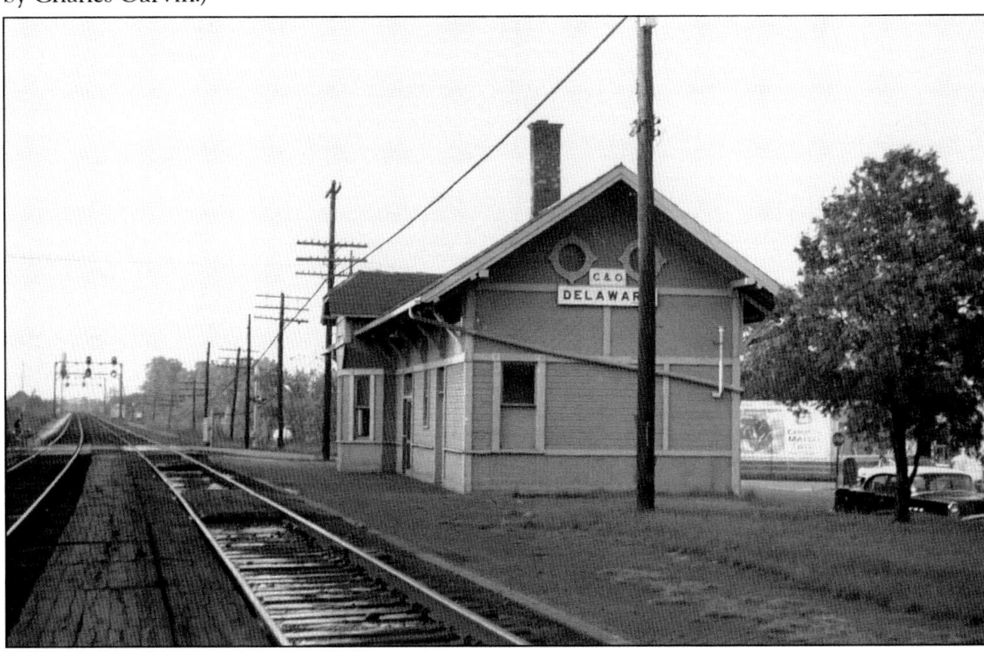

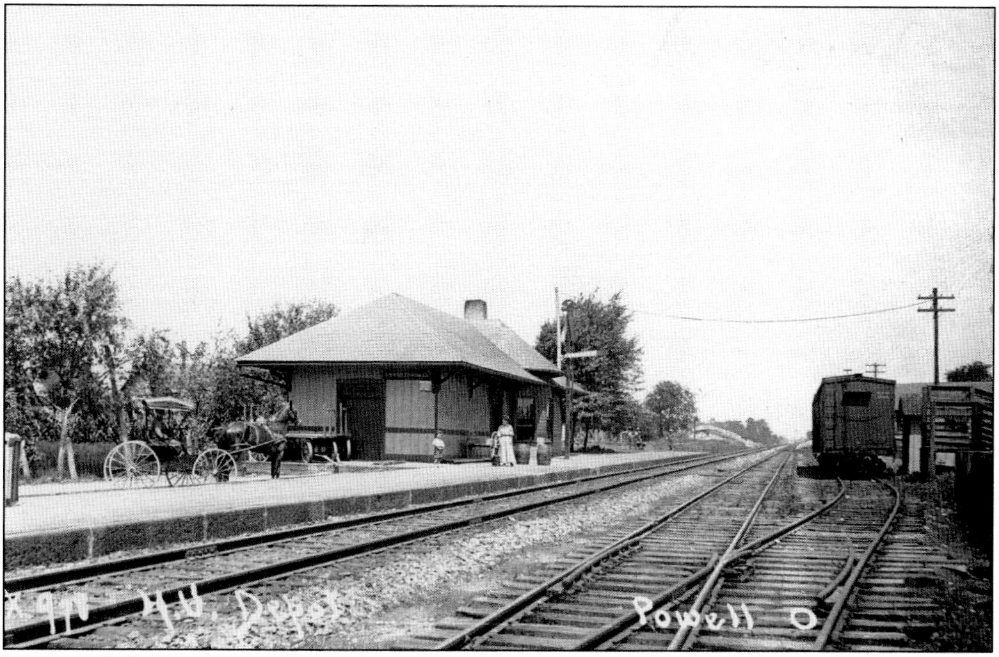


Between Delaware and Powell, the CHV&T had an 1895 depot at Hyatts and a telegraph office two miles north of Powell. Hyatts depot was retired in 1945. Powell's second depot, shown in the *c.* 1907 views above and below, was erected by the CHV&T in 1893, replacing an 1876 C&T depot. This design was apparently unique to the line; no other CHV&T depot had both a rounded operator's bay window and a rounded waiting room. Powell was demoted to a non-agency in 1952. It was retired by the C&O in October 1961. (Author's collection.)

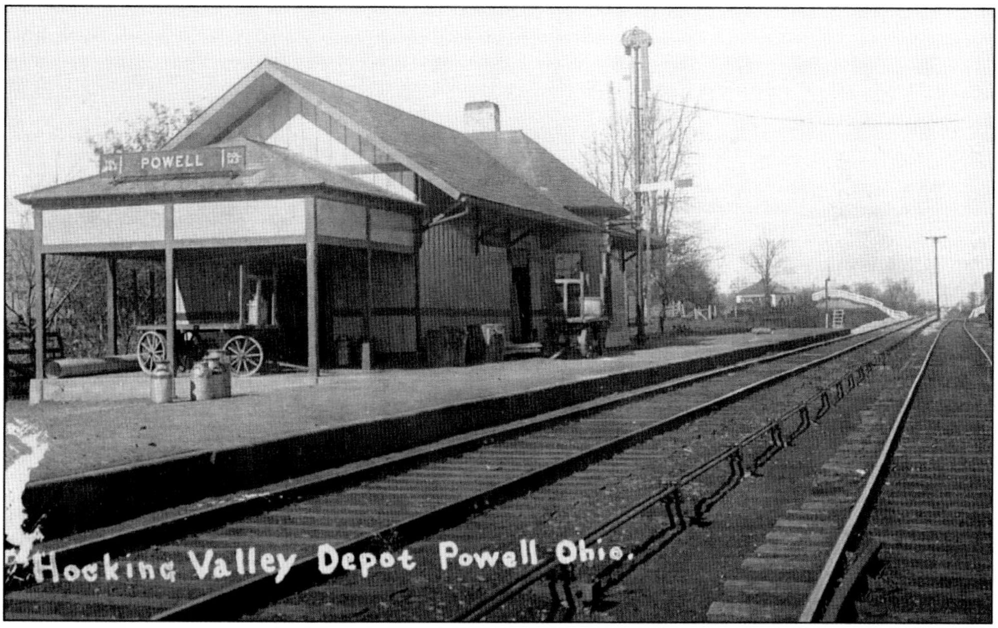

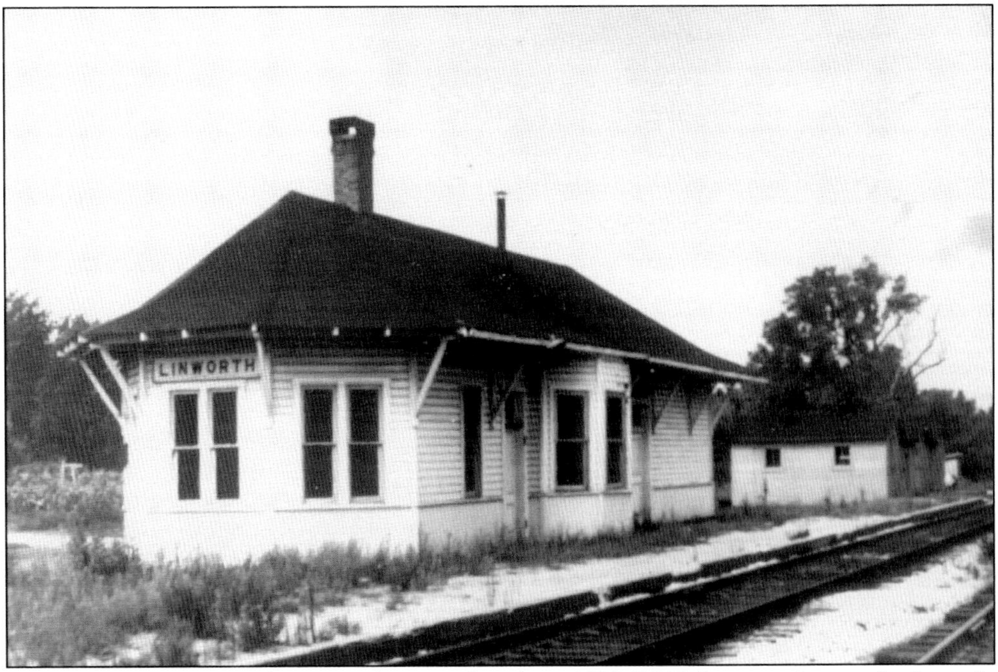


This CHV&T 1895 combination depot replaced an 1876 C&T depot at Linworth, formerly Elmwood. The depot sat just north of Ohio 161. The last passenger train to stop was in 1952. The depot closed in 1961 and was torn down in January 1965. (Author's collection.)

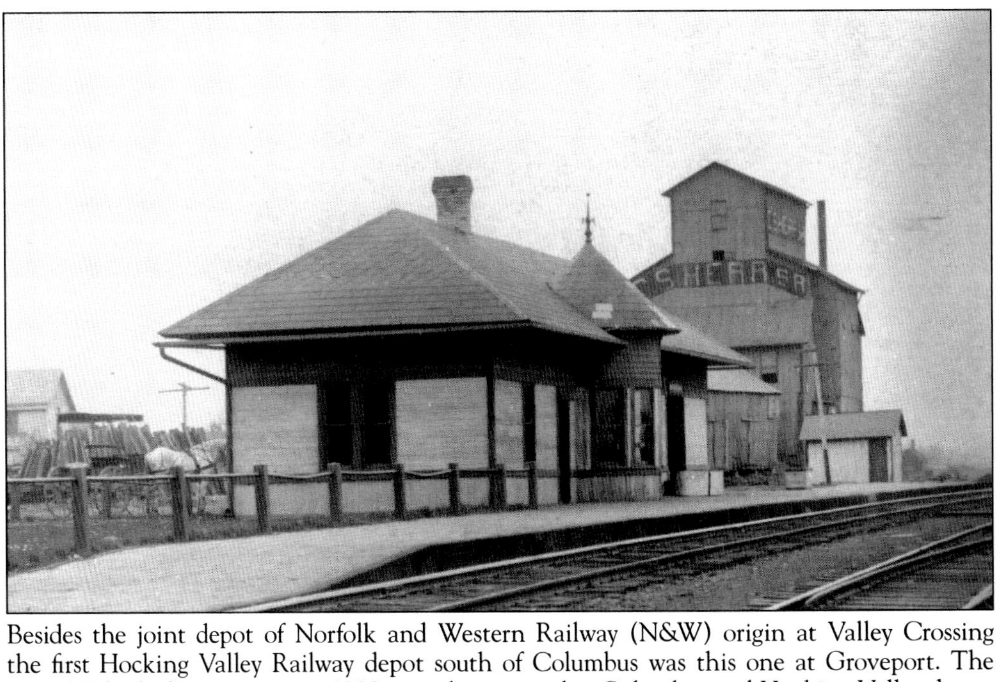

Besides the joint depot of Norfolk and Western Railway (N&W) origin at Valley Crossing the first Hocking Valley Railway depot south of Columbus was this one at Groveport. The CHV&T built this structure in 1898 to replace an earlier Columbus and Hocking Valley depot. The C&HV reached Groveport in June 1868. The depot was closed by the C&O in 1964. (Author's collection.)

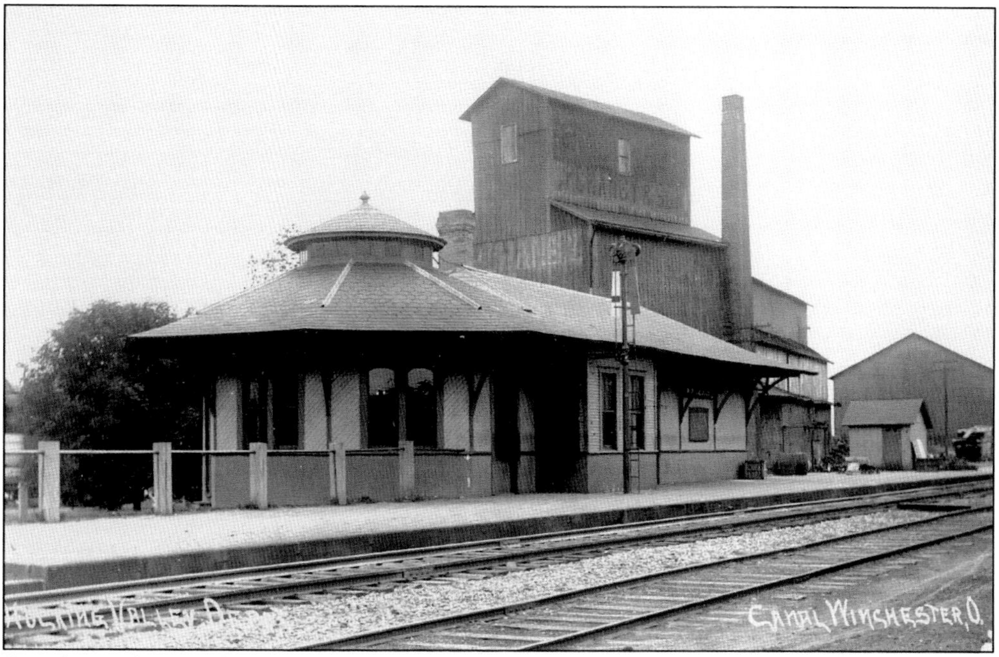


Canal Winchester's first C&HV depot was destroyed by fire October 11, 1894. The CHV&T wasted no time in replacing the depot, opening the combination depot seen above and below by early 1895. These *c.* 1907 views show both the passenger and freight ends of this unique depot. The angled waiting room and round cupola are distinctive. Schoolboys found the depot platform irresistible. Many locals rode the train into nearby Columbus for shopping, jobs, and entertainment. The agency closed in late 1971, but this depot survived to undergo restoration. It now houses the local historical society. (Author's collection.)

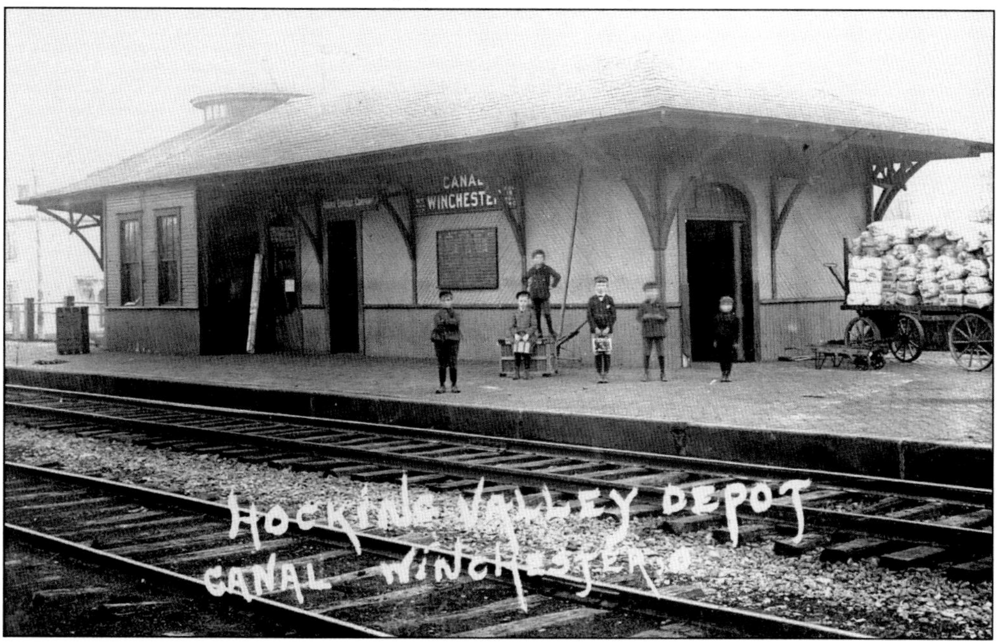

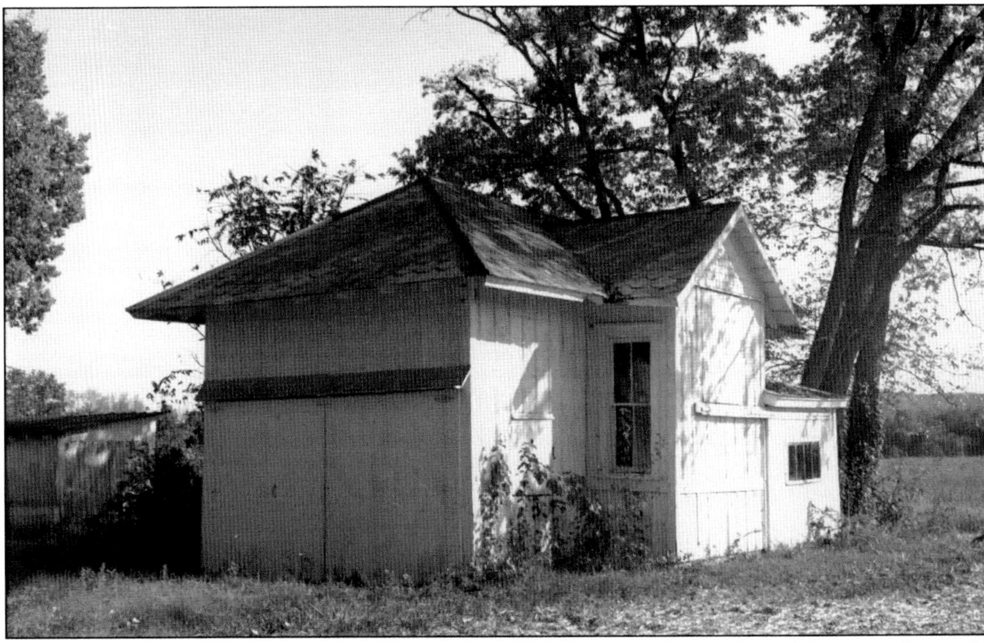

The first depot of this early canal town was built by the C&HV. A replacement depot for Lockville came in 1905 when the Hocking Valley Railway erected this small structure, seen in 2000. The depot was closed in December 1938 and was shortly moved nearby by a local farmer. The building remains in storage use. (Photograph by the author.)

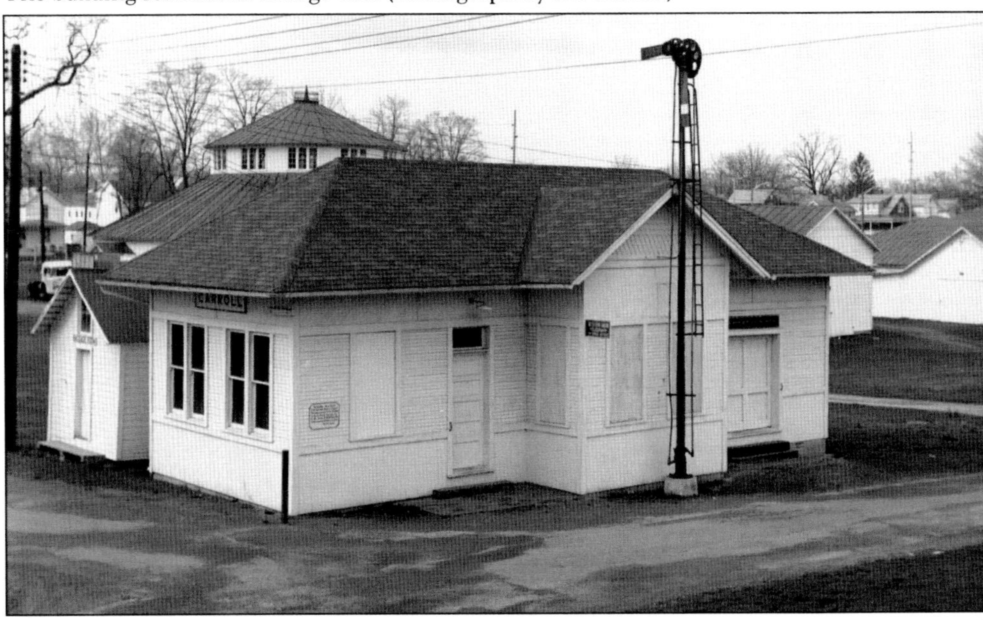


This 1974 photograph also shows a second-generation depot located at the next station south of Lockville. Carroll's first depot, built in 1871, burned in 1905. This depot was apparently a Hocking Valley Railway modification of the remains of the original depot. The depot was closed as an agency in 1958, sold in 1963, and moved from the trackside in 1966. It ended up at the Fairfield County fairgrounds in Lancaster, one of the earlier cases of depot preservation in the state. (Photograph by the author.)

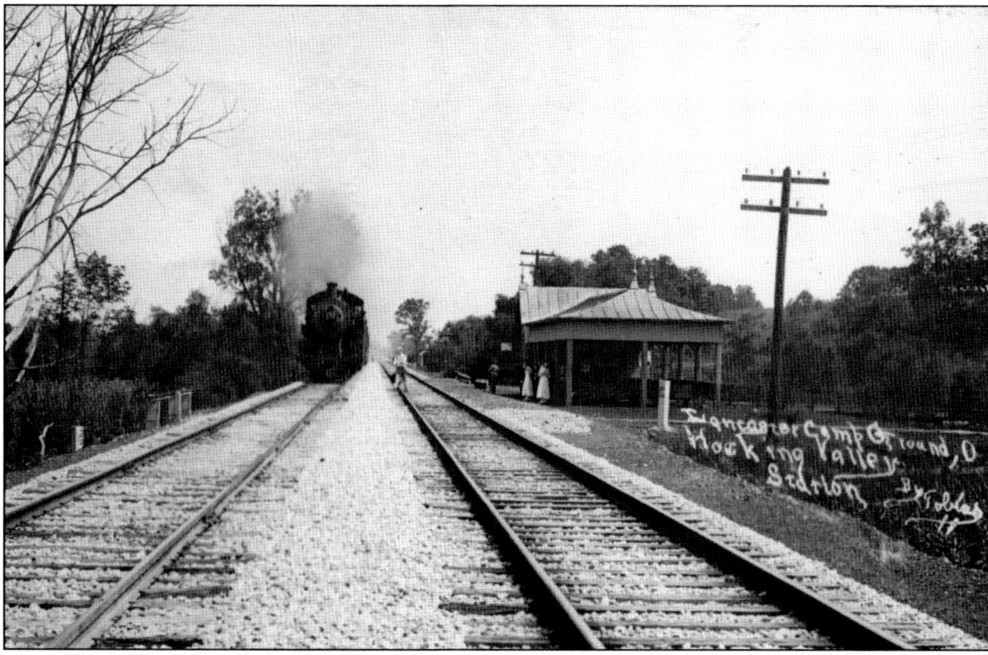


This is a *c.* 1910 view of the small CHV&T depot at Lancaster Camp Grounds, north of Hookers. This began as Buckeye Park, a place for Gay Nineties summertime outings. The railroad eliminated this as a stop in 1924, and the depot quickly disappeared. Further south was a depot at Hookers, an important water stop on the Hocking Valley. (Gary D. Rolih collection.)

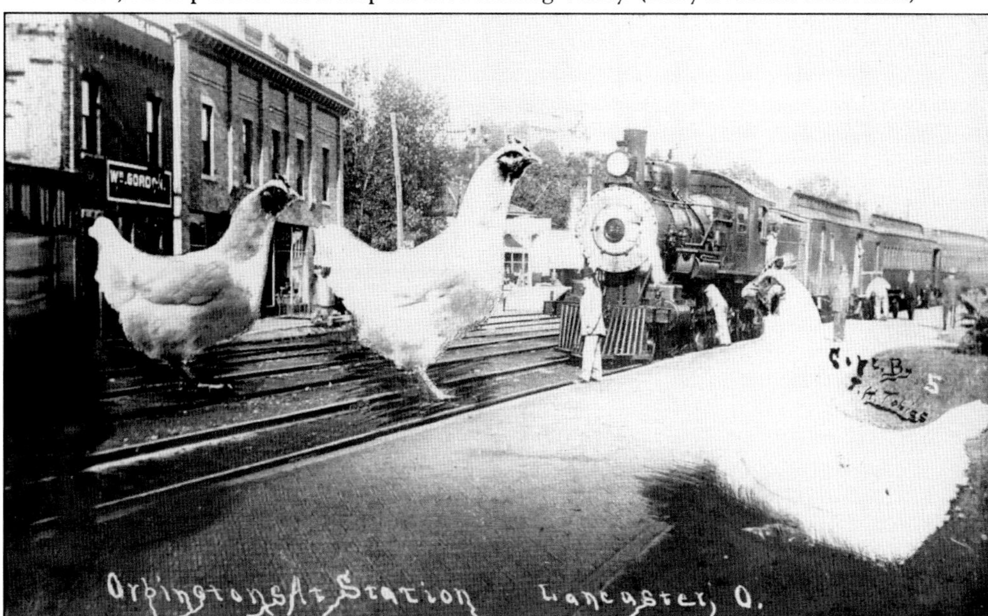


The C&HV opened frame passenger and freight depots at Lancaster in January 1869. The C&HV was the second line to enter town and had separate facilities from the Cincinnati, Wilmington and Zanesville Railroad, which had been there since 1854. When it came time to upgrade, the two railroads agreed on a union station. Farming remained a major activity in Fairfield County as evidenced by this spoof on the depot platform. (Author's collection.)

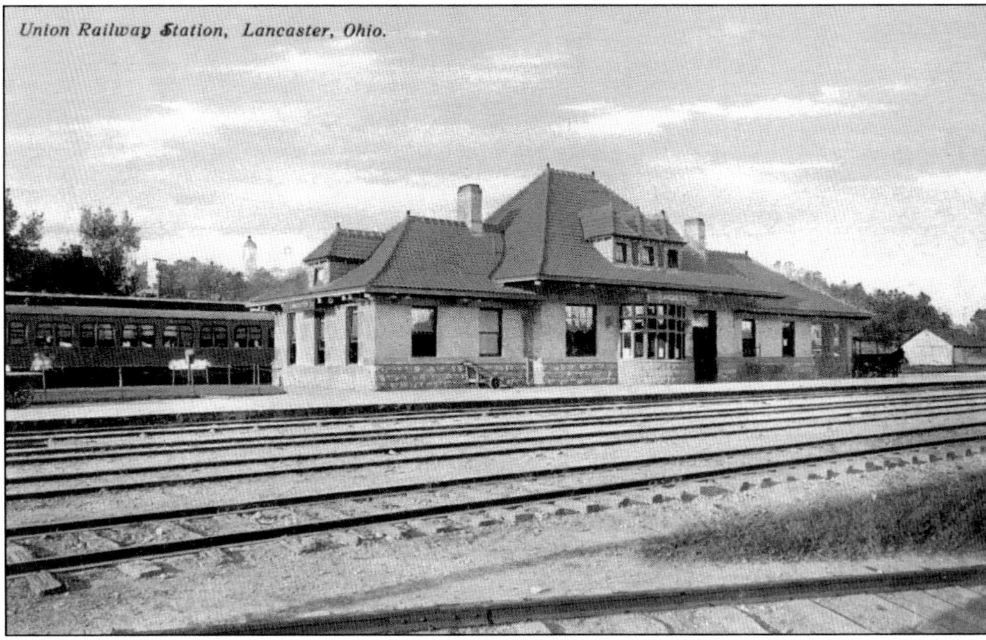


Lancaster Union Station opened in 1900. The above c. 1912 view shows the PRR side of the building; the Hocking Valley Railway trains used the tracks on the far side. The PRR discontinued its passenger service to Lancaster May 20, 1933, but the C&O continued to use it until December 31, 1949. The C&O moved its offices to the freight station, below, seen in 1971. The union station met the wreckers in 1960. The freight station was closed in June 1983. (Above, author's collection; below, photograph by the author.)

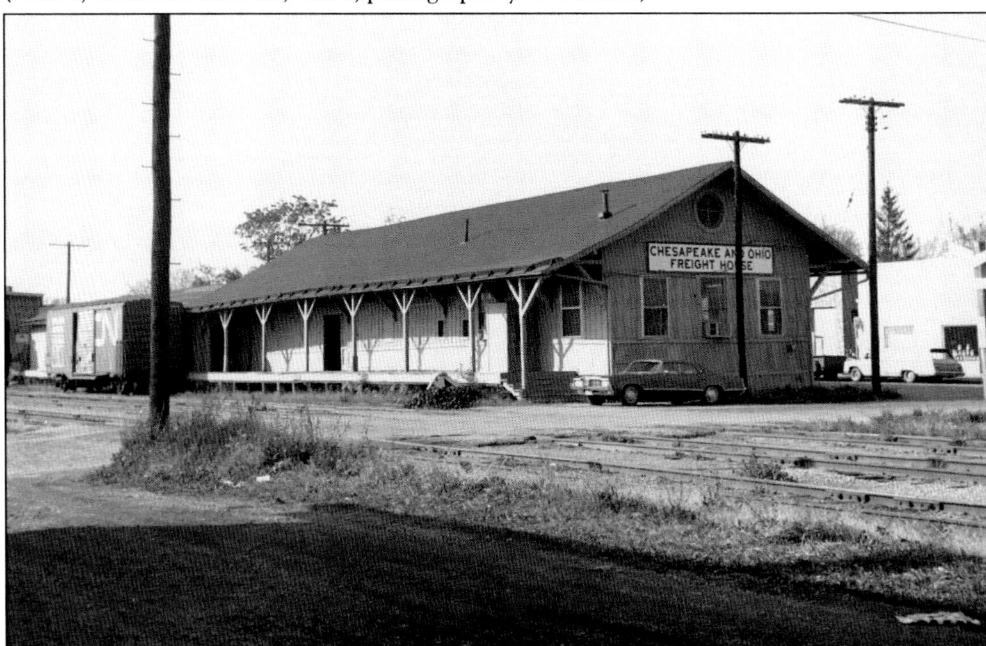

# *Three*

# New York Central Lines

In 1836, the Cleveland, Columbus and Cincinnati Railroad (CC&C) incorporated; but it was 1851 before the line opened between Cleveland and Columbus by the way of Shelby, Galion, and Delaware. The Bellefontaine and Indiana Railroad began construction on a line from Galion to Union City to connect with an Indiana line. The CC&C gained a route to Springfield when the former Springfield, Mount Vernon and Pittsburgh Railway (chartered in 1852) failed and the CC&C received the portion of this route built in 1862 from Delaware to Springfield by the way of Marysville. In 1868, the CC&C joined with the Bellefontaine and Indiana Railroad (Galion to Indianapolis) to form the Cleveland, Columbus, Cincinnati and Indianapolis Railroad. In 1889, this became the Cleveland, Cincinnati, Chicago and St. Louis Railway (CCC&StL), known as the Big Four.

The Springfield and London Railroad was completed between London and Springfield by 1853. After a number of name changes it became the Columbus, Springfield and Cincinnati Railroad in 1869. The gap between London and Columbus was filled in late 1871. In 1889, this line also became part of the CCC&StL. The Big Four became part of the vast New York Central System in 1930.

The Big Four engineering offices produced a series of standard depot plans and many of the predecessor line depots were replaced in the 1890s. Big Four interlocking and telegraph towers were distinctive. The ground level of the tower was often a cast-iron open framework, which supported a rectangular frame tower cabin. These were erected at all junctions and at regular intervals along the lines.

The Ohio Central Railroad, which became the Toledo and Ohio Central Railroad (T&OC) in 1885, began service between Toledo and Corning in 1882. The T&OC then took over the Toledo, Columbus and Cincinnati Railroad and finished its line from Kenton to Columbus, where it connected with the former Ohio Central's Columbus branch, in 1893. The old southern portion of the Columbus, Sandusky and Hocking Railroad also fell under T&OC control as the Z&W in 1902. The T&OC was molded into the NYC between 1910 and 1938. Today Norfolk Southern operates remaining T&OC tracks south of Columbus, while CSX operates what is left north of Columbus.

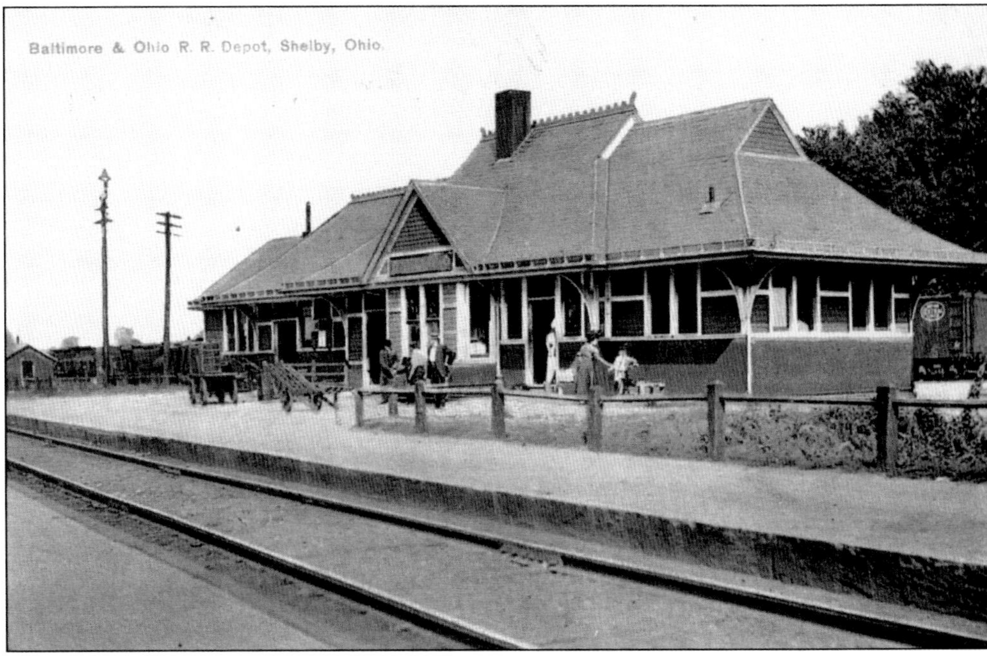


About 55 years separates these two photographs of the joint Big Four–B&O depot at Shelby Junction just north of downtown Shelby. Although the above c. 1910 view is labeled the B&O station, it is a standard plan Big Four structure. This junction was one of the earliest crossings of railroads, around 1851, west of the Allegheny Mountains. The original union depot was a sprawling frame building with rooms and dining hall. It was destroyed by fire in the 1880s and eventually replaced by this depot, seen in 1966. (Above, author's collection; below, photograph by Charles Garvin.)

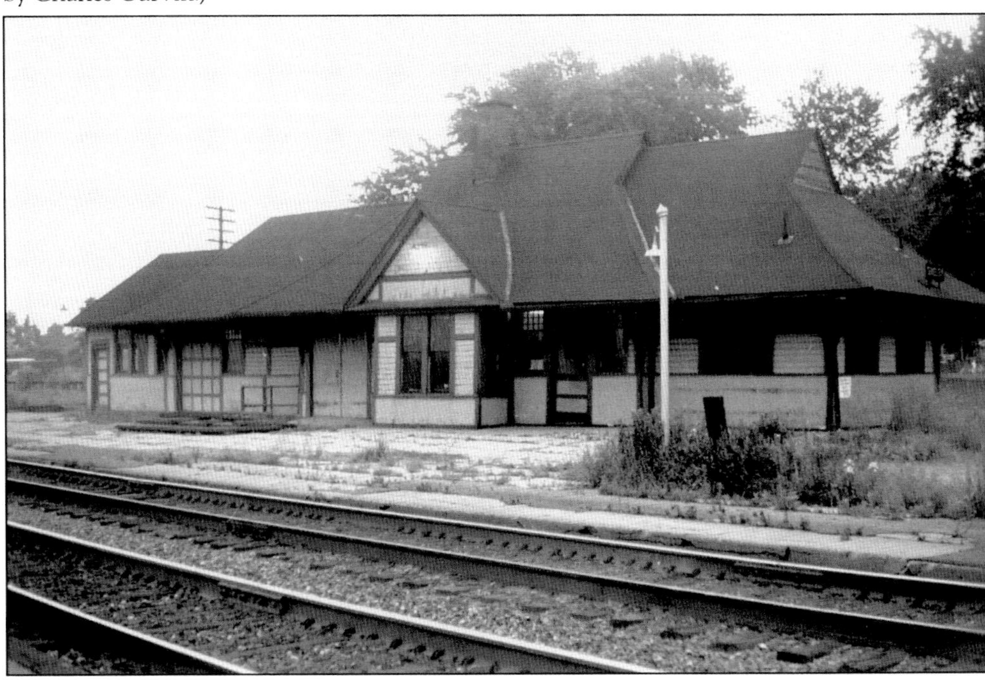

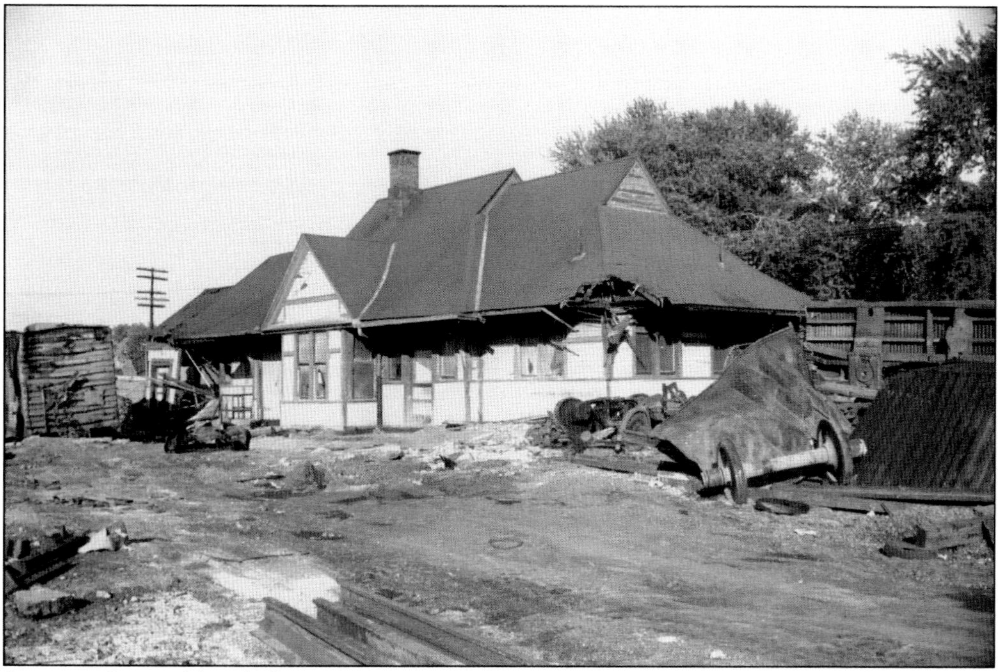

Junction depots, like Shelby Junction, were occasionally the scene of derailments. The above photograph from 1969 shows the freight train accident of the fall of 1969, which sent freight cars into the building and led to the eventual removal of the building. Only the Shelby Junction interlocking tower, diagonally across the tracks from the depot, remained in the 1970s, seen here in 1969. The tower survived a scare in July 1977 when a tornado passed above the building. Shelby tower was dismantled in 1983 and the remains taken to Wakeman for future reassembly. (Photographs by Charles Garvin.)

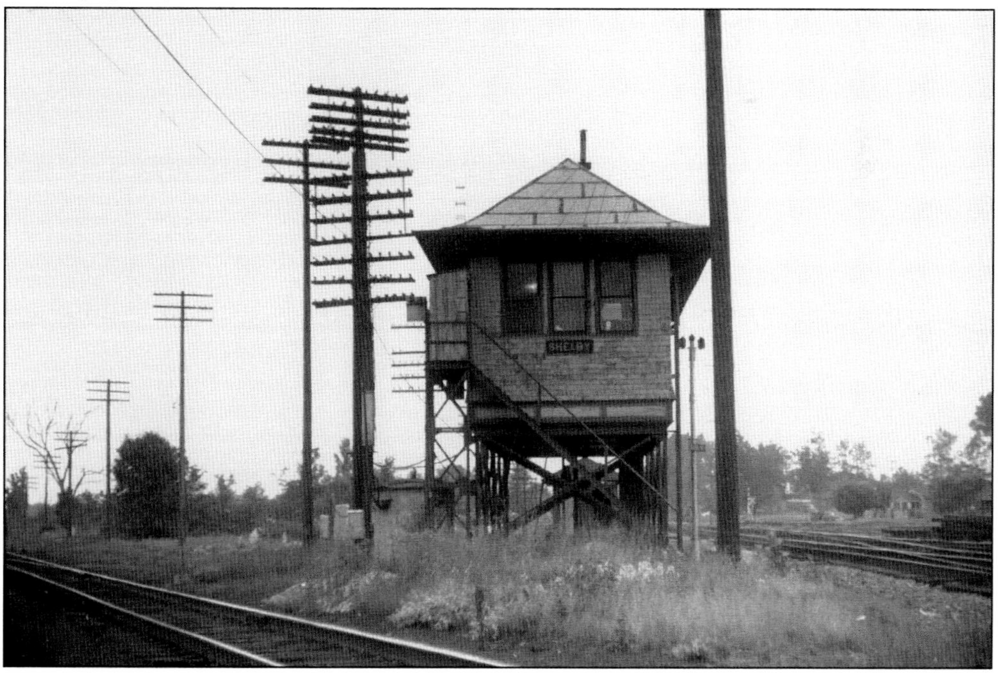

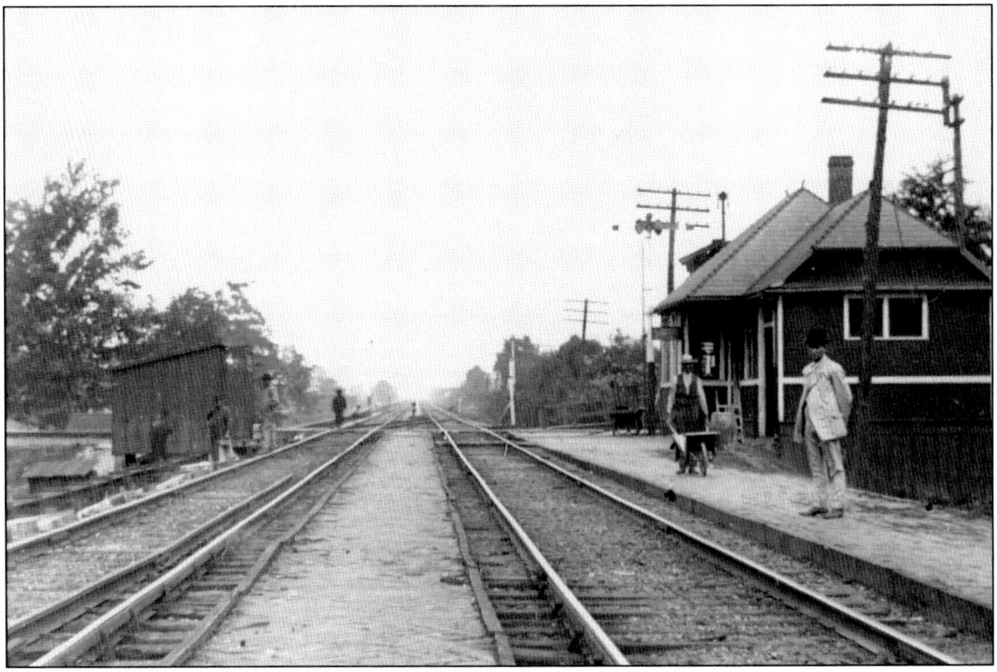

This picture is believed to be at Vernon where the Big Four crossed the PRR line to Toledo. Note the similarities in architecture between this combination depot and the Shelby building. Gandy dancers are busy at work in this *c.* 1907 postal view. The depot has been gone since the mid-1900s. (Author's collection.)

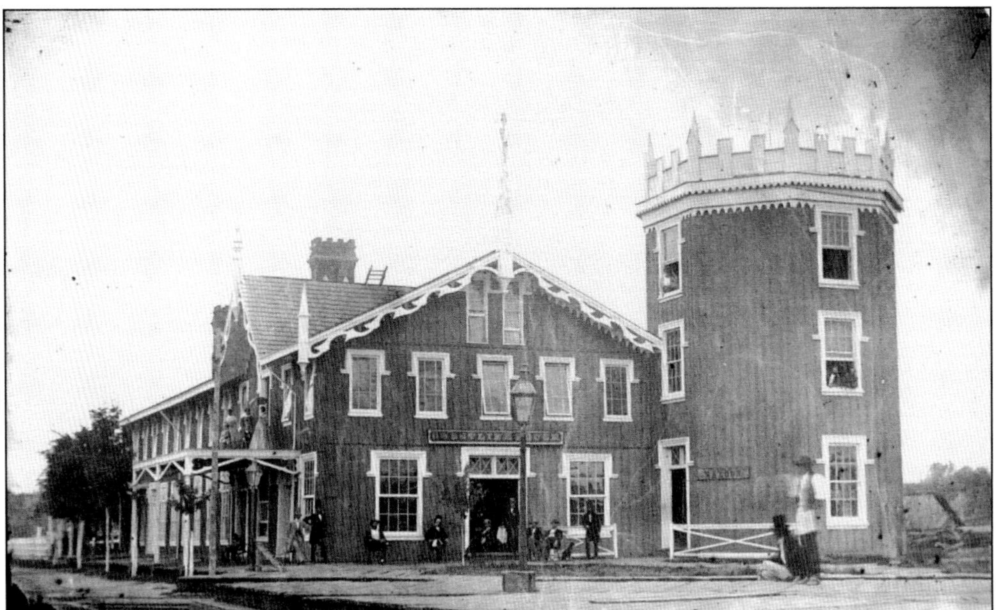

Across from the old frame 1853 union station at Crestline where the CC&C crossed the Ohio and Indiana Railroad, later the Pittsburgh, Fort Wayne and Chicago Railway, was the Crestline House—a railroad hotel and dining room. The hotel dates from the 1850s. (Author's collection.)

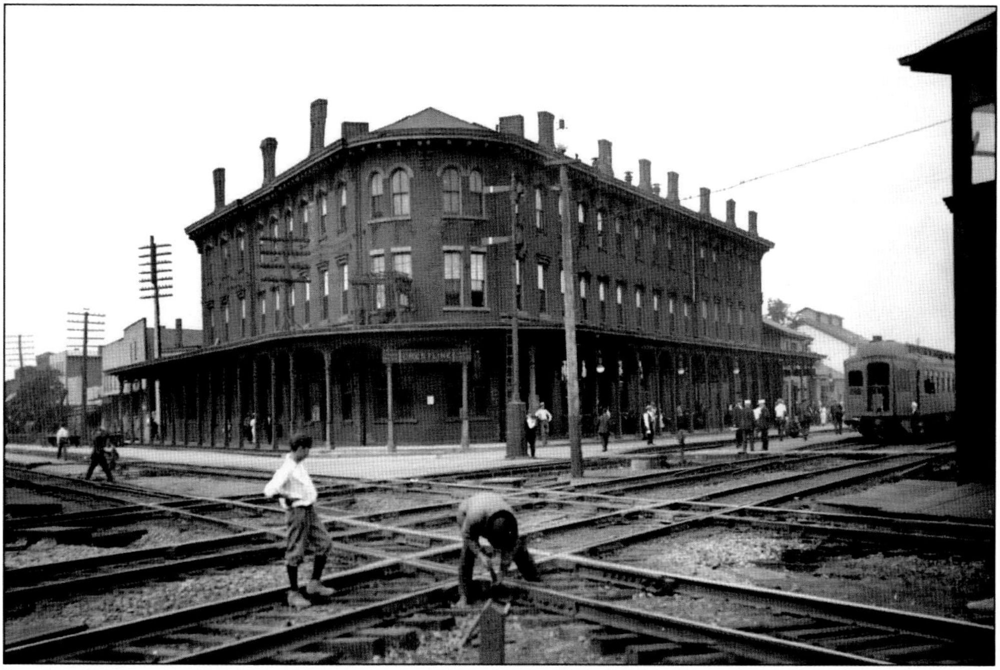

In the 1860s, the Big Four began to use this impressive PRR passenger depot at the junction in Crestline. The PRR had a huge presence in Crestline; just to the west was a major engine terminal. In the above early-1900 scene, a boy apprentice observes a track worker tightening a track plate, and members of the train crew and passengers are on the platform awaiting the departure of the next train. By the mid-1900s, the depot had been reduced to one story, as shown in the 1968 photograph below. The frame interlocking tower was also replaced with a brick one, which still remains. (Above, author's collection; below, photograph by the author.)

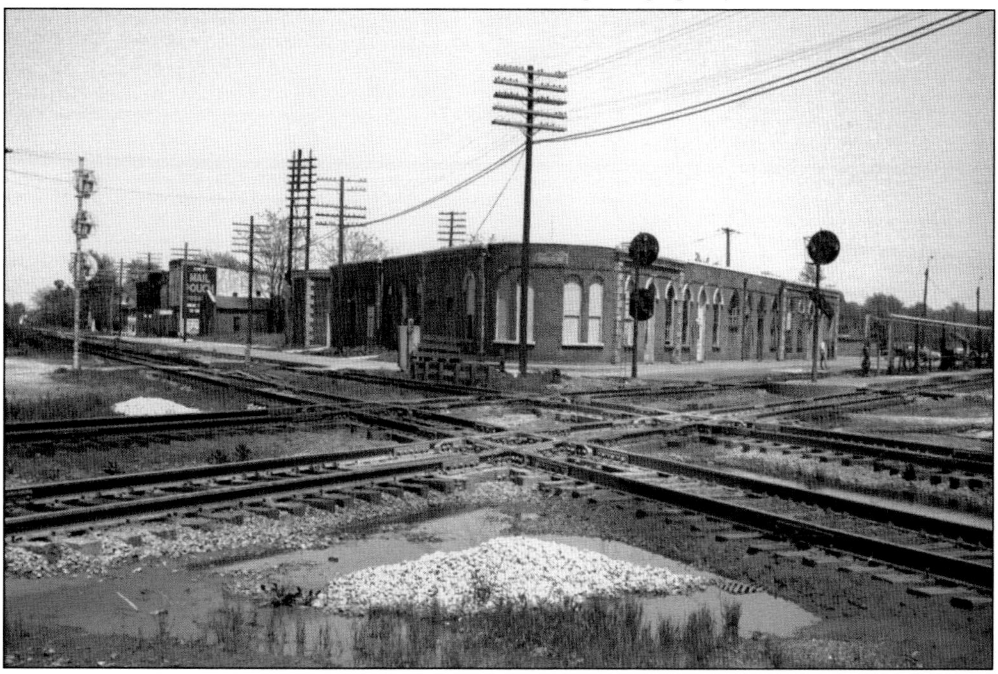

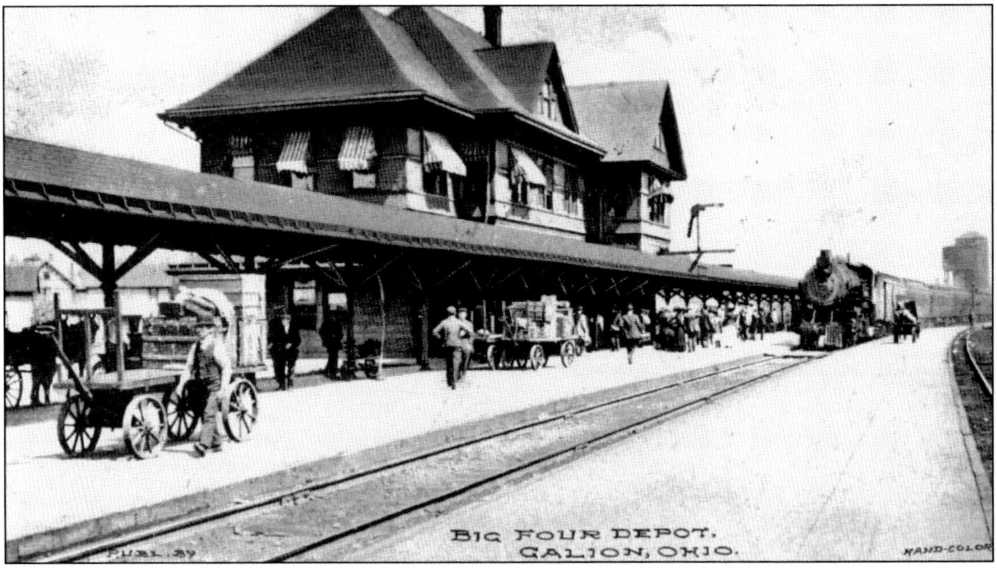


The next town, Galion, was to the Big Four what Crestline was to the PRR. The Big Four maintained an engine terminal, note the water tanks in the distance, near its impressive dimension stone and frame passenger depot, dating to 1900. The second floor housed railroad offices. Around 1909, a train is arriving from Cleveland. The image below presents a quieter scene, taken in 1973. The depot remains one of the architectural gems of the city. (Above, author's collection; below, photograph by Charles Garvin.)

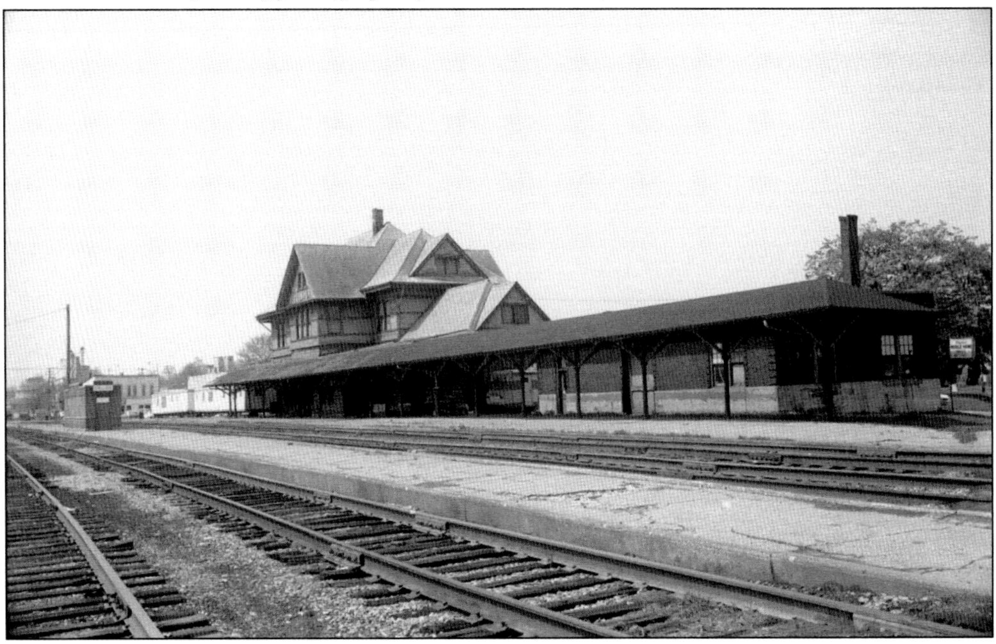

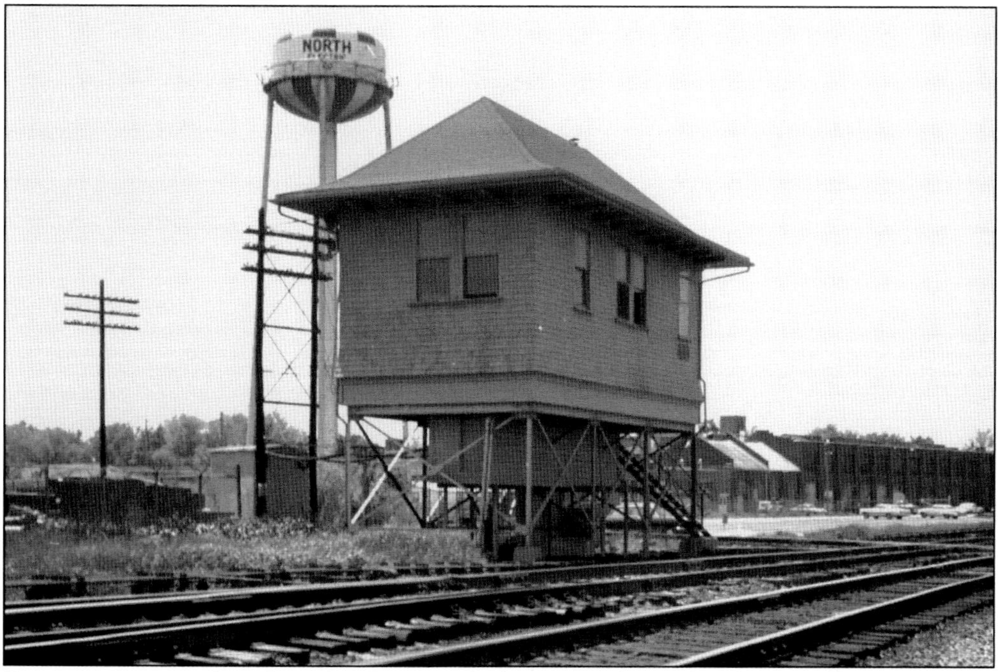


Burt tower was another classic Big Four interlocking tower located at the crossing with the Erie Railroad in Galion. The tower was still active in this 1968 image. (Photograph by the author.)

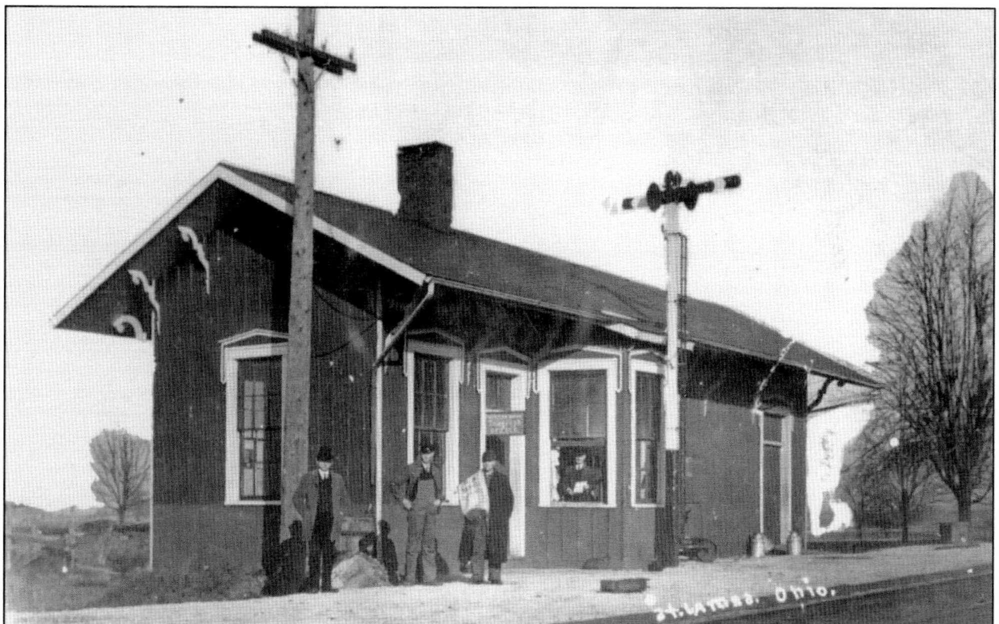

South of Galion the first station stop by locals was at St. James. The depot is typical of many built along the Big Four lines. The order board indicates there is business for the next train. The uniformed agent is in the operator's bay; one of his assistants is holding a mail bag. The depot was no longer an agency by 1949 and was eventually moved off-site. (David P. Oroszi collection.)

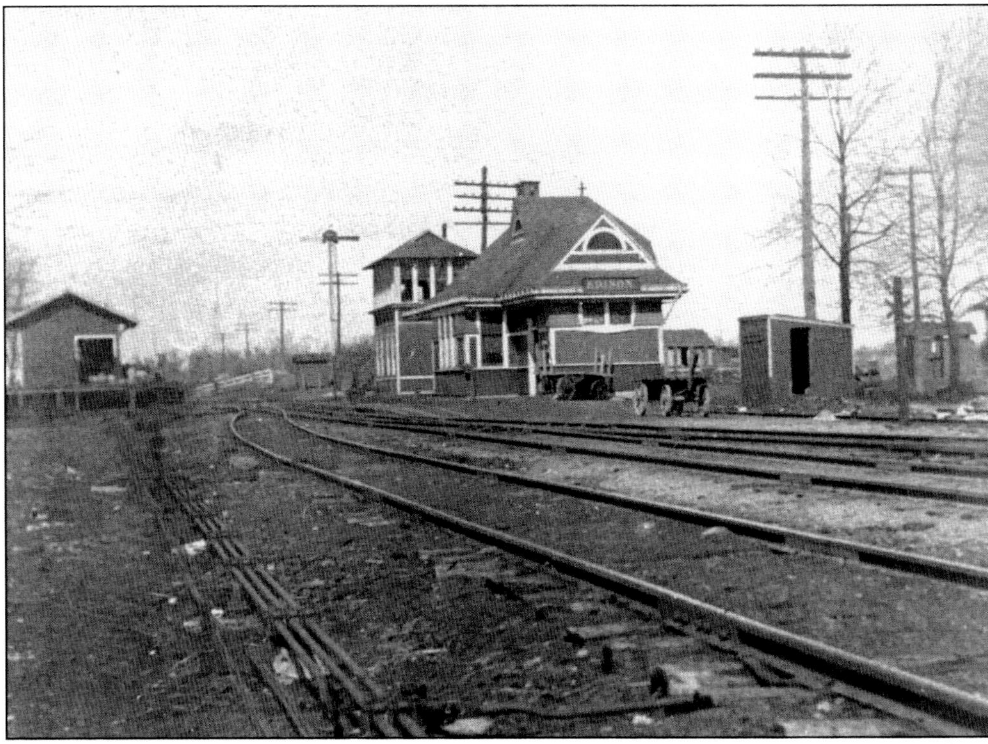

Another junction, this time with the T&OC, was at Edison, formerly Gilead Station. Above around 1908 is a classic design Big Four depot and a T&OC design interlocking tower. A freight house is seen to the left. Below is a 1919 street-side view of the Edison depot. At this point, the Mount Gilead Short Line Railroad carried passengers the short two and a half miles into Gilead, which had been bypassed by the Big Four. The depot was razed in 1966; the tower was still there in 1969, however abandoned. (Above, author's collection; below, T&OC photograph, Allen County [Ohio] Historical Society collection.)

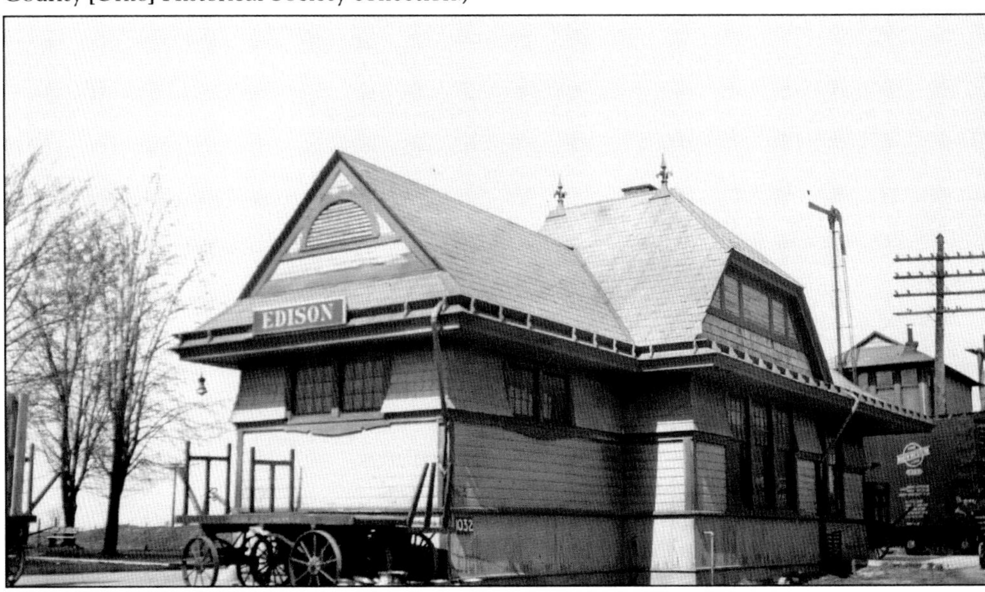

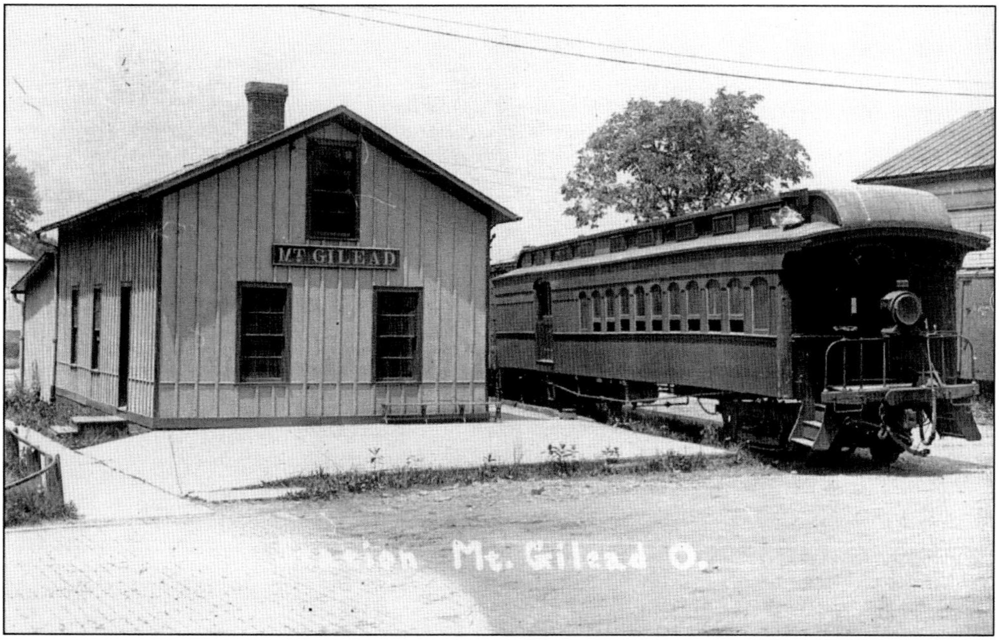


The city fathers of Mount Gilead were miffed that their town had been left off the original route of the CC&C in 1851 and organized the Mount Gilead Short Line Railroad in 1879 to build a line from downtown Mount Gilead to Gilead Station, later Edison. Above is the old frame depot around 1907 built by the Big Four, which leased the city-built line. Below is the depot, photographed in 1938, that replaced it in 1924 at the cost of $12,600. The short line ceased running its own trains in 1929 and leased its track to the NYC. The NYC closed the depot in 1959. The brick-frame depot now houses municipal offices. (Above, author's collection; below, photograph by Eldon Neff, David P. Oroszi collection.)

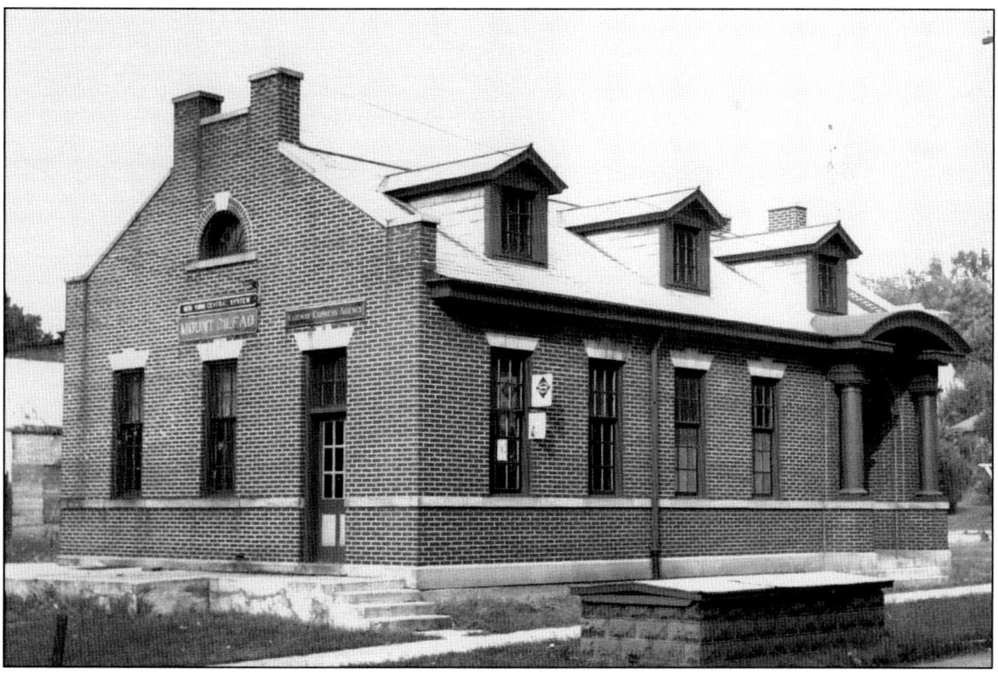

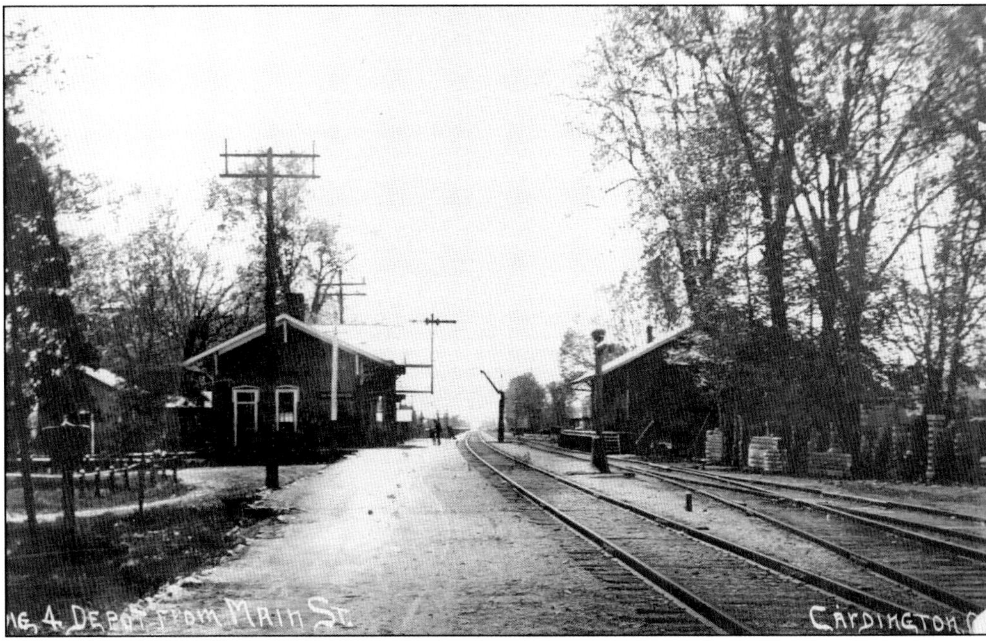


Another depot design is exhibited by the passenger depots at Cardington (above) and Ashley (below). Note that the order boards are not freestanding but instead project from the bay window. Both depots are passenger facilities; separate freight houses were nearby. Cardington was also a water stop; note the water penstocks between the tracks. A crowd awaits the arriving train at Ashley around 1910. Ashley closed in 1955; followed by Cardington a few years later. Only the freight houses existed by the 1960s. (Author's collection.)

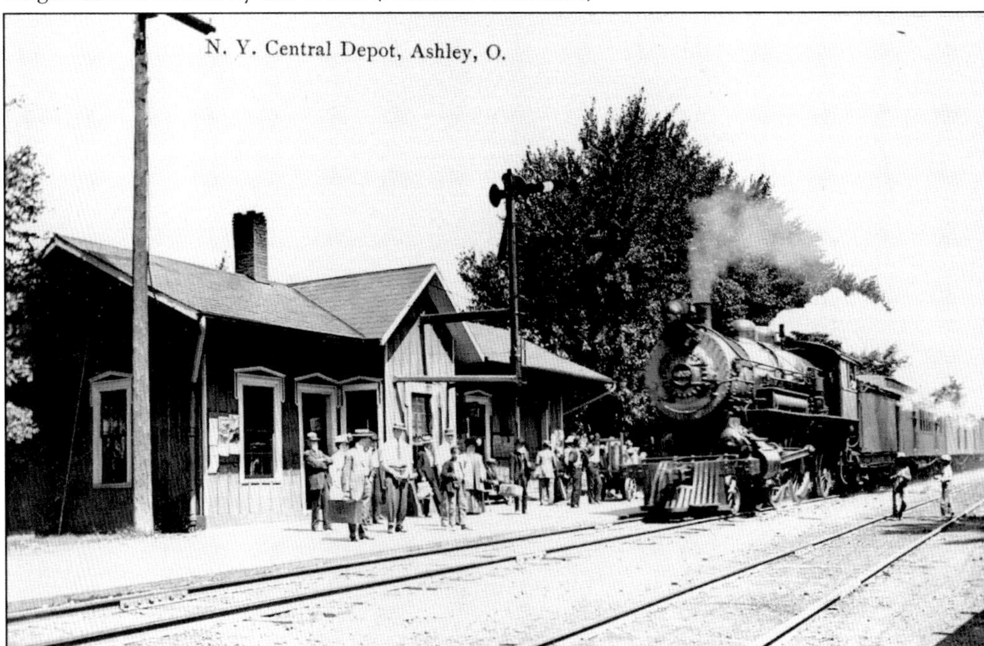

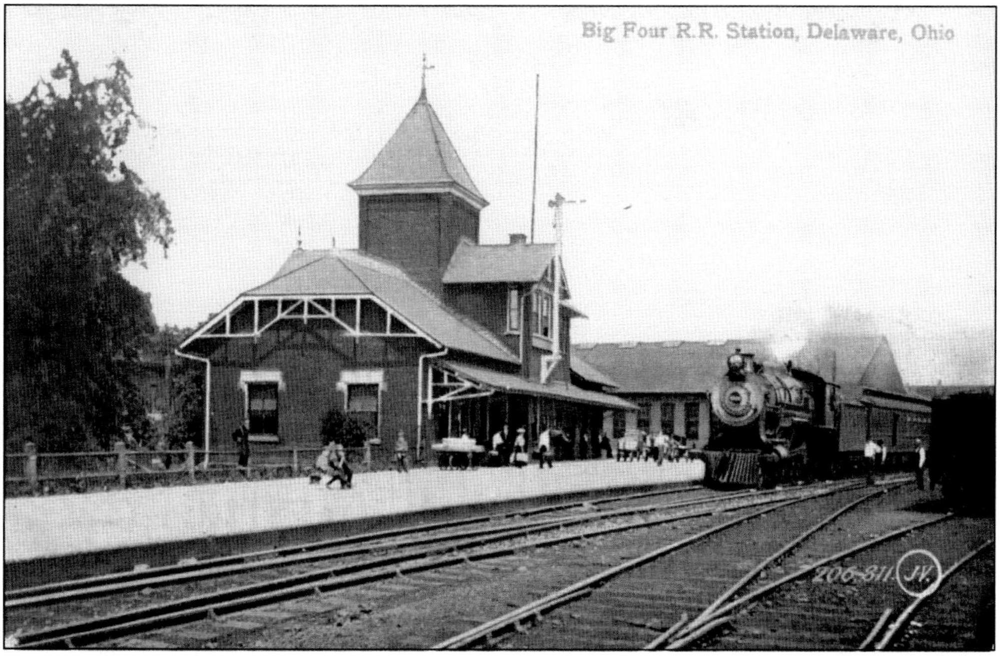


The CC&C reached Delaware in the early 1850s. The first depot was a frame building. The Cleveland, Columbus, Cincinnati and Indianapolis Railroad built the brick edifice, shown here, in 1887. Around 1910, a southbound passenger chugs into the station. Out of view beyond the railroad shop buildings in the background was a roundhouse and other buildings of the local engine terminal. (Above, David P. Oroszi collection; below, author's collection.)

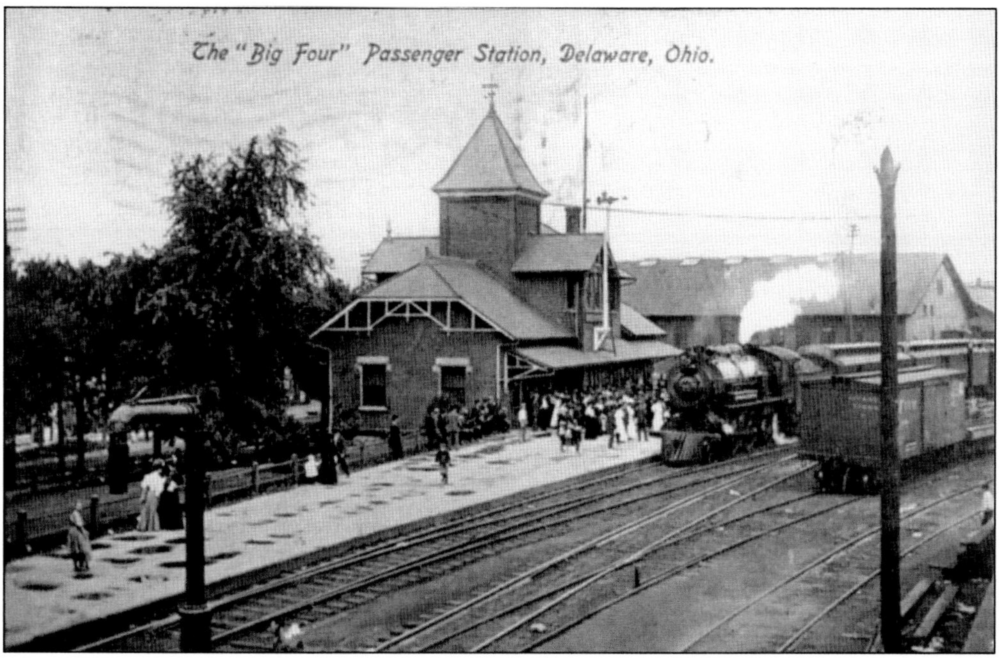

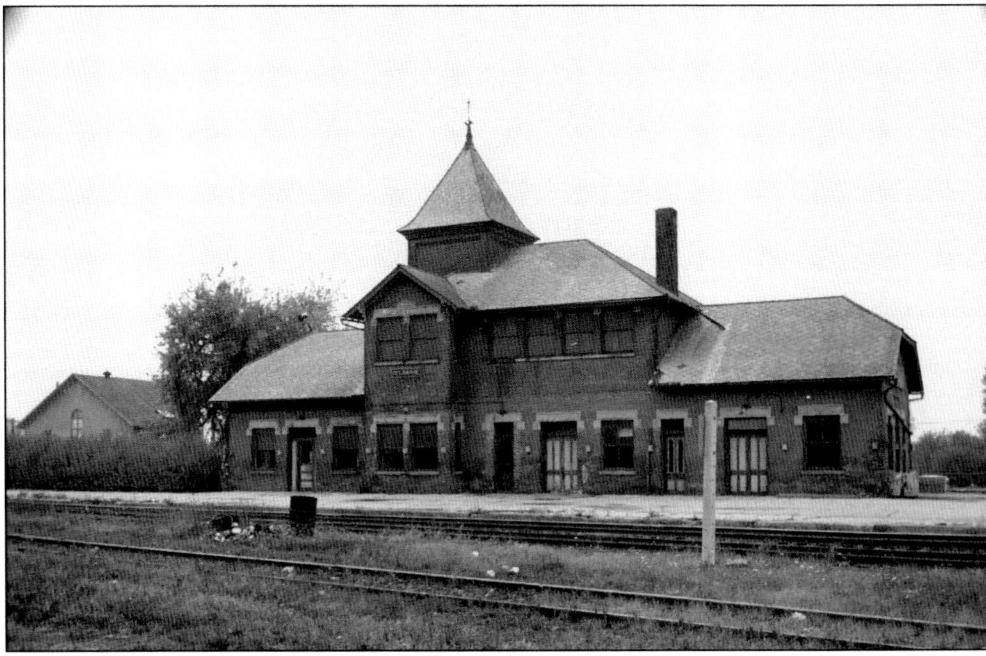

Around 1922, alterations were made to Delaware's Big Four passenger depot and a freight cutoff was built east of town. By the 1960s, the passenger depot was relegated to freight service; note its designation as a freight station in the 1965 view above. Across the tracks was the freight house (shown below in 1969). In later years, this served as a Railway Express Agency office. Although research is still underway, this appears to be the original CC&C depot built in the 1850s. The passenger depot has been home to a florist shop for many years; the freight house has also been preserved. (Above, photograph by Charles Garvin; below, photograph by the author.)

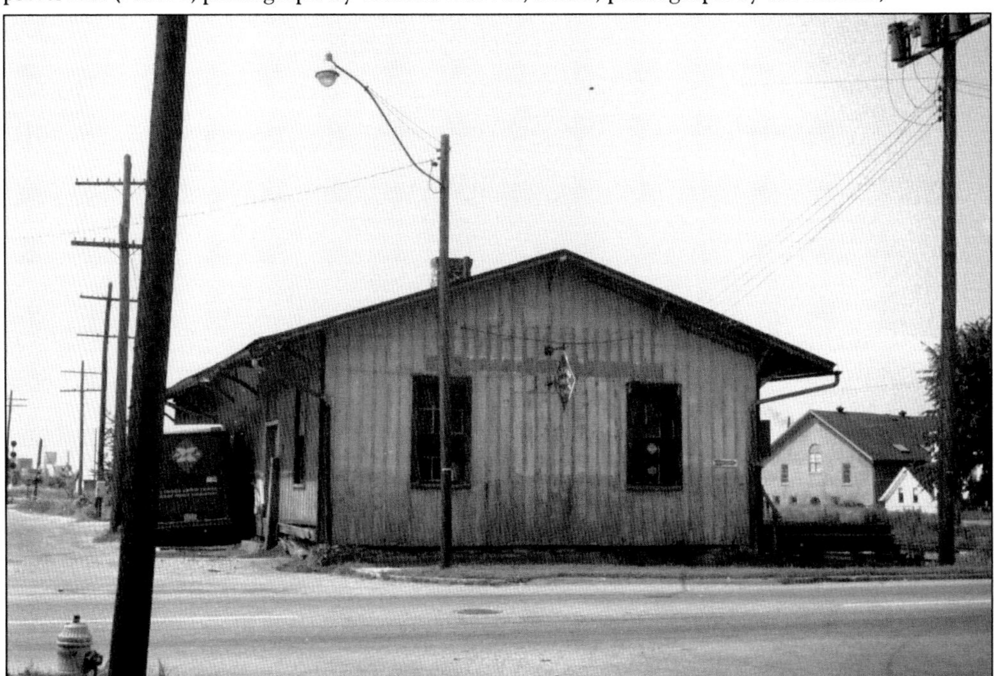

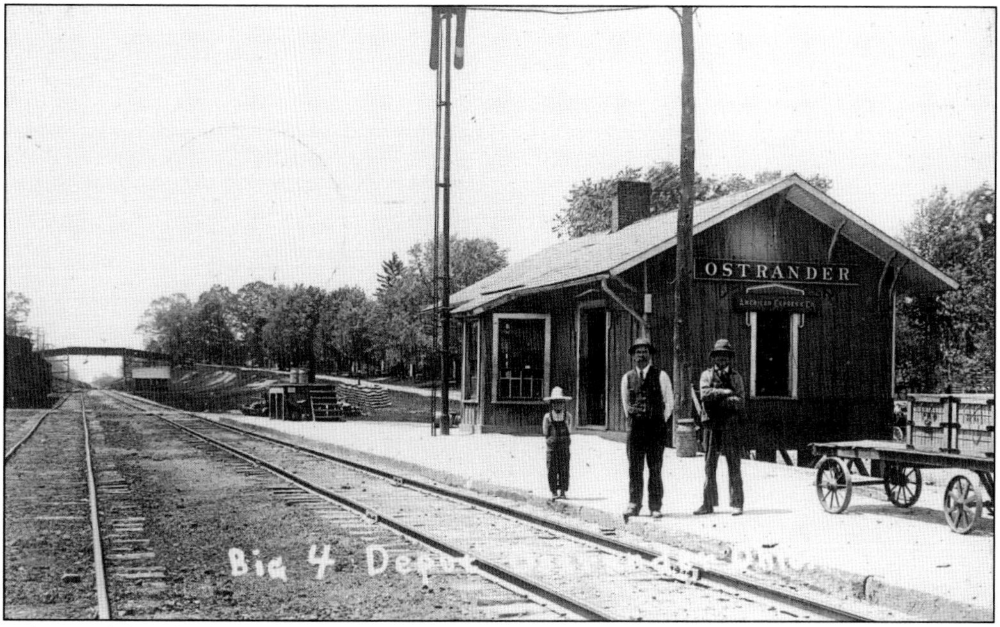


White Sulphur had a small frame combination depot; unfortunately a picture has not been located. Next was Ostrander. The agent is flanked by his helpers in this early-1900s postcard view. Looking closely at the building under the town board, one can see the hand stenciled letters "Ostrander" painted directly on the board-and-batten wall. This depot was closed by the NYC in 1960, sat abandoned in the mid-1960s, and has since disappeared. (Author's collection.)

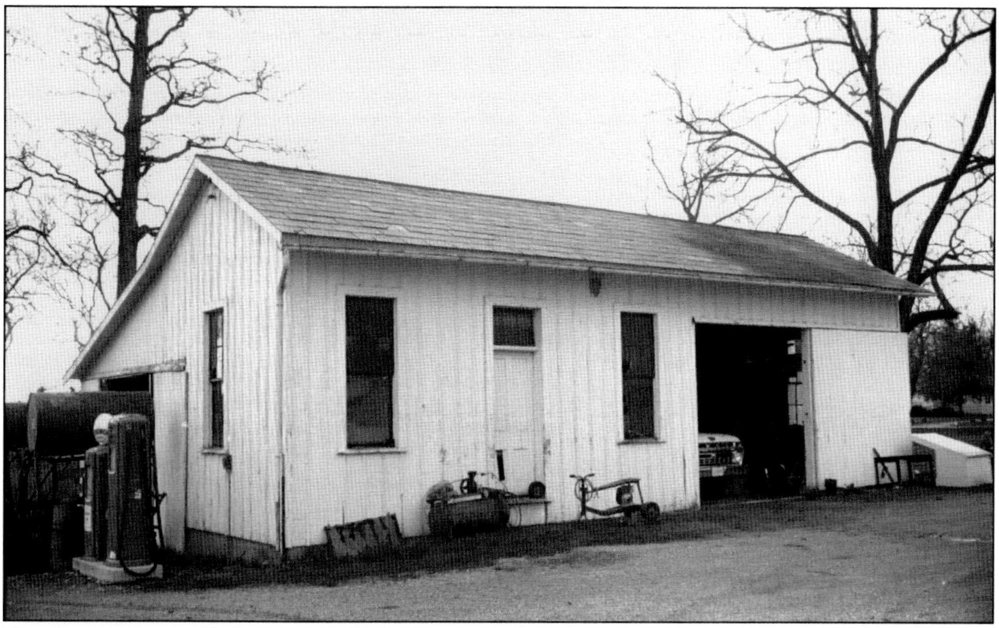

New Dover, originally Dover, also had a frame combination depot. Its passenger agency was closed in 1929. The Big Four had used a gasoline-powered motorcar for passengers between Delaware and Springfield in the early 1900s, but switched to pulling a single coach at the end of a freight train in 1928. Everything is gone now along the Delaware Branch, but the New Dover depot, shown here in 1969, exists as a private storage building. (Photograph by Charles Garvin.)

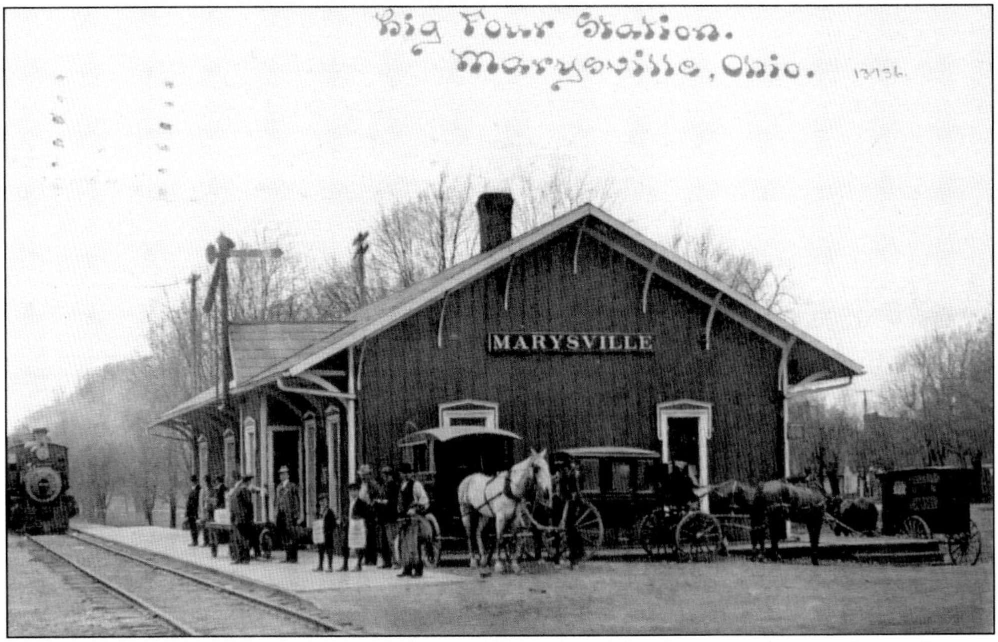


Marysville had a larger combination depot. Above, hotel hacks await the traveling salesmen and other visitors that need a ride into the city. Compare the activity in the early 1900s to the desolation of the early 1960s below. After the NYC closed the depot in the late 1950s, it was used as a warehouse for a number of years. The Big Four depot was gone by the mid-1960s. (Above, Jeff A. Spencer collection; below, photograph by Bernard Kern.)

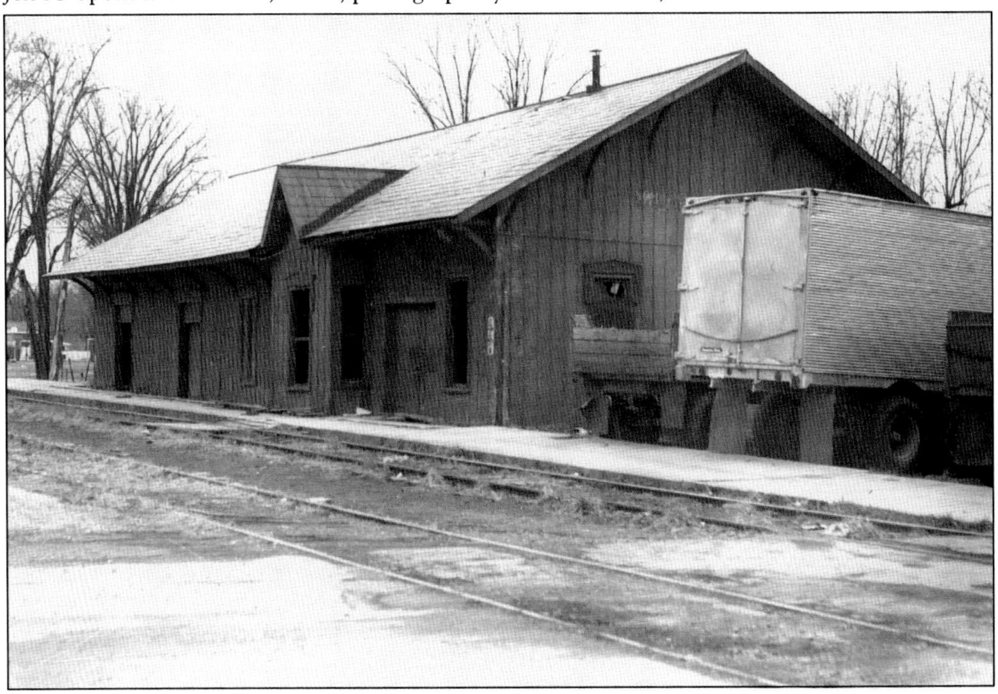

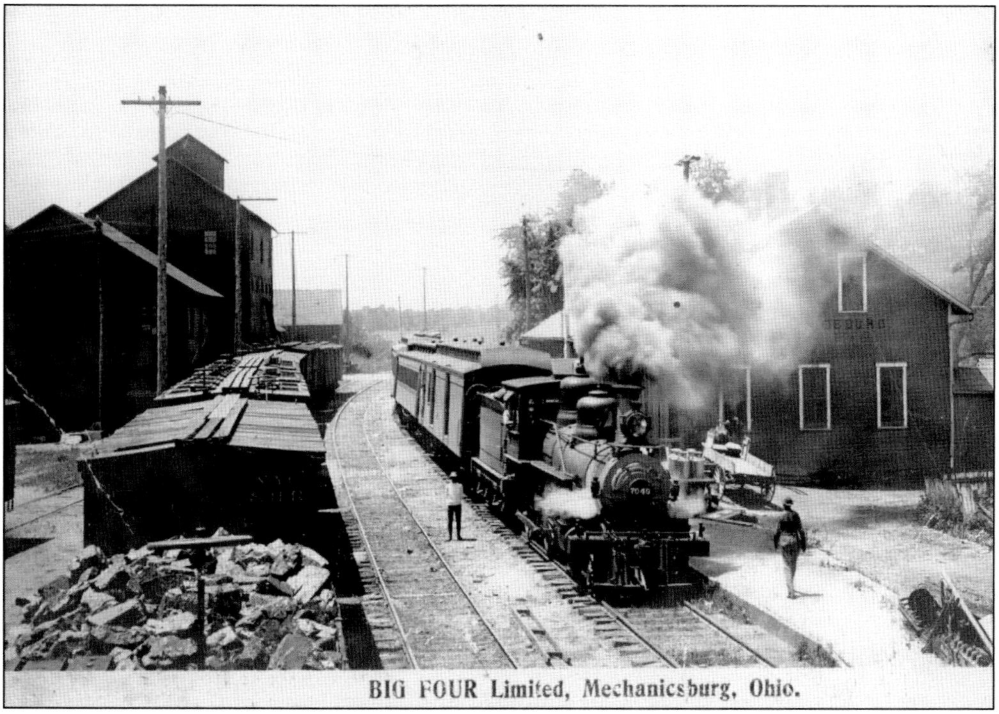


Big Four locomotive No. 7040 at the head of the Springfield–Delaware local chugs out of Mechanicsburg around 1910. The Mechanicsburg depot was of an older design and was never replaced. It was removed by the late 1960s. (Author's collection.)

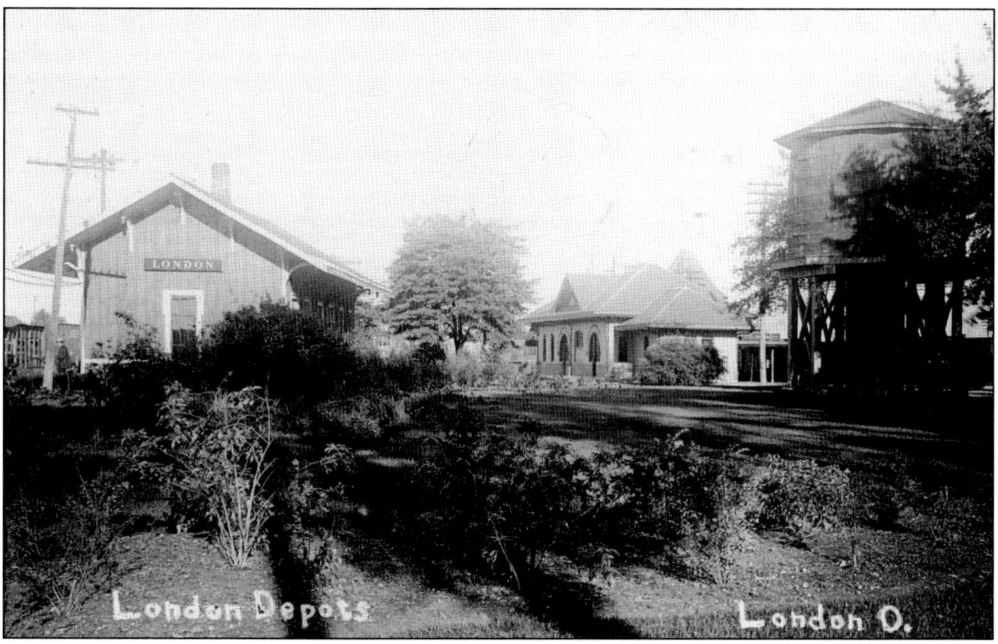


London was on the Big Four line between Springfield and Columbus. The Big Four depot is on the left, while to the right is the PRR depot and water tank. Reportedly, the Big Four depot was destroyed in a train derailment in the mid-1900s. (Author's collection.)

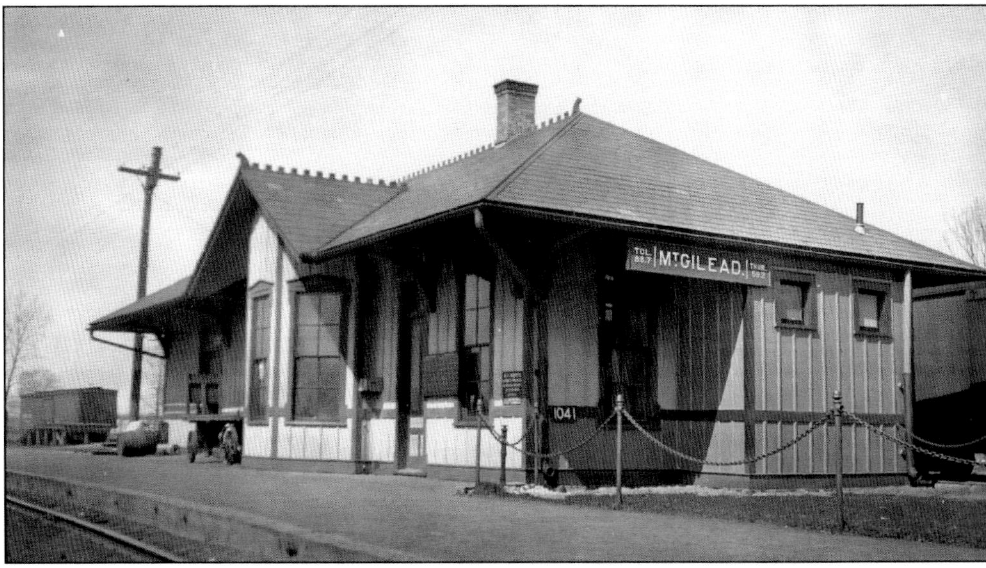


This 1882 depot was built to Ohio Central Railroad standard plans for a county seat or community of similar stature. A near identical structure still stands at Granville. The Mount Gilead building was torn down after the NYC took over the T&OC and Big Four lines; the NYC maintained the brick former Mount Gilead Short Line depot. It is seen here in 1919. (T&OC photograph, Allen County [Ohio] Historical Society Collection.)

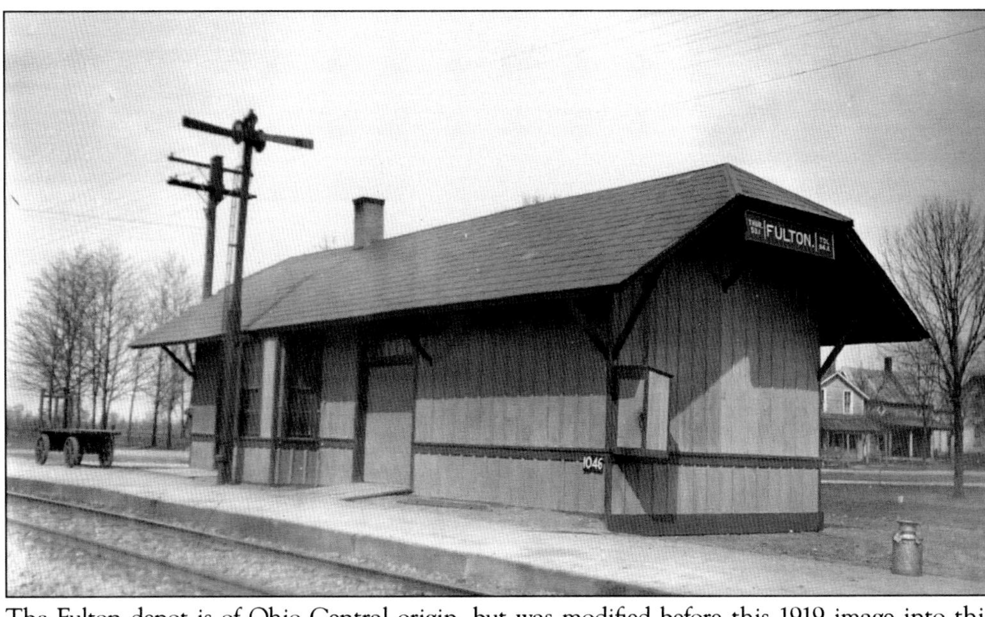


The Fulton depot is of Ohio Central origin, but was modified before this 1919 image into this pleasing half-hipped roof design. It probably closed in the 1950s. Since then it was relocated off-site to private property. (T&OC photograph, Allen County [Ohio] Historical Society Collection.)

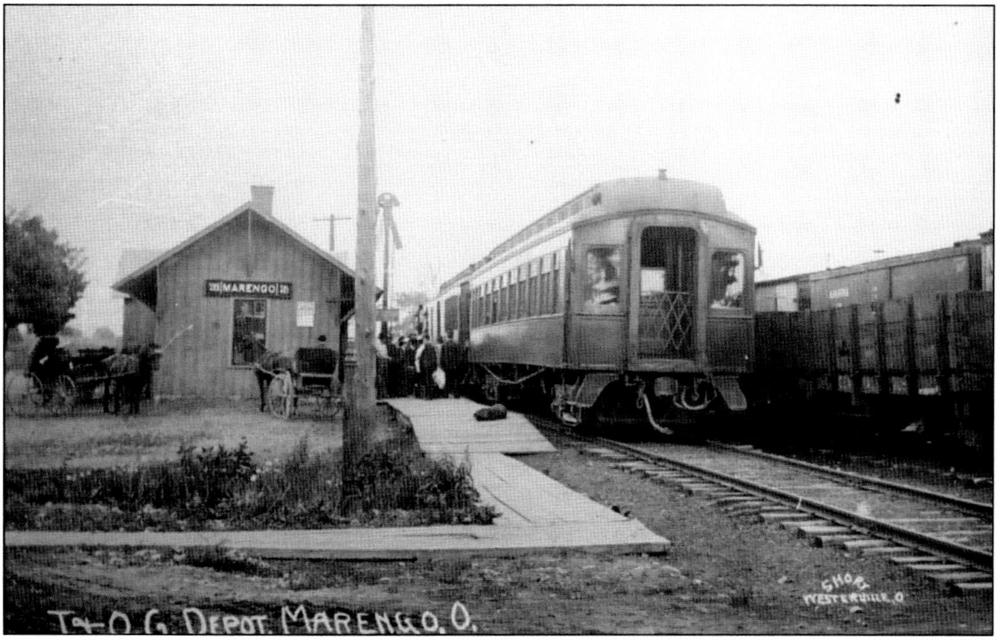

Marengo's depot is typical of the original 1882 depot plan for a small town. The Fulton depot was of this design, also. The Marengo depot closed in the 1950s and was apparently torn down. (Author's collection.)

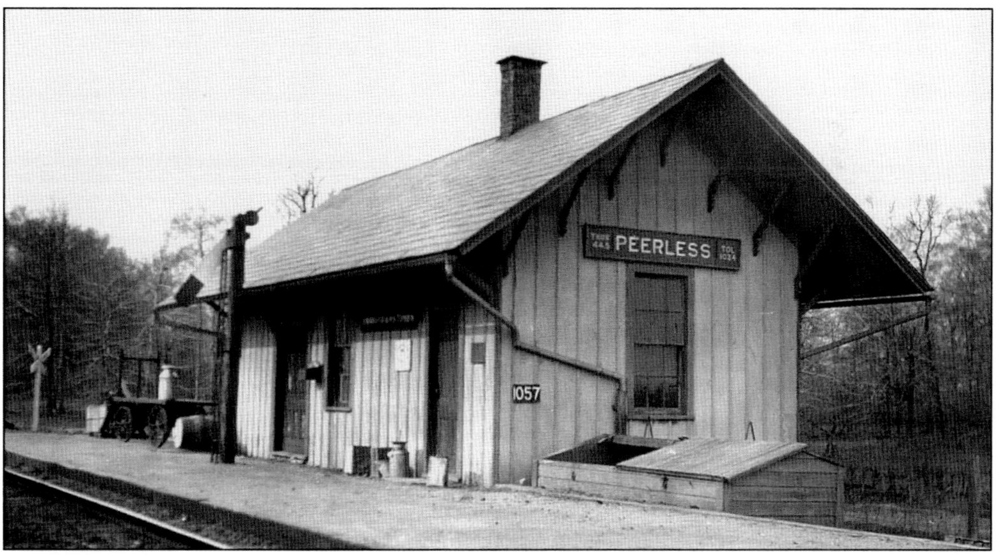

The next depot south on the Ohio Central was this one at Peerless. The short semaphore signal was to signify if a station stop was necessary for the local. The agent did not issue train orders by the date of this photograph in 1919. Peerless was closed by the NYC in 1956 and removed shortly afterward. (T&OC photograph, Allen County [Ohio] Historical Society Collection.)

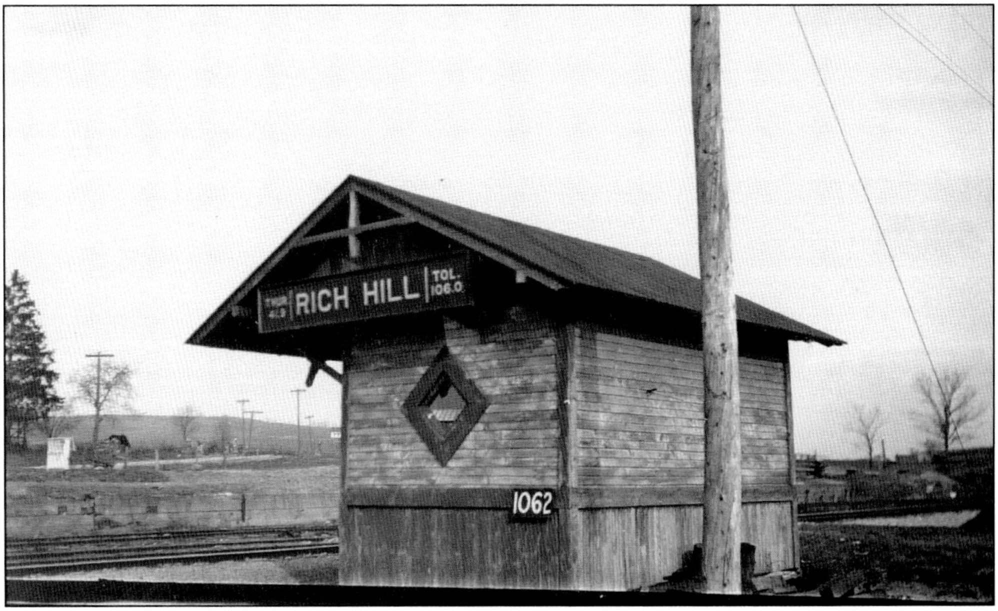


This small three-sided shelter had been a flag stop throughout its existence at Rich Hill. By the time of this 1919 photograph, passenger use was negligible. (T&OC photograph, Allen County [Ohio] Historical Society Collection.)

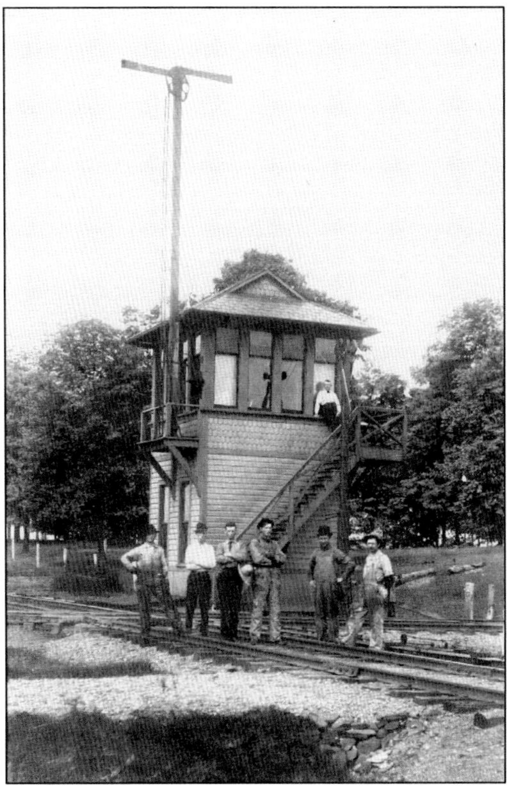

The tower operator and track crew posed for the photographer at the interlocking tower near Centerburg, where the Ohio Central Railroad crossed what was to become the Cleveland, Akron and Columbus Railroad. The tower was built by the Ohio Central around 1882 and removed by the 1960s. (Author's collection.)

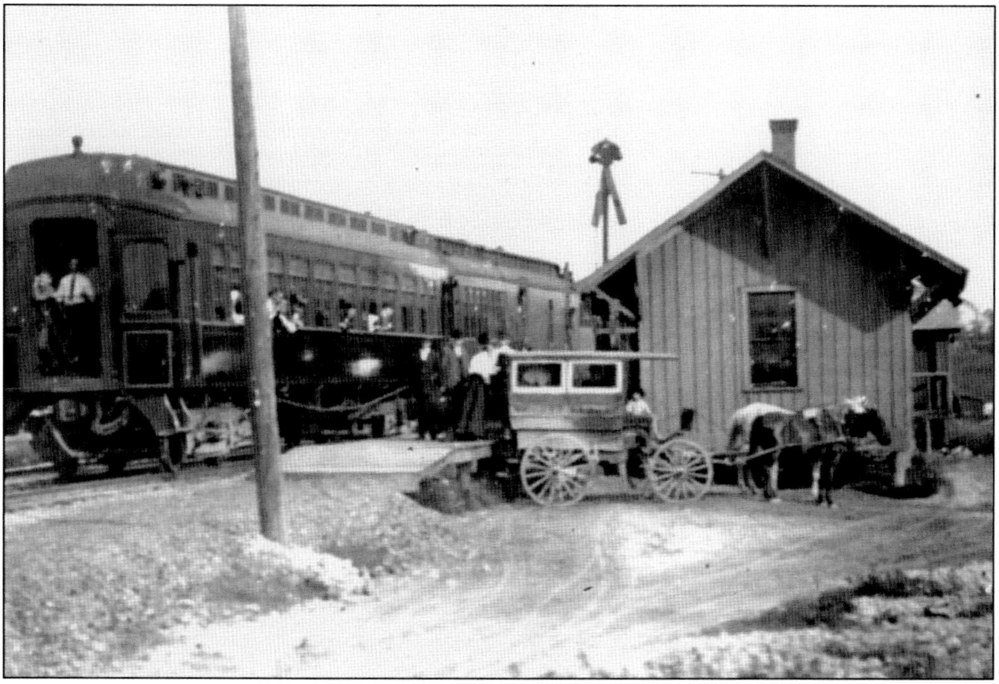

Here is a good example of the depot modernization plan of the T&OC. Above is the 1882 version of the Centerburg Ohio Central depot. Below is the modified early-1900 version. The only major external change is the roof rebuilding and new paint scheme. At this time the depots also gained indoor plumbing and electricity. The depot was closed in 1956, but remains as a business. (Author's collection.)

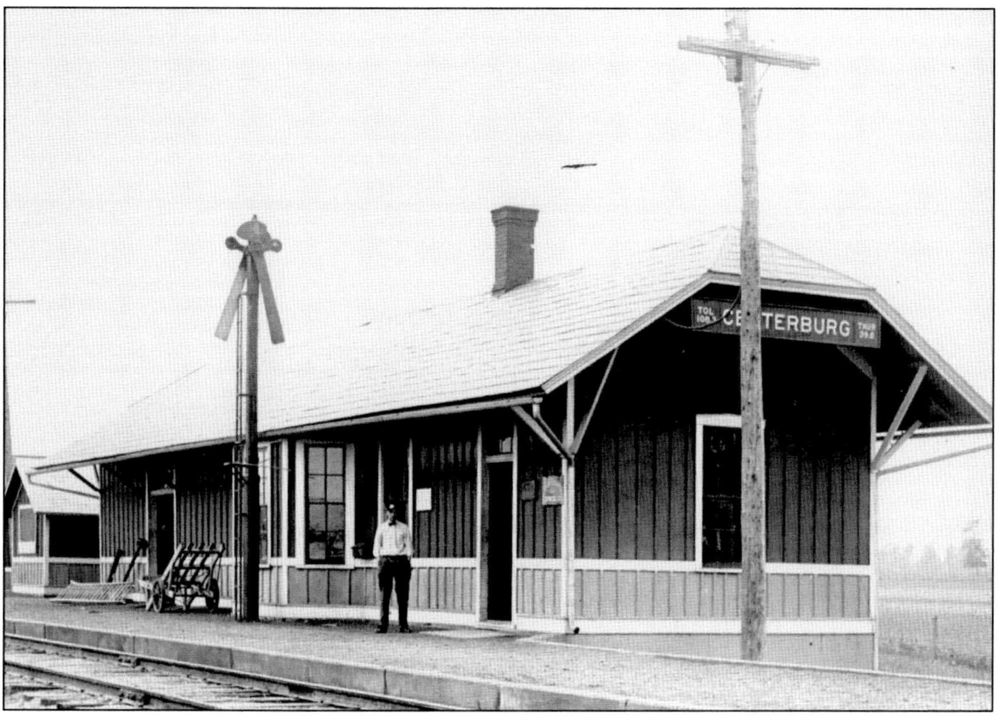

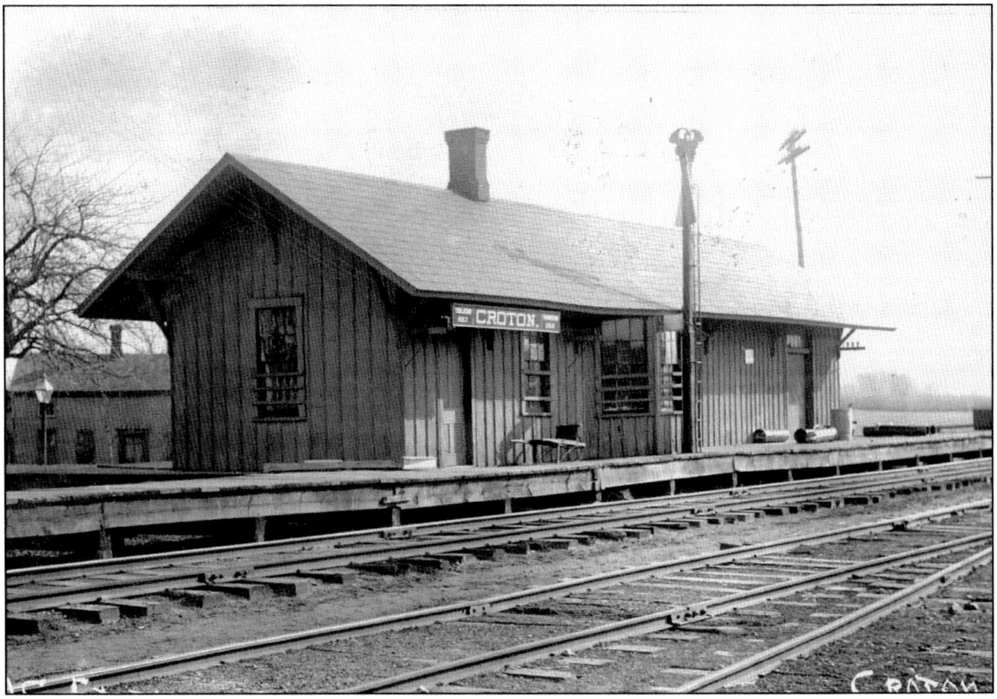


Croton also serves as an example of the depot reconstruction. Above is the original 1882 Ohio Central Railroad structure and below is the updated version. Note that the old depot had a raised plank platform and protective bars on the windows. Croton became a non-agency station in 1959. The depot was moved two miles into the country in the 1940s and converted into a house. (Author's collection.)

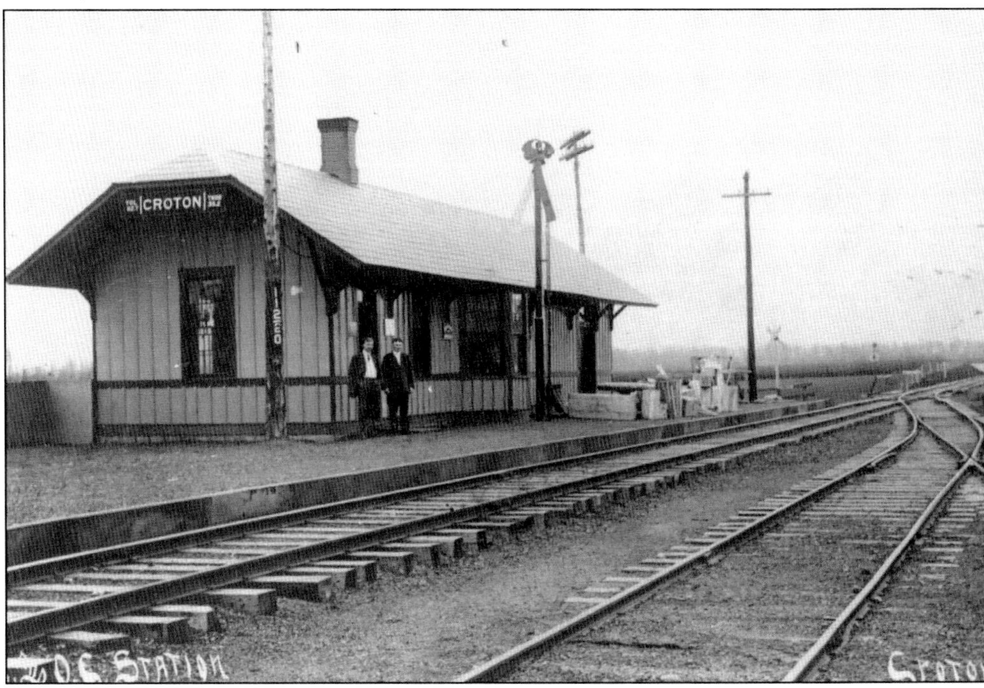

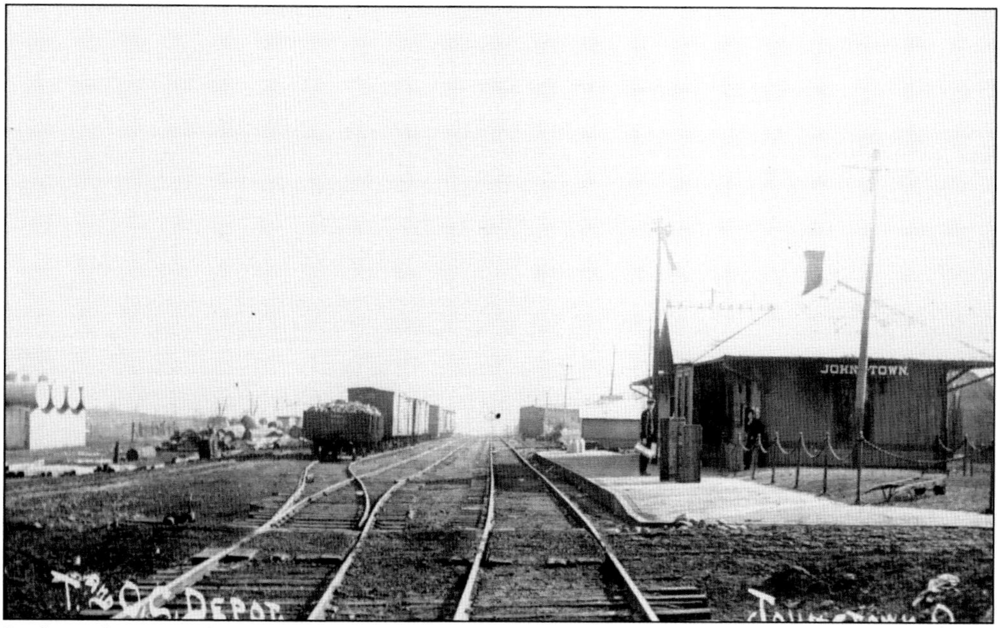

In the early 1900s, the Ohio Central had a storage track just beyond its depot in Johnstown. This depot is built to the same plan as Mount Gilead and Granville. At some point, an addition was tacked on to the freight end. Although the tracks are gone, the depot remains in commercial use; for many years it was an antique shop. (Author's collection.)

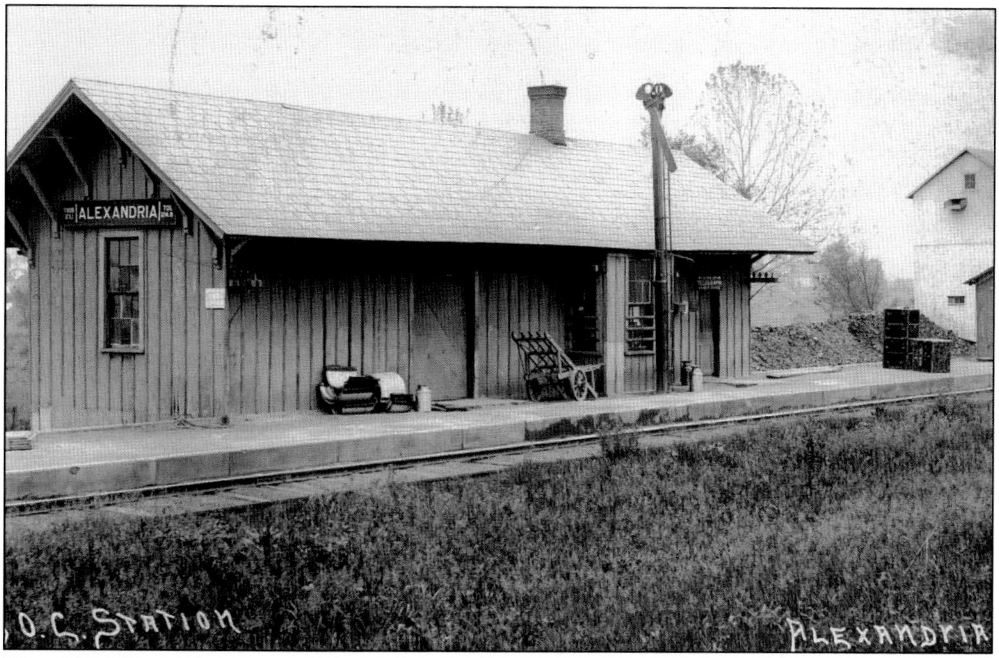


The Ohio Central depot in Alexandria dates to 1882. The postcard photographer picked a quiet period around 1907 to record this image. Alexandria was never modified and became a non-agency in 1950. Later the depot was moved to a lot in town where it was under restoration in 2000. (Author's collection.)

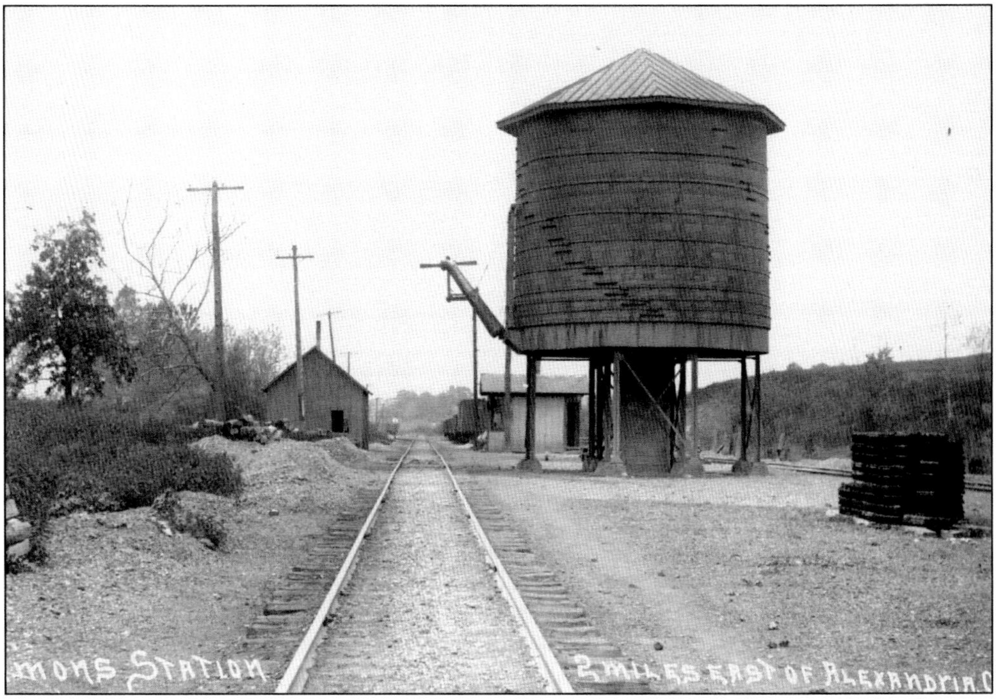


Clemons was a water and train order station halfway between Alexandria and Granville. The wooden water tank is fed from the pump house across the track. Behind the tank is the operators shack. All are long gone. (Author's collection.)

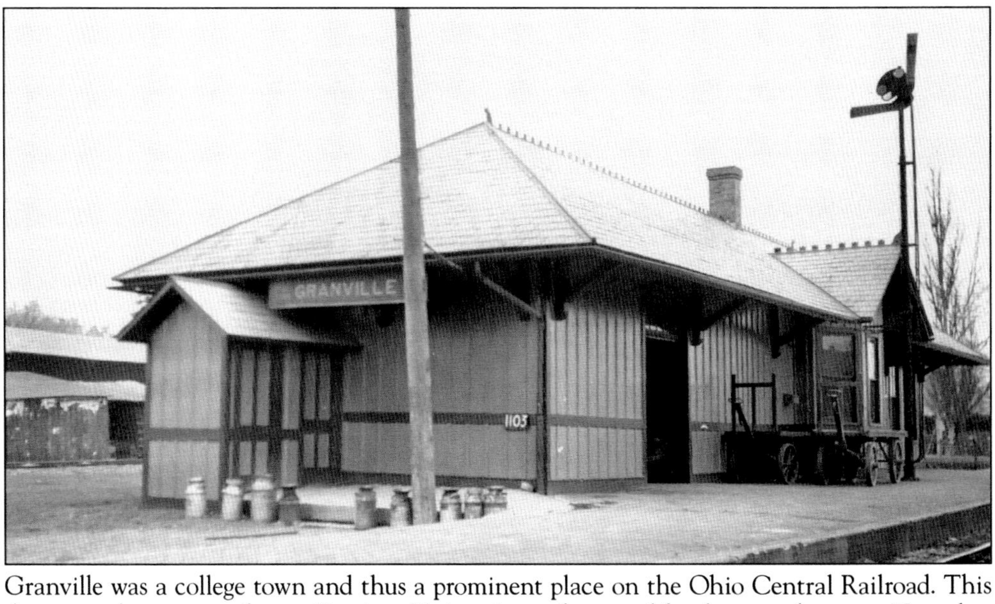


Granville was a college town and thus a prominent place on the Ohio Central Railroad. This depot saw the passage of many Denison University students and faculty over the years. Note that it was built to the same plan as Mount Gilead and Johnstown. The agency was closed in 1959. Luckily the depot is restored and in commercial use on South Main Street. (T&OC photograph, 1919, Allen County [Ohio] Historical Society Collection.)

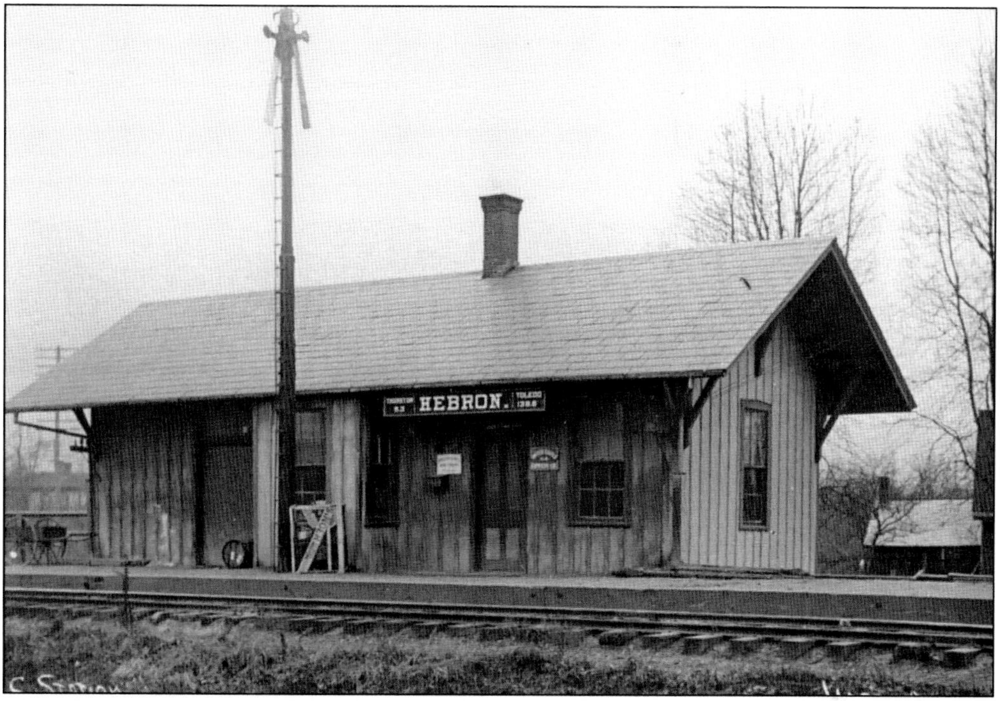


The Ohio Central built this standard plan depot at Hebron in 1882. The crate contains a new Singer sewing machine. The agency closed in the 1950s, and the building has since been razed. (Author's collection.)

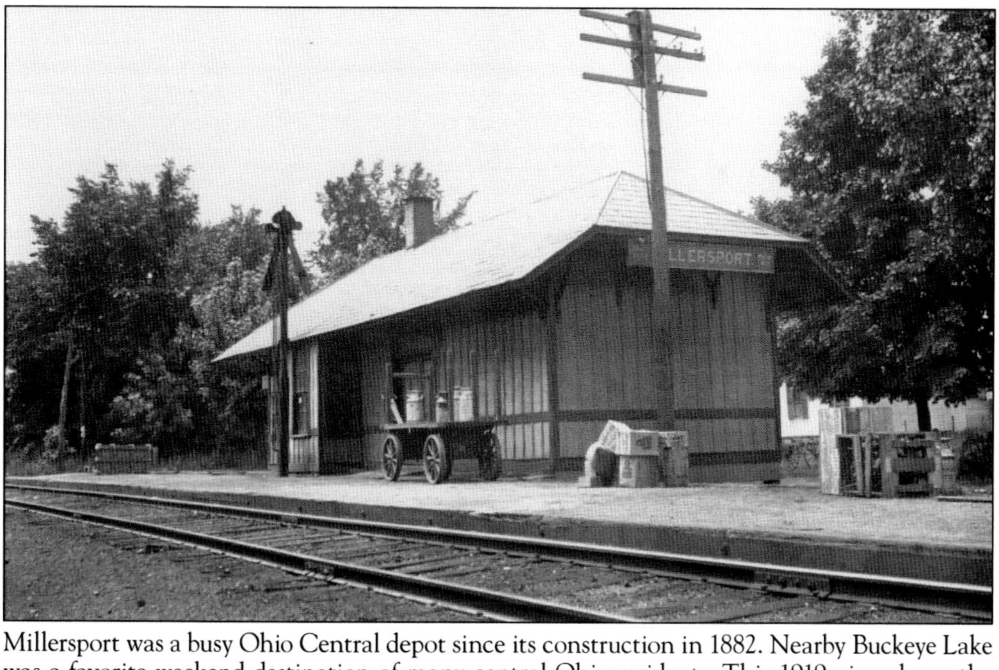

Millersport was a busy Ohio Central depot since its construction in 1882. Nearby Buckeye Lake was a favorite weekend destination of many central Ohio residents. This 1919 view shows the depot as modified by the T&OC. The agency closed by 1952. The depot was relocated in town around 1955. (T&OC photograph, Allen County [Ohio] Historical Society Collection.)

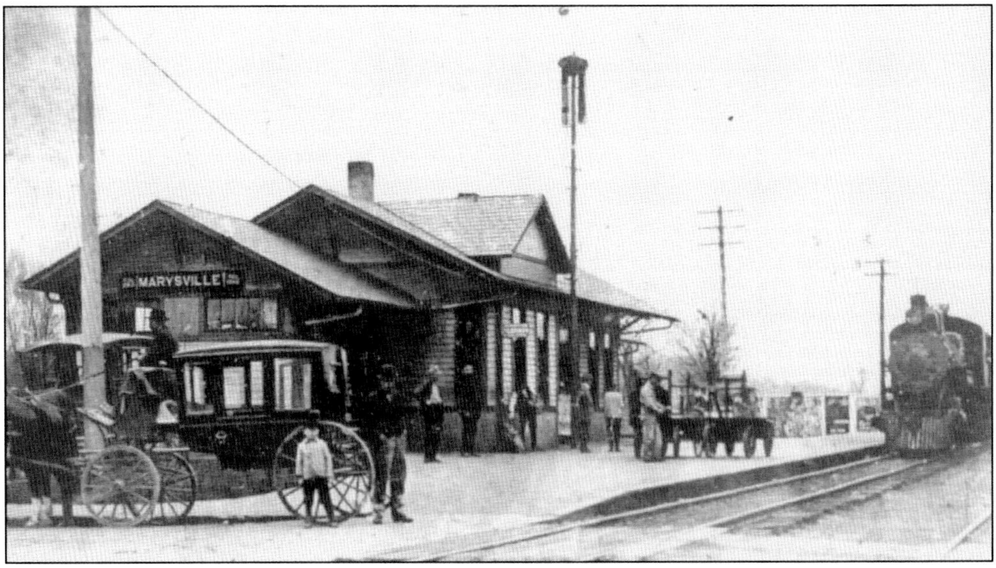


The T&OC completed a line through Marysville to Columbus in 1893. These views show the passenger depot in about 1907 above and in 1919 below. A separate freight house sat across the tracks. The depots were torn down in the 1960s. (Above, author's collection; below, T&OC photograph, Allen County [Ohio] Historical Society Collection.)

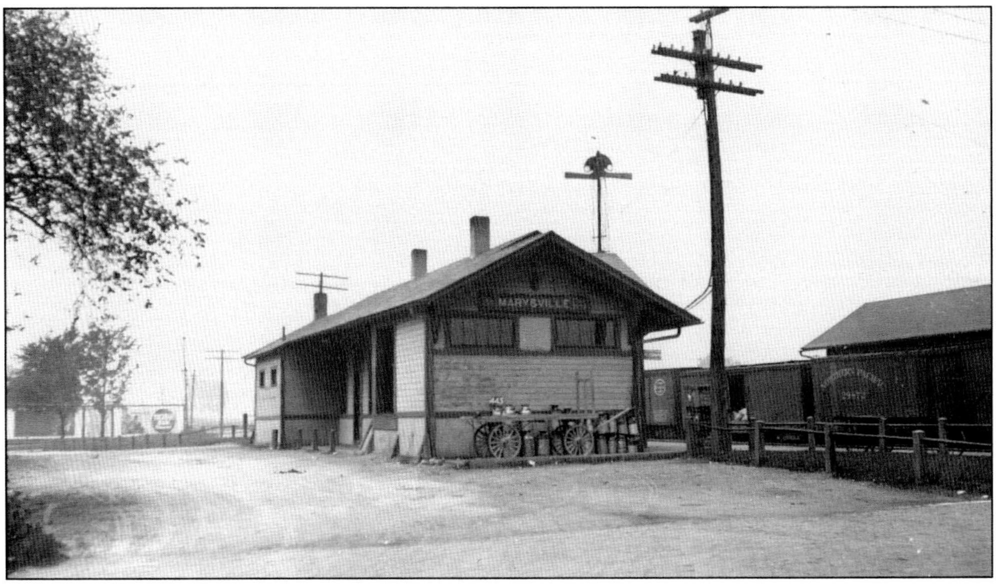

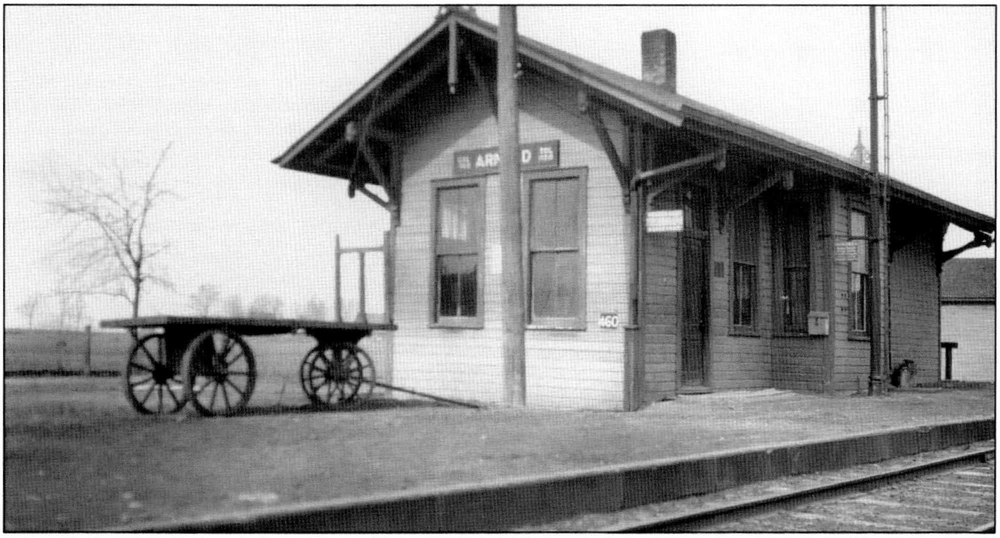


The T&OC combination depots at Arnold and Kile differ mainly in roof and eave decoration; otherwise they were built from the same plan. Both were non-agency stations by 1949 and have been gone for many years. They are seen here in 1919. (T&OC photographs, Allen County [Ohio] Historical Society Collection.)

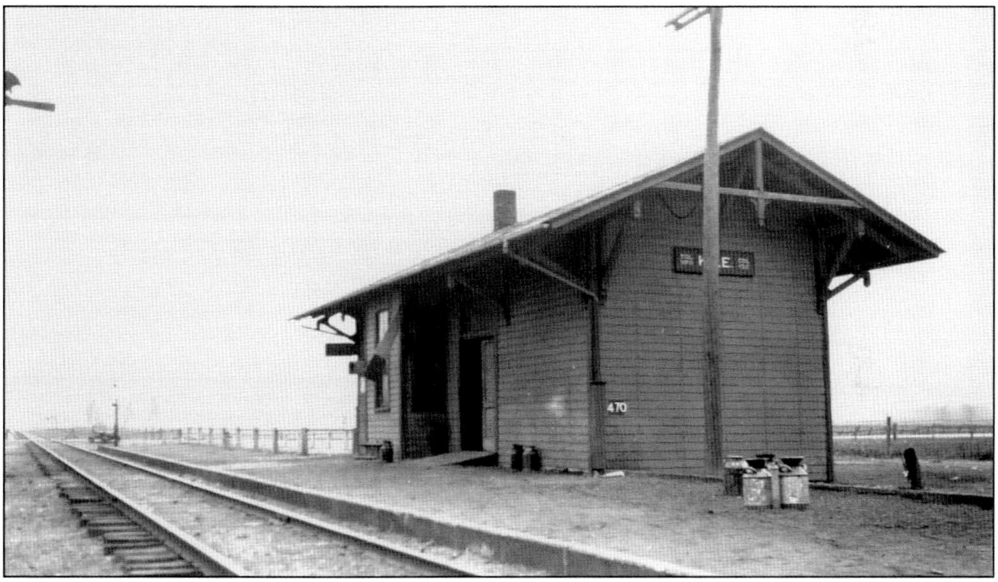

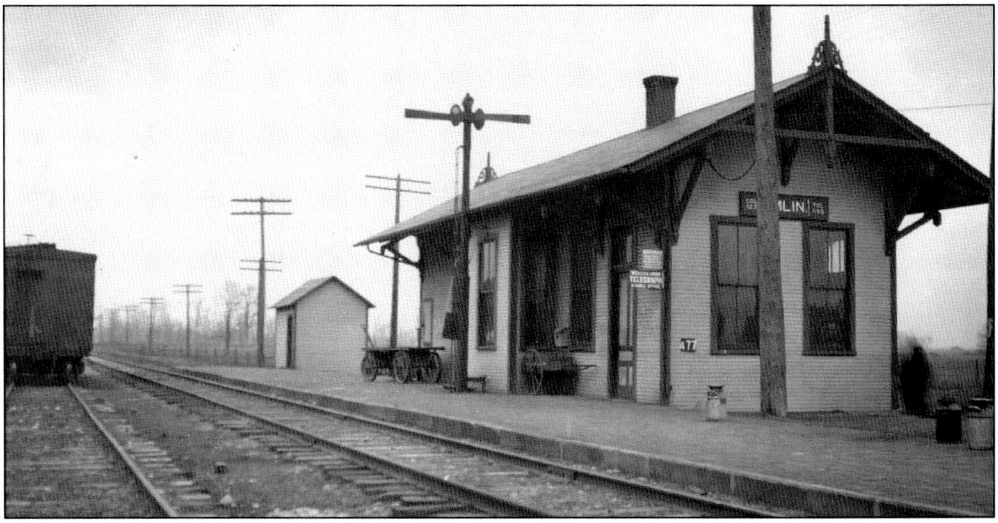


Amlin's T&OC depot, seen here in 1919, is still another variation of this standard plan. Note the lower blade on the order board to signal a station stop and the upper signal indicating train orders. Like Arnold and Kile the agency was closed by 1949 and later razed. (T&OC photograph, Allen County [Ohio] Historical Society Collection.)

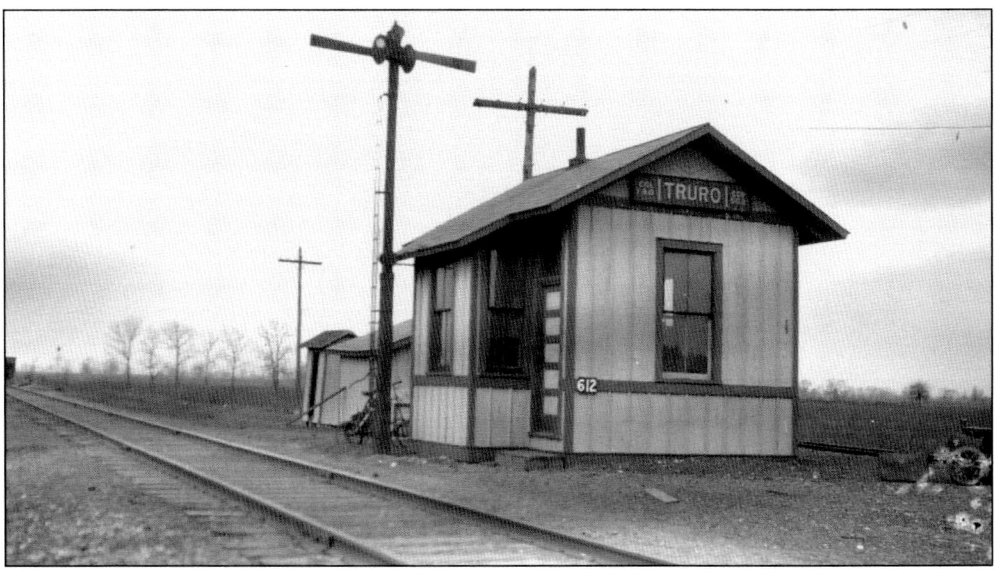


The wide-open farmland surrounding the Truro depot in 1919 has now been replaced by Interstate 70 and suburban Columbus. This small depot still stood until 1974. (T&OC photograph, Allen County [Ohio] Historical Society Collection.)

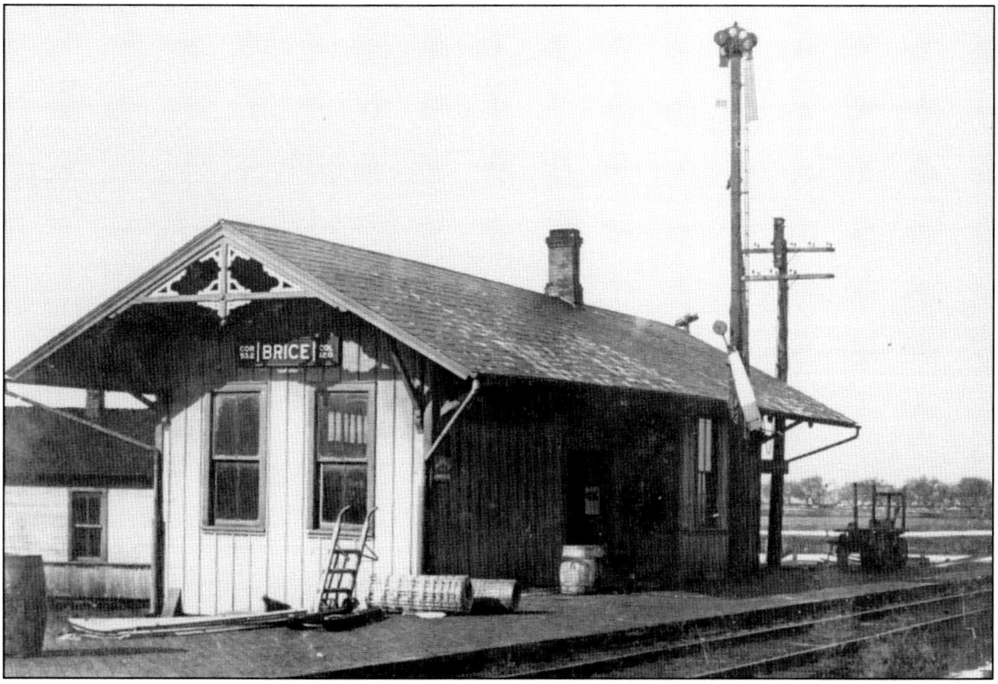


The Brice depot dates to 1882 when the Ohio Central Railroad built its line to southern Ohio. The unique feature was the ornate gable. Brice's depot was relocated and placed in commercial use after the agency closed in the late 1950s. It was dismantled and reconstructed on the northwest side of Columbus around 2001 as the Depot Conference Center. (David P. Oroszi collection.)

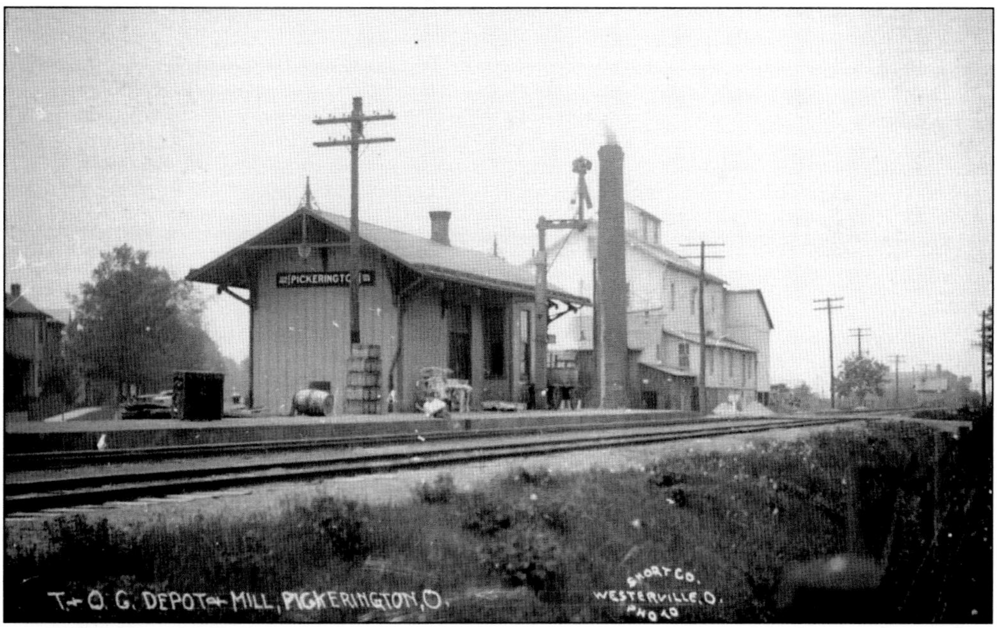


The Ohio Central erected this depot at Pickerington in the 1880s. The depot has the early ornate finials and gable decorations characteristic of the T&OC. It closed as an agency in 1958. It remained trackside as a storage facility until it was immaculately restored in the 1990s. A restored section house is adjacent. (Author's collection.)

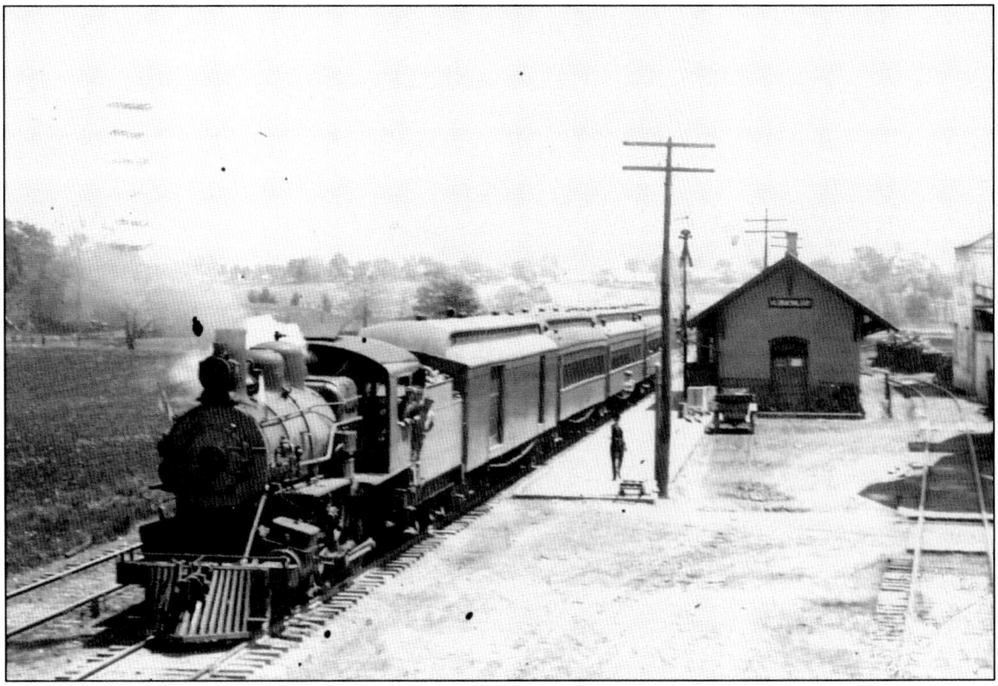

These two depots were only a couple of miles apart when built in the late 1880s. Basil, above, was the only small-town combination depot on the entire T&OC line built of brick; while Baltimore, below, was of typical frame construction. It is likely the Basil depot was constructed by the Swiss immigrants of the town in order to have the railroad stop in their community. Basil was closed in July 1948. The towns were merged in the late 1940s as Baltimore. Both depots are long gone. (Author's collection.)

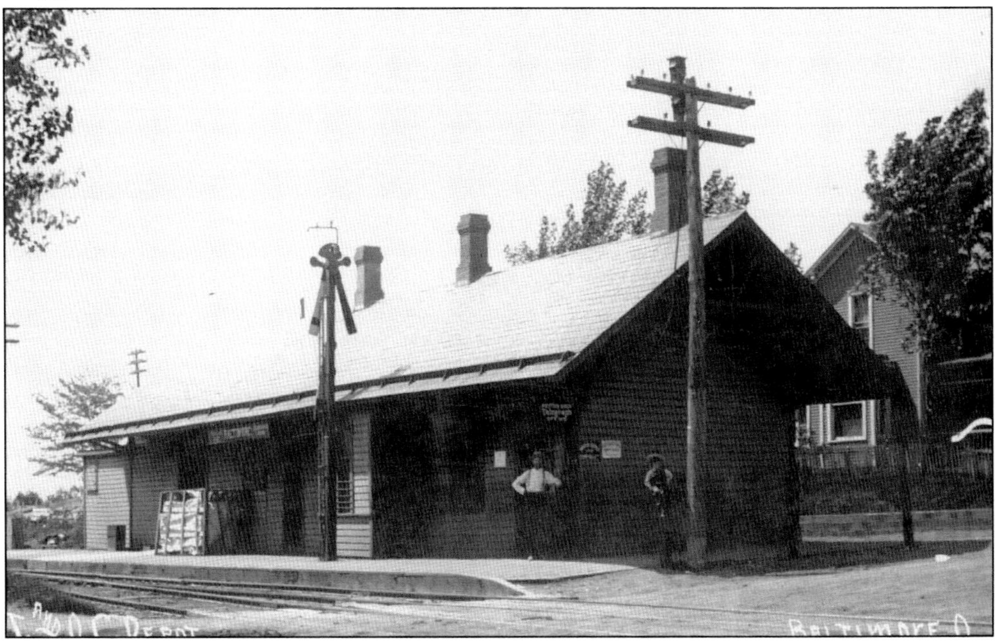

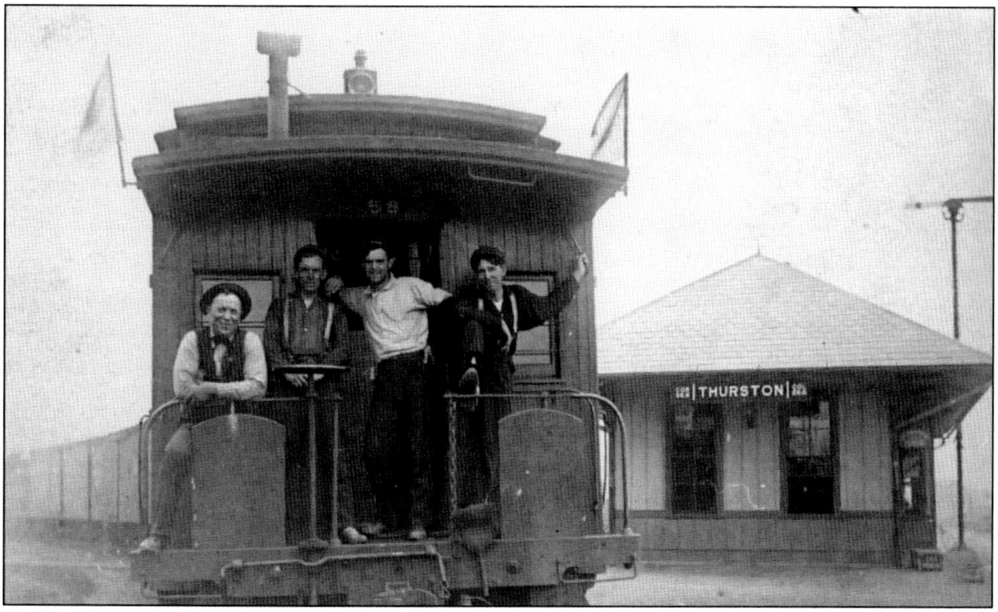


Thurston was a major junction on the T&OC where the Ohio Central Railroad's branch to Columbus and the Z&W joined the Ohio Central main line from Toledo to Corning. This frame passenger depot served all lines. Above, railroad workers pose on the coach platform of the local train around 1907. The two-story building behind the depot in the lower view from 1919 was a popular railroad hotel. Passenger service between here and Bucyrus was discontinued in May 1933. By the 1960s, the junction was quiet; about all that remained was a small frame freight house. (Above, author's collection; below, T&OC photograph, Allen County [Ohio] Historical Society Collection.)

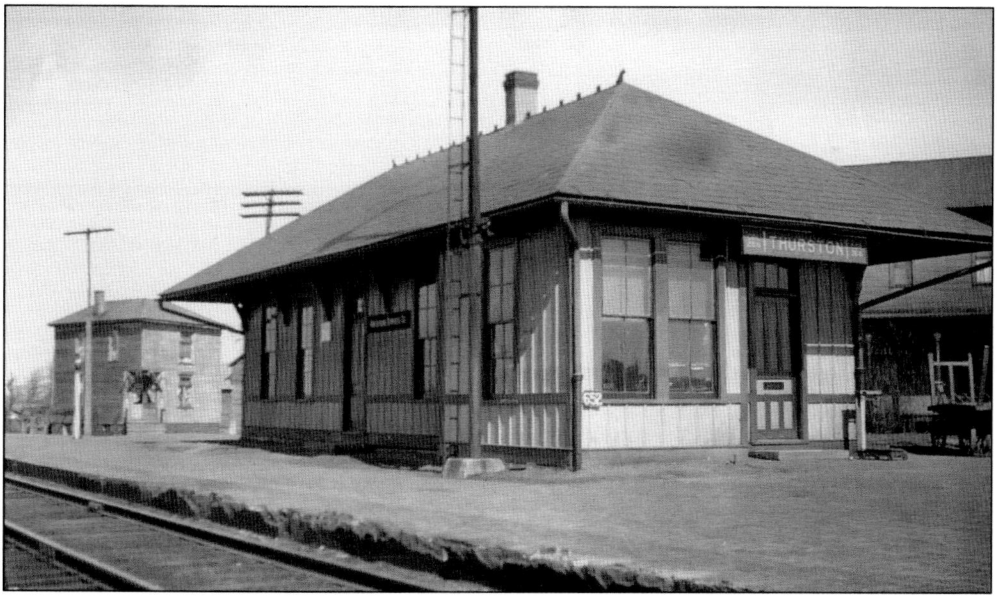

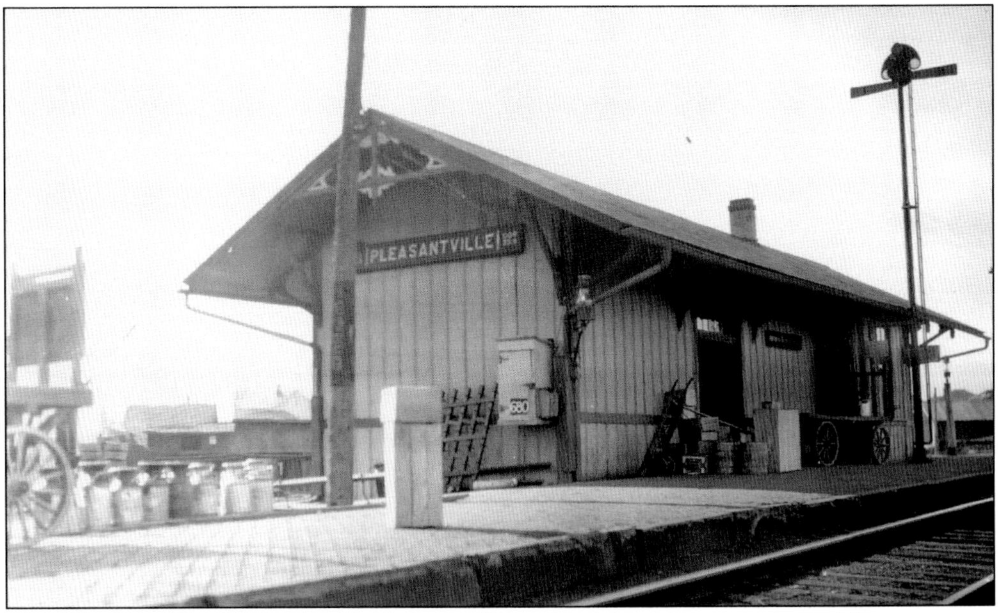


An otherwise rather plain depot at Pleasantville in 1919 has ornate turned wood decorations in the gables. The NYC closed the agency in 1958. The depot has long since disappeared. (T&OC photograph, Allen County [Ohio] Historical Society Collection.)

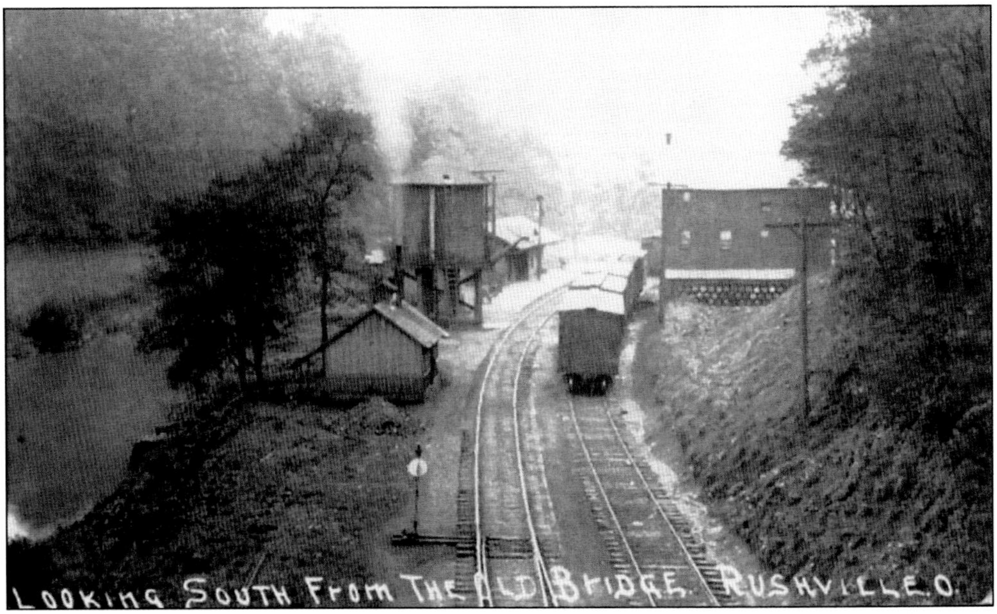


Rushville's T&OC depot was located in the valley of Little Rush Creek about halfway between West Rushville and Rushville. In 1907, the railroad facilities included the pump house, water tank, and combination depot. The NYC removed the agent in 1950, and the depot was razed long ago. (Fairfield County Historical Society Collection.)

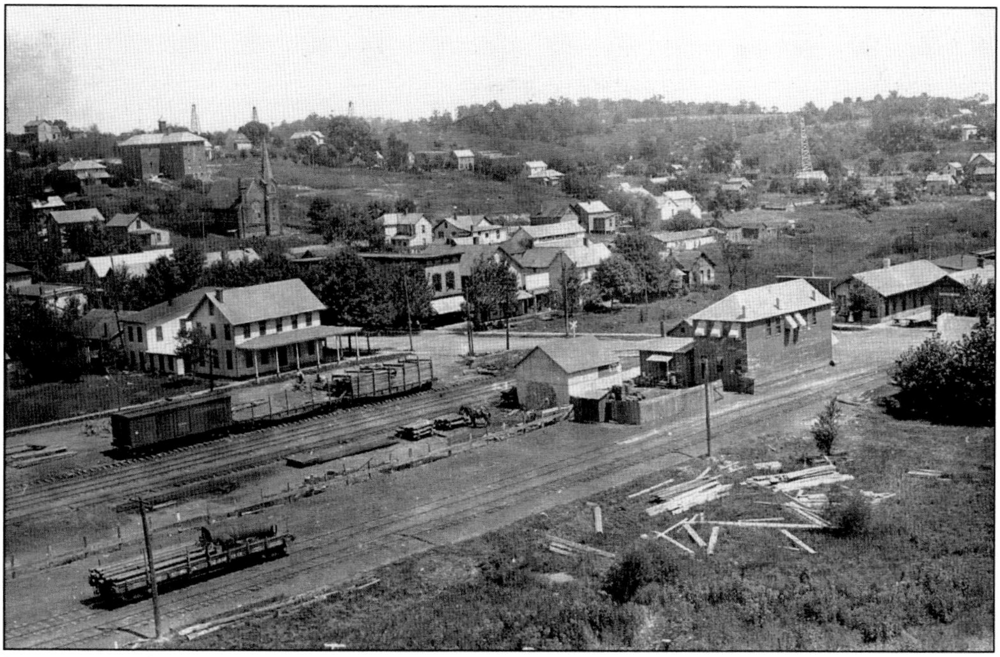

Junction City became an oil boom town around 1910. This aerial view shows the Cincinnati and Muskingum Valley (C&MV), later PRR, and B&O depots on the far right. The T&OC used the C&MV depots at both Junction City and New Lexington. The NYC agent was removed from Junction City in 1966. Today the depots are gone. (Author's collection.)

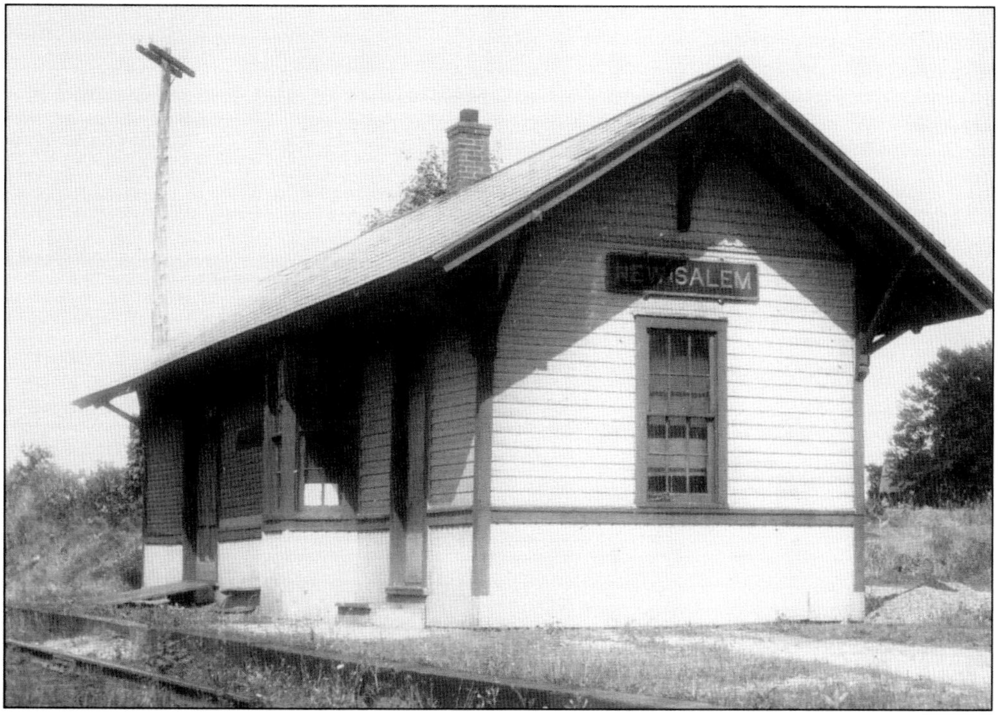


The Z&W maintained this depot at New Salem, seen here in 1948. The NYC closed it in 1958. It has been relocated and is in private storage use. (Photograph by Bernard Kern.)

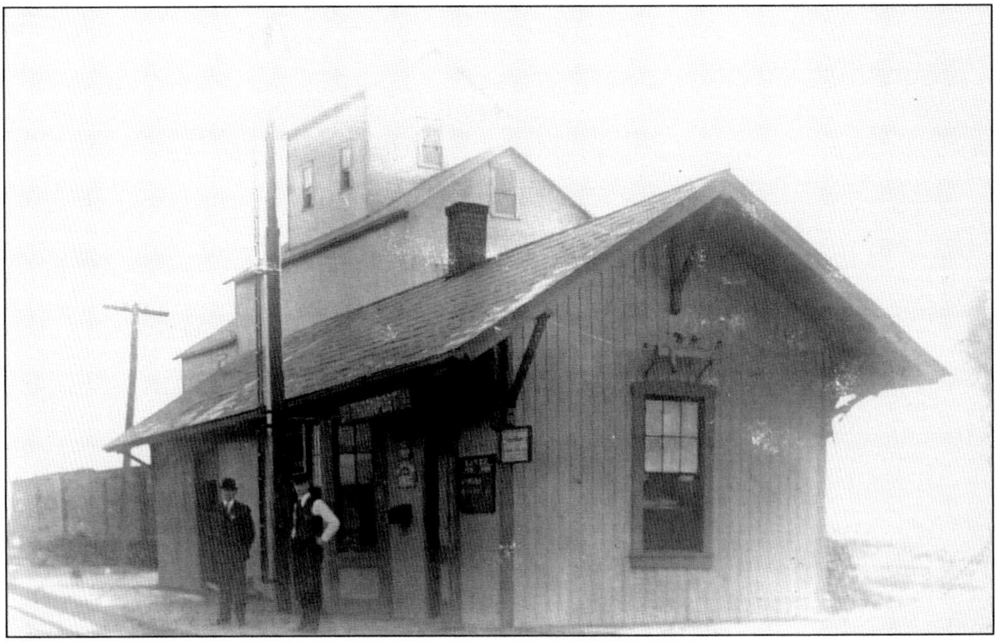

This Z&W depot served the nearby communities of Thornville and Thornport and has variously been called Thornville and Thornport. The agent and perhaps a railroad official pose for a postcard photographer in this c. 1908 view. Regular passenger service was reduced to one mixed train each way in May 1928. (Author's collection.)

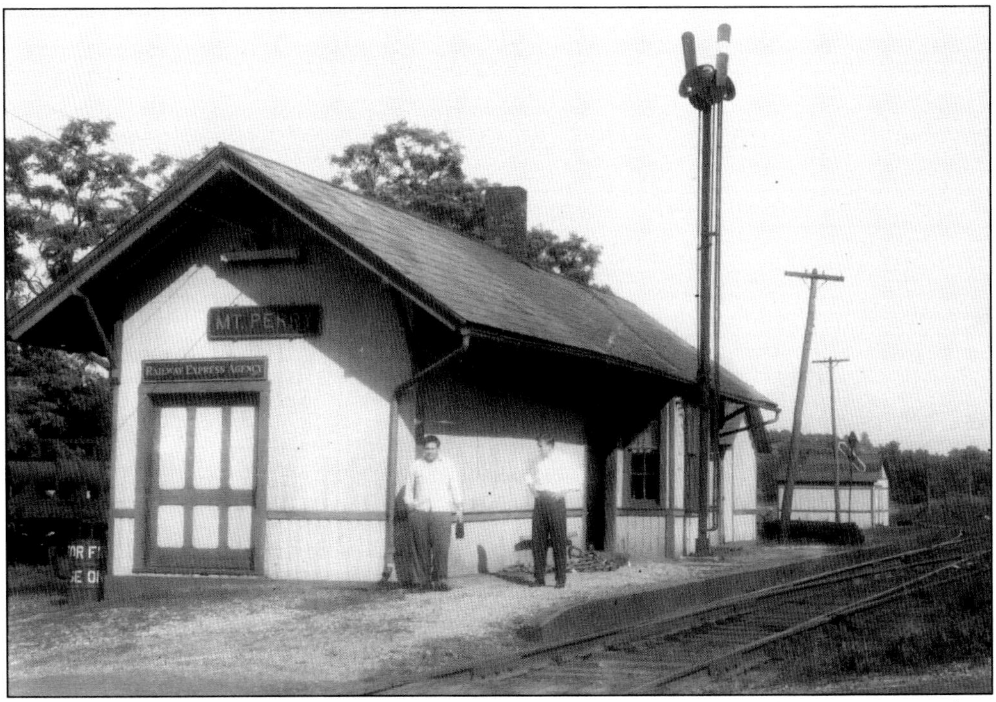


The Z&W depot at Glenford sat across the tracks from the B&O depot; both are pictured on page 31. Further down the line was Mount Perry, shown here in 1948. The depot was closed by the NYC in 1956 and later demolished. (Photograph by Bernard Kern.)

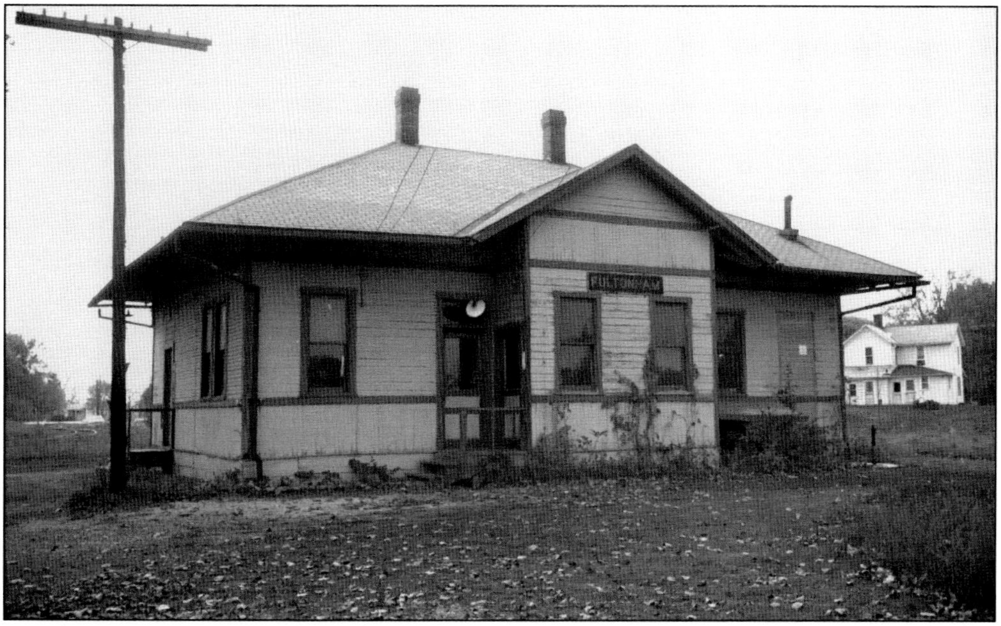


Seen here in 1967, at Fultonham, the Z&W connected with the line south to the coalfields. The depot was in the middle of the wye. The depot was used as a yard office during the Penn Central era and has since been removed. (Photograph by Charles Garvin.)

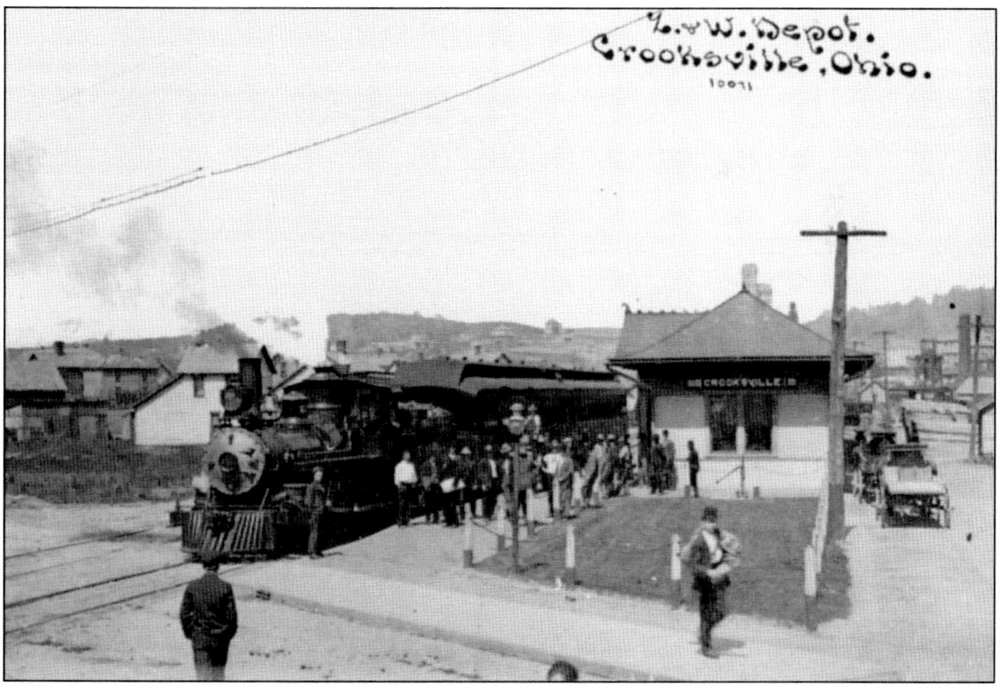


Around 1910, the Crooksville Z&W passenger depot was a busy place. By the 1970s, little trace of this building could be found. (Author's collection.)

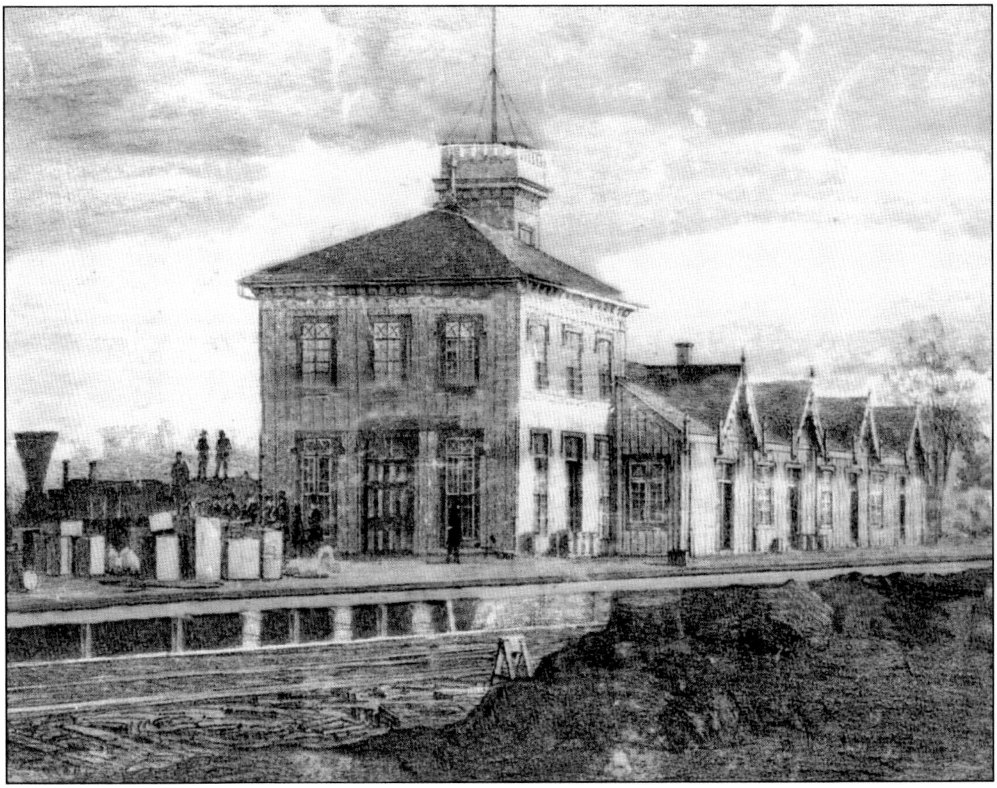

An early depot was built at the crossing of the Mansfield and Sandusky City Railroad (later SM&N) and the Pittsburgh, Fort Wayne and Chicago Railway (PFtW&C) and served Mansfield from the 1850s into the 1960s. It later became the site of a B&O interlocking tower. Below, a freight train is in the siding as a passenger train slows for Mansfield Union Station around 1906. The depot was built in 1869 at the crossing of the PFtW&C and Atlantic and Great Western Railroad (later the Erie Railroad), a little south of the depot shown here. (Sherman Room Photograph Collection, Mansfield Richland County Public Library.)

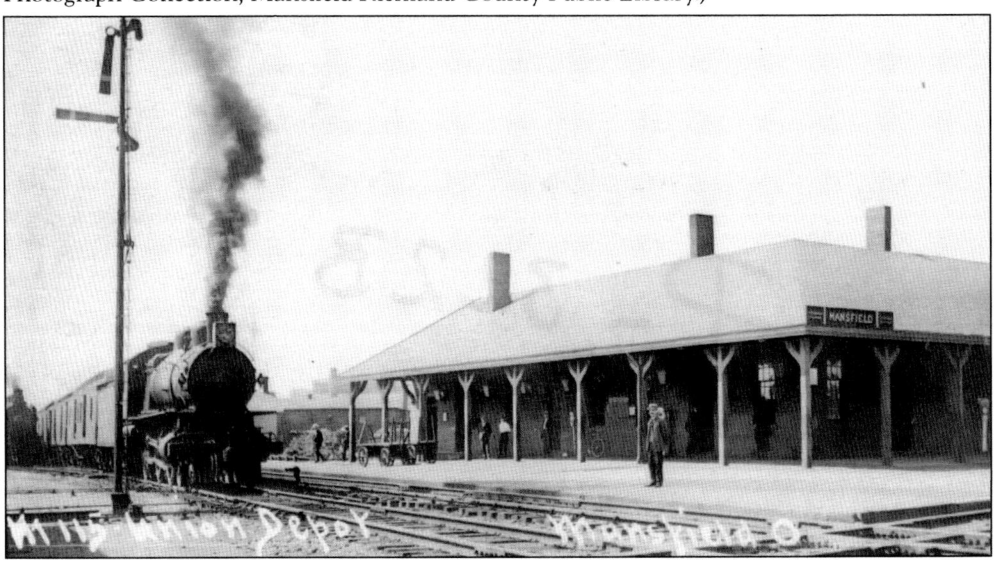

# *Four*

# PENNSYLVANIA LINES

The Columbus and Xenia Railroad completed a line from Xenia to Columbus in 1850. The Columbus and Xenia was formally leased by the Little Miami Railroad in 1868. The Cincinnati, Wilmington and Zanesville Railroad, completed in 1851, stretched from Morrow on the Little Miami Railroad to Zanesville on the Central Ohio Railroad. After financial difficulties, the line became the Cincinnati and Muskingum Valley Railroad (C&MV) in 1870. The Steubenville and Indiana Railroad (S&I) completed a line from Steubenville to Newark in 1855, but ran out of money to build its own line into Columbus. The financially strapped corporation eventually worked out a deal to share the Central Ohio Railroad's tracks between Newark and Columbus. All became part of the Panhandle, or Pittsburgh, Cincinnati and St. Louis Railway, under PRR control in 1869.

By 1855, Pittsburgh and Fort Wayne, by way of Mansfield, were connected by the Ohio and Pennsylvania and Ohio and Indiana Railroads. Financial problems led to the usual reorganizations and name changes. The line was called the PFtW&C when it was formally leased by the PRR in July 1869. In 1868, the Columbus, Chicago and Indiana Central Railway (CC&IC) operated trackage from Columbus to the Indiana border at Union City. The CC&IC already had a line connecting Columbus with Indianapolis. More consolidations led to the Pittsburgh, Cincinnati, Chicago and St. Louis Railroad in 1916, all under the control of the PRR.

In 1869, the Cleveland, Mount Vernon and Delaware Railroad was formed to extend the line of the former Cleveland, Zanesville and Cincinnati Railroad (CZ&C) from its terminal at Millersburg southwest to Columbus. The extension was completed by 1873. The CZ&C was reorganized as the Cleveland, Akron and Columbus Railroad in 1885. The Cleveland, Akron and Columbus and the C&MV merged in 1911. The Columbus, Sandusky and Hocking Railroad, which connected Columbus with Lake Erie at Sandusky, opened in 1895 as the Columbus and Sandusky Short Line. The PRR acquired the northern portion of the bankrupt line in 1902; the portion that ran southeast of Columbus to Shawnee became part of the NYC and operated as the Zanesville and Western Railroad. Later the N&W acquired the line north of Columbus.

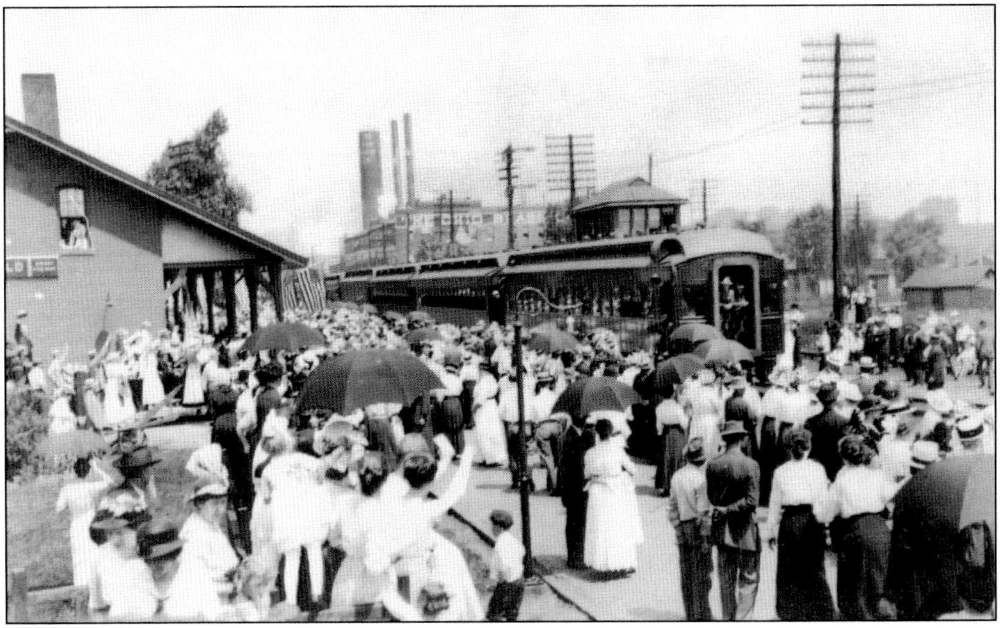

The union station was witness to many important events in Mansfield. Above, in 1912 William Jennings Bryan stopped during his campaign for president. Below, tributaries to the Mohican River flood the station grounds in 1913. The Erie Railroad and the PRR ran over 30 trains through the depot around 1900. (Above, Sherman Room Photograph Collection, Mansfield Richland County Public Library; below, author's collection.)

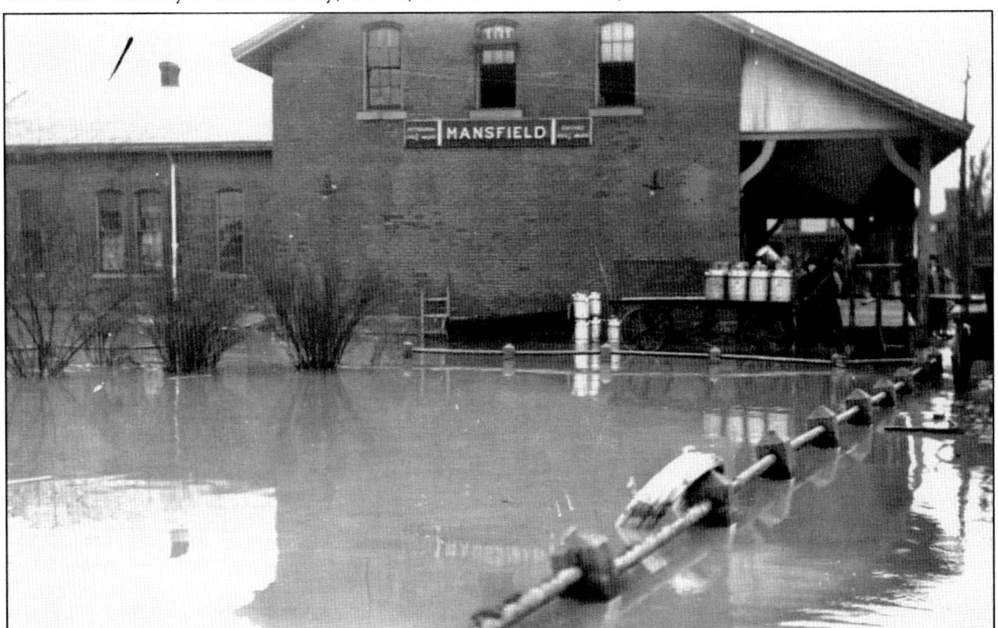

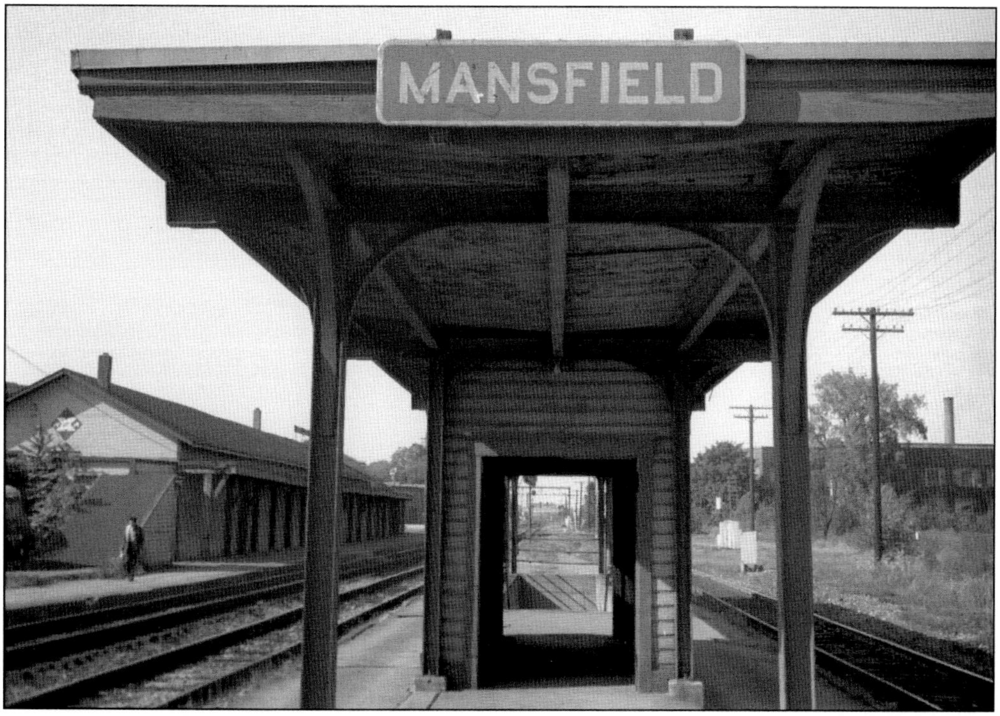


The PRR remodeled the union station in 1941. Seen above, in 1968, one of the many improvements was a subway so that passengers could reach the far tracks in safety. A small heated enclosed shelter was also built for westbound passengers. Inside (below) the depot was completely rearranged. This view shows the PRR and Erie ticket counter, part of the main waiting room, and the yet-to-be-stocked newsstand. (Above, photograph by the author; below, Sherman Room Photograph Collection, Mansfield Richland County Public Library.)

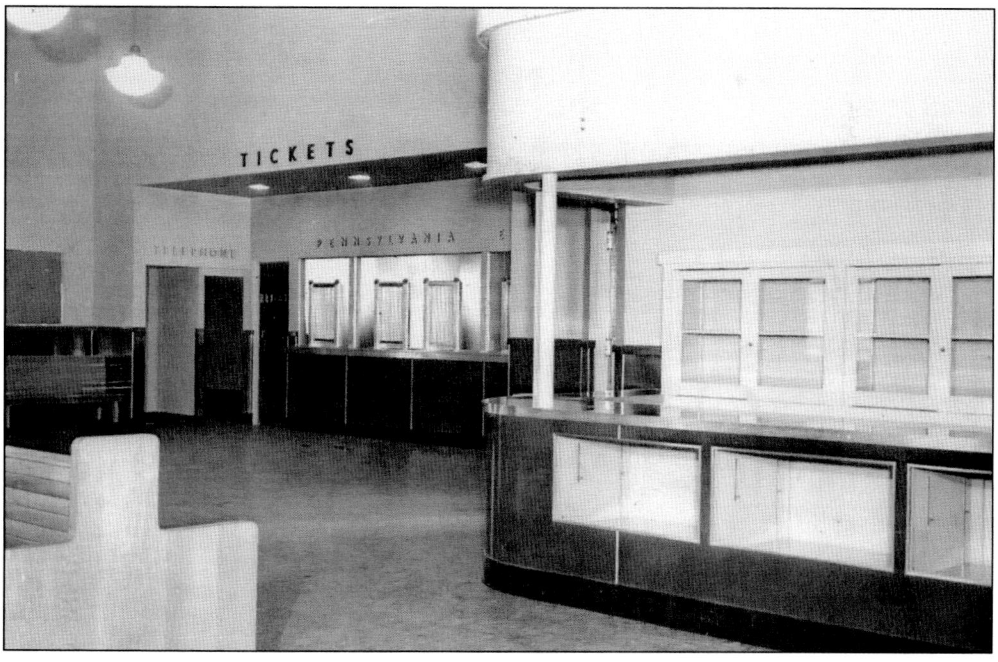

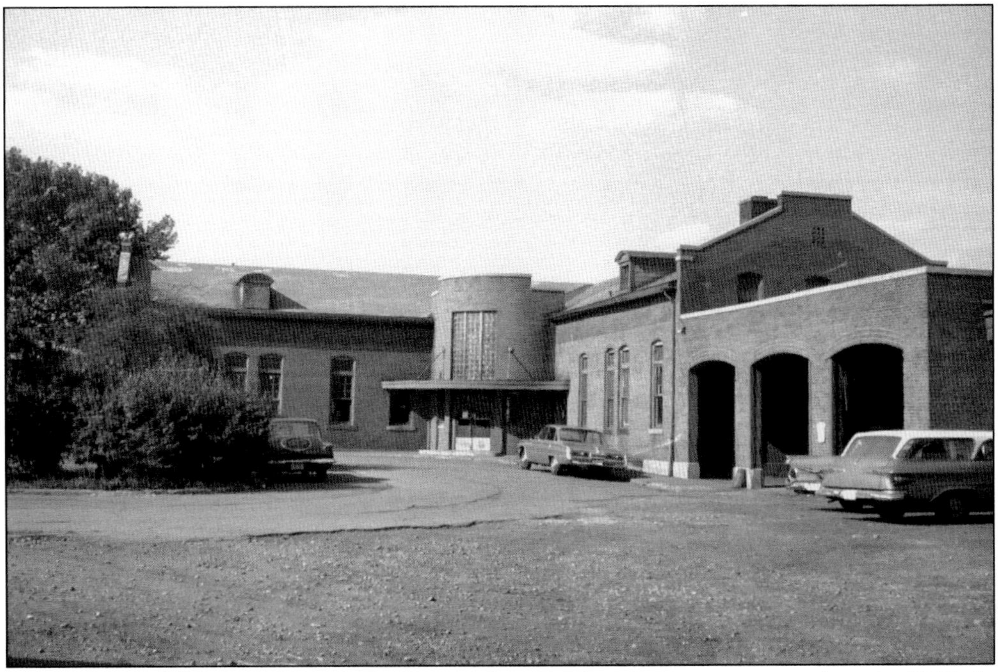

The exterior of the union station also received a complete makeover, as seen here in 1968. By 1950, train traffic at the depot had greatly declined. The last passenger train left the station April 30, 1971. Unfortunately this once-grand structure was razed. (Photograph by the author.)

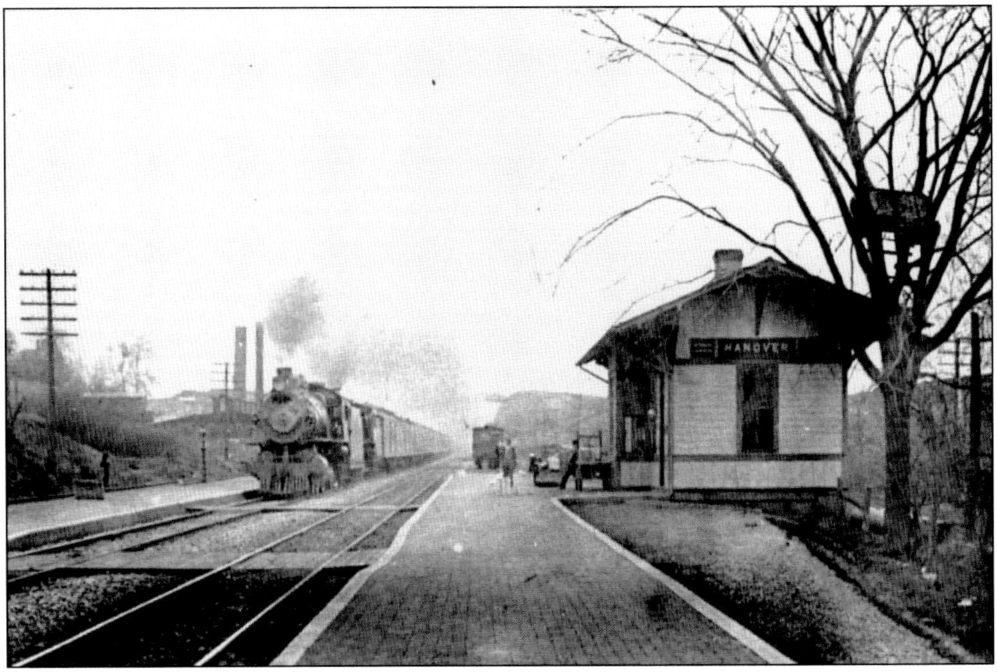


The PFtW&C had a combination depot at Frazeyburg, however it was gone by the late 1960s. The depot closed in 1963, however, a passenger train had not stopped since 1953. The depot was shortly torn down. Pictured is the PRR standard-design depot at Hanover, the next station west, which was closed in 1963. Nearby was VI signal tower. (Jim Henry collection.)

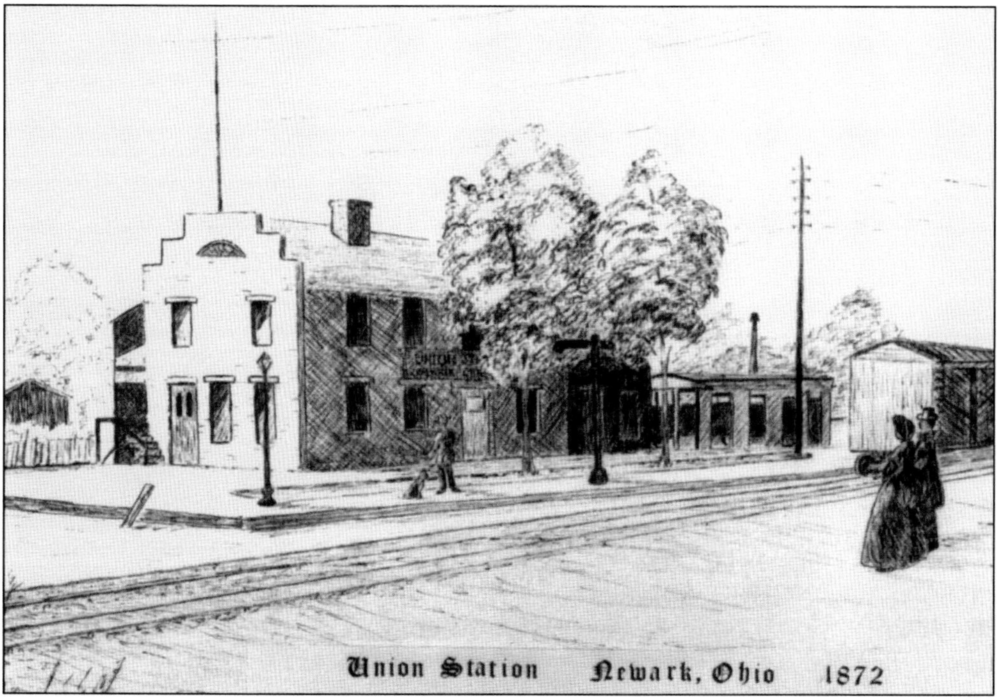


The above depot served the Central Ohio Railroad (later B&O) and the PFtW&C at Newark and was the predecessor to the B&O and Pittsburgh, Cincinnati and St. Louis Railway (PC&StL) depots built in the late 1800s. In 1880, the PC&StL opened the passenger depot, below, on Walnut Street. (Author's collection.)

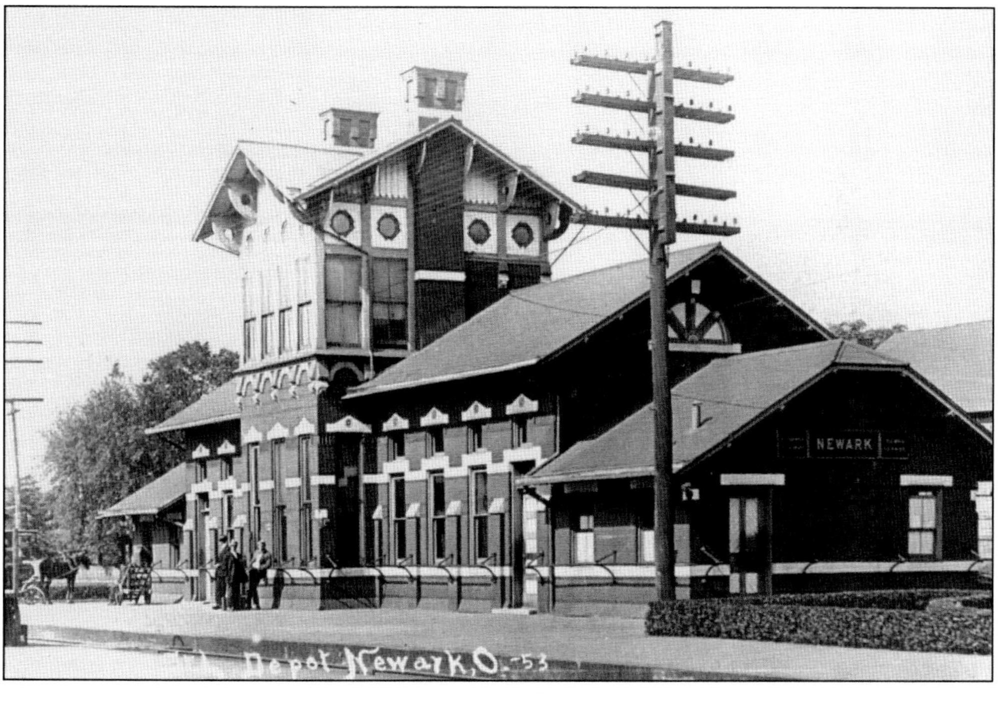

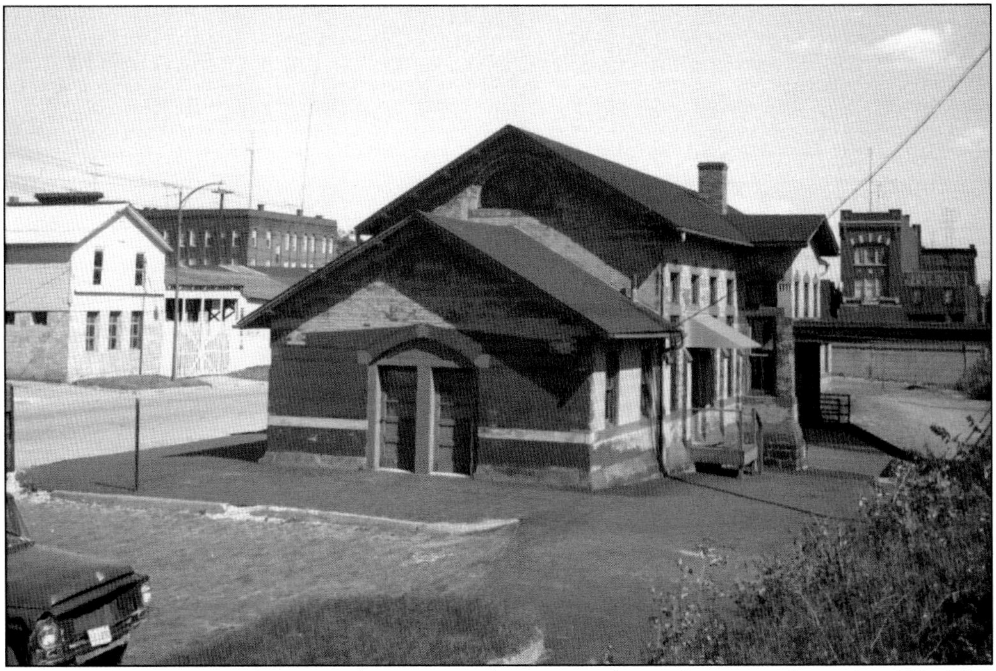

Photographed in 1970, the Newark passenger depot was a busy place into the early 1950s. The tracks had been elevated through Newark in 1930, and passengers reached the platform by an elevator shown in the photograph below. Also the ornate tower for railroad operators had been removed. The depot closed in 1963 and later housed a restaurant. In 1997, it was purchased by a local foundation and restored. (Photographs by the author.)

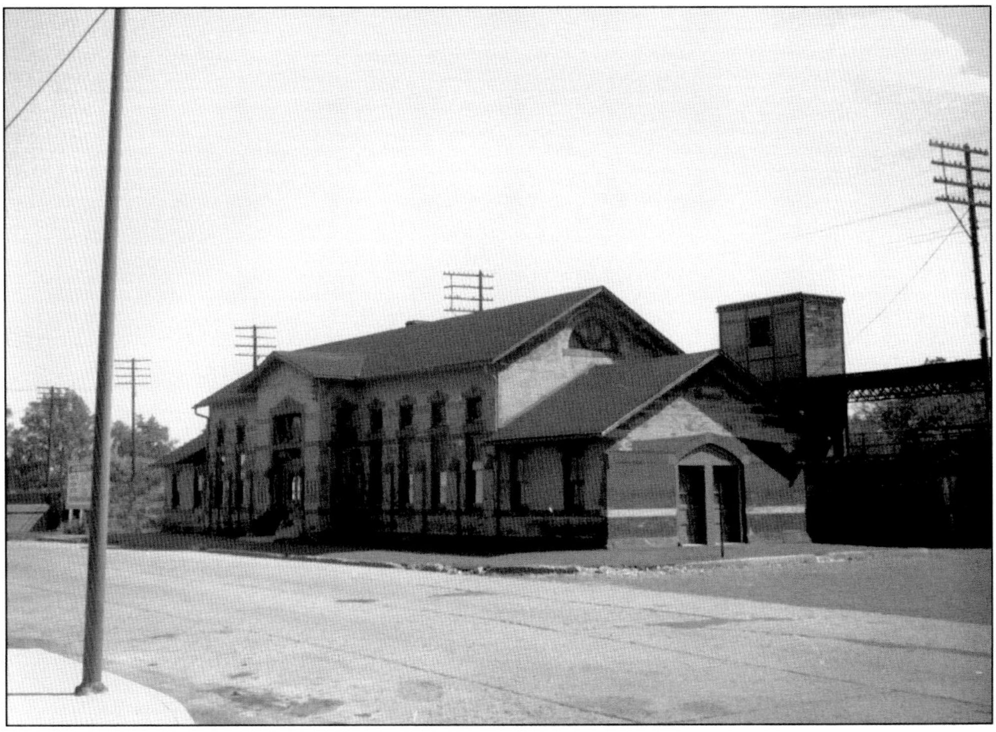

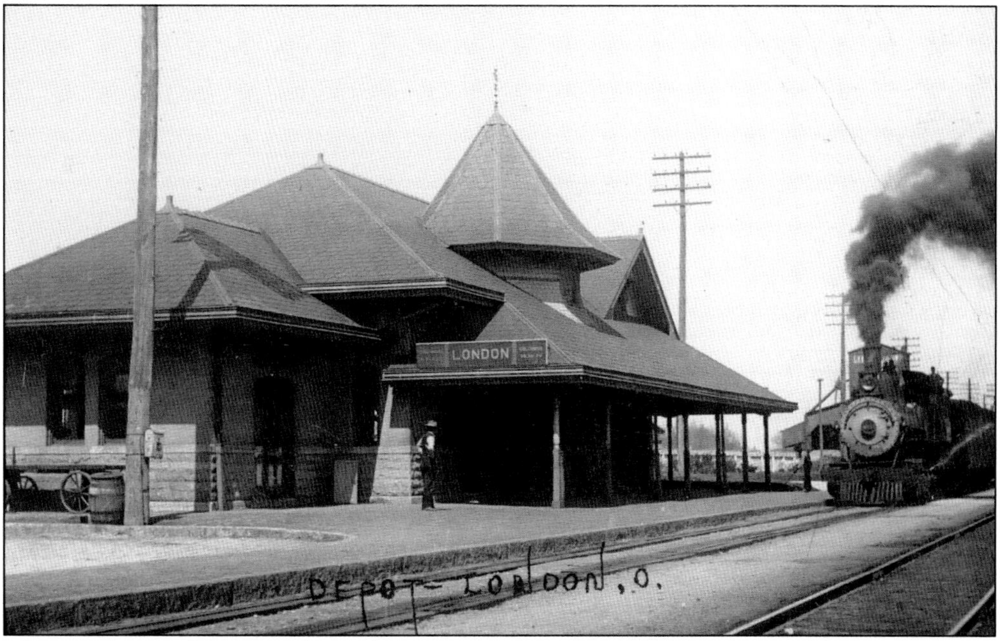


The PC&StL used the B&O depots between Newark and Columbus. The Pittsburgh, Cincinnati, Chicago and St. Louis Railroad (PCC&StL), or its predecessor, had an unusual shape brick depot at West Jefferson. The original London depot was a frame barnlike building built in the early 1850s by the Columbus and Xenia–Little Miami line. The PCC&StL built this brick passenger depot at London. A separate freight house was nearby. The grounds around the depot were well maintained with flower gardens perhaps in competition with the nearby CCC&StL depot. The depot closed in 1963. The photograph below was taken in 1968. At the Madison County Historical Society in London is the relocated PCC&StL depot from Florence. (Above, author's collection; below, photograph by Charles Garvin.)

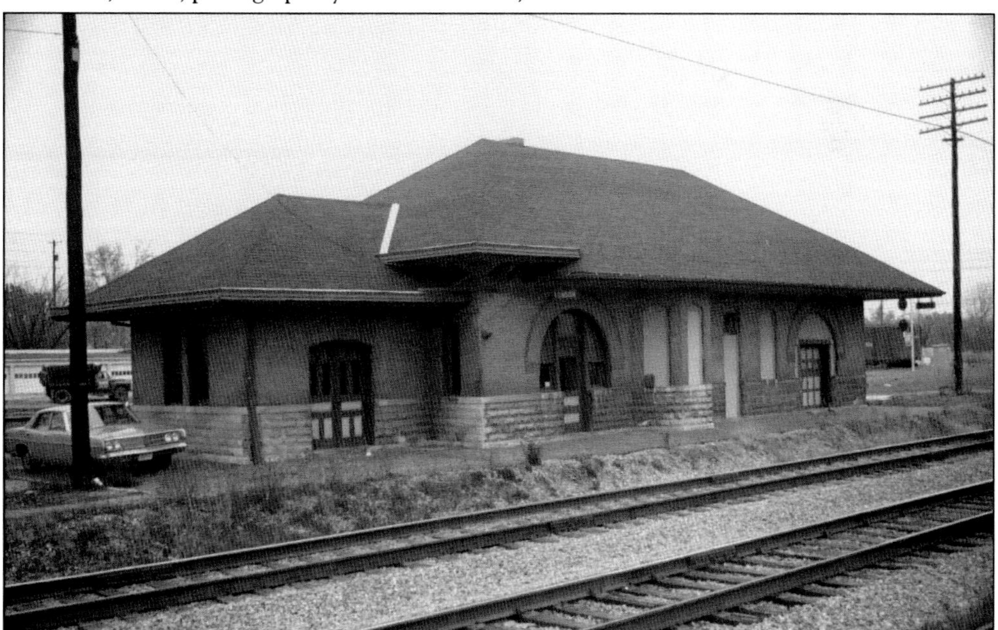

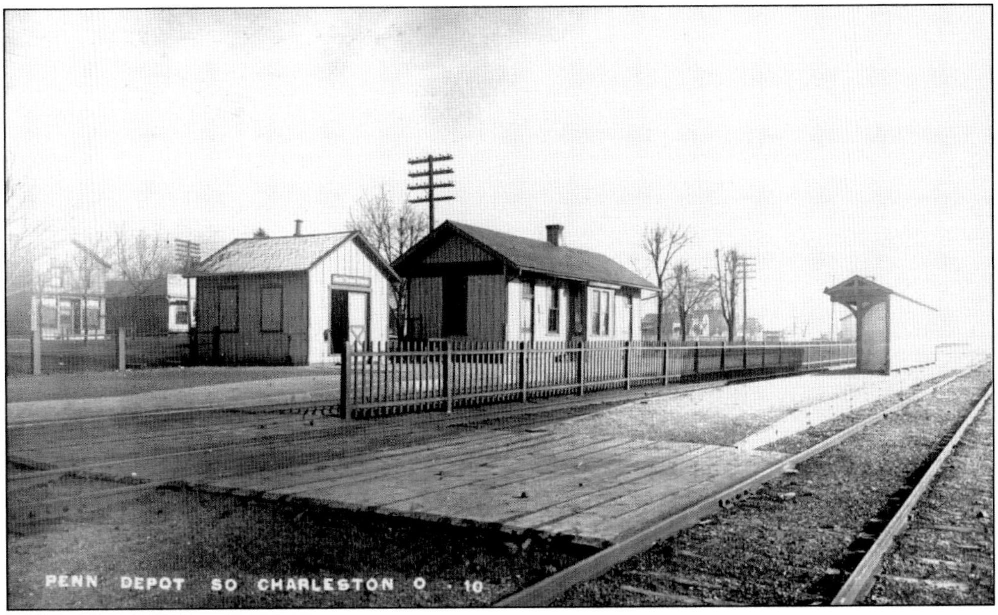


Above is an earlier PCC&StL depot at South Charleston; below is the *c.* 1906 replacement. Note that the new depot has the same platform as its predecessor. Down the track at the Detroit, Toledo and Ironton Railroad crossing was a standard design PRR interlocking tower. The depot closed in 1966, but the depot and tower were still there in 1971. (Above, author's collection; below, Gary D. Rolih collection.)

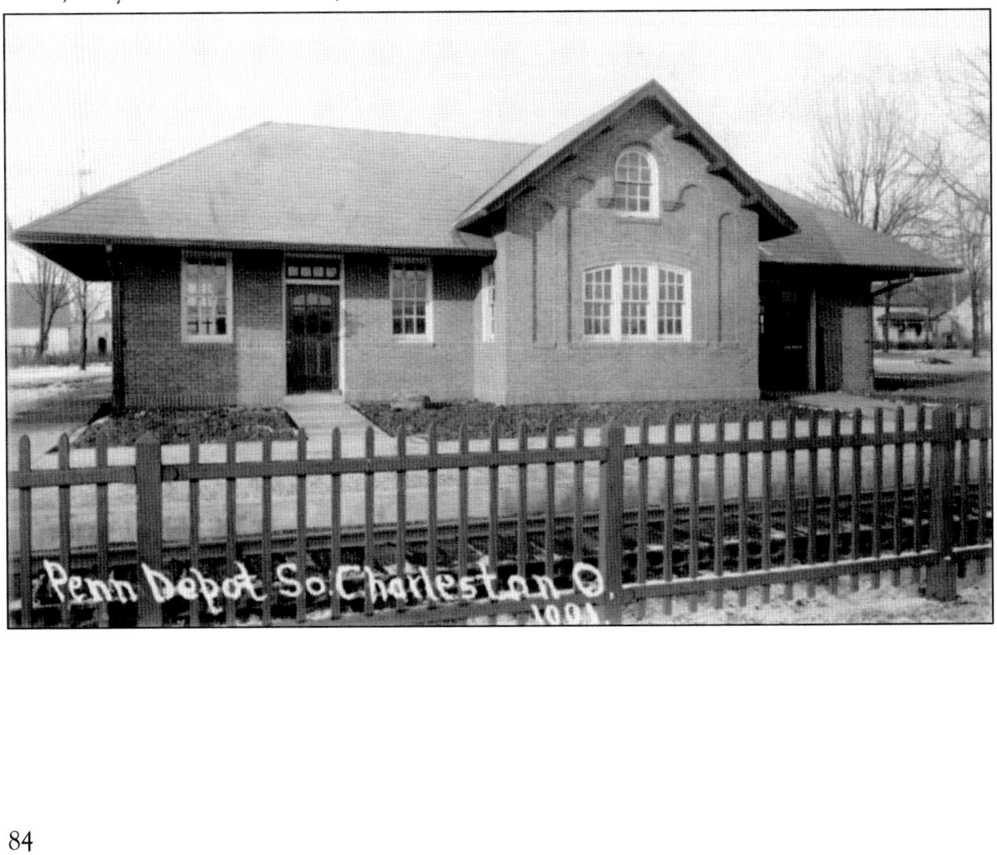

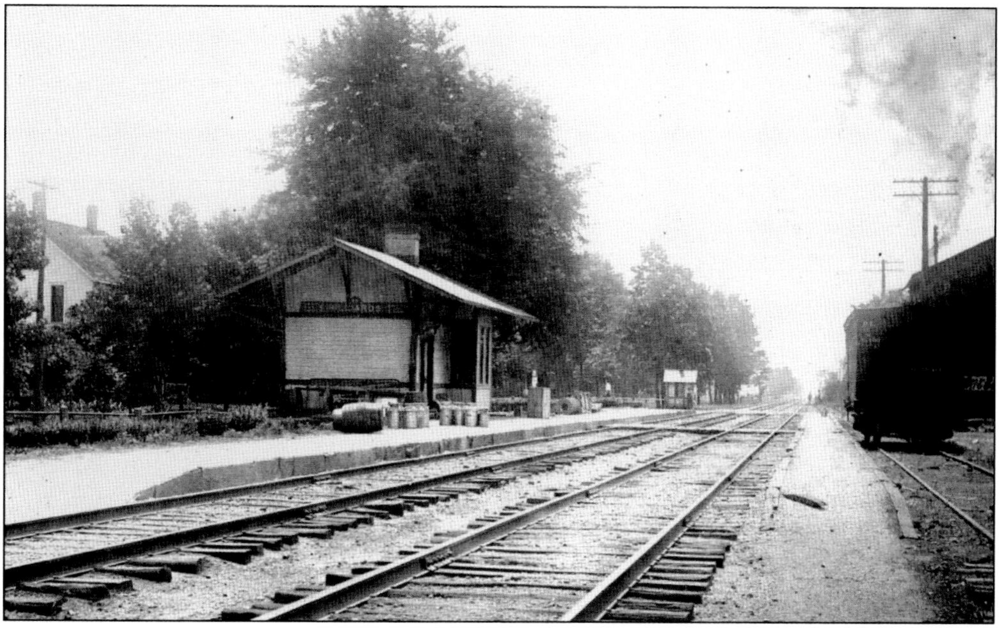

Northwest of Columbus on the Piqua line is Hilliards. This is one common style used on the entire PCC&StL. Hilliards was just a small country community when this postcard was made. Now it has been consumed by the urban sprawl of Columbus. The depot was closed in 1963 or 1966 and has since been relocated to the Franklin County fairgrounds and restored. (Author's collection.)

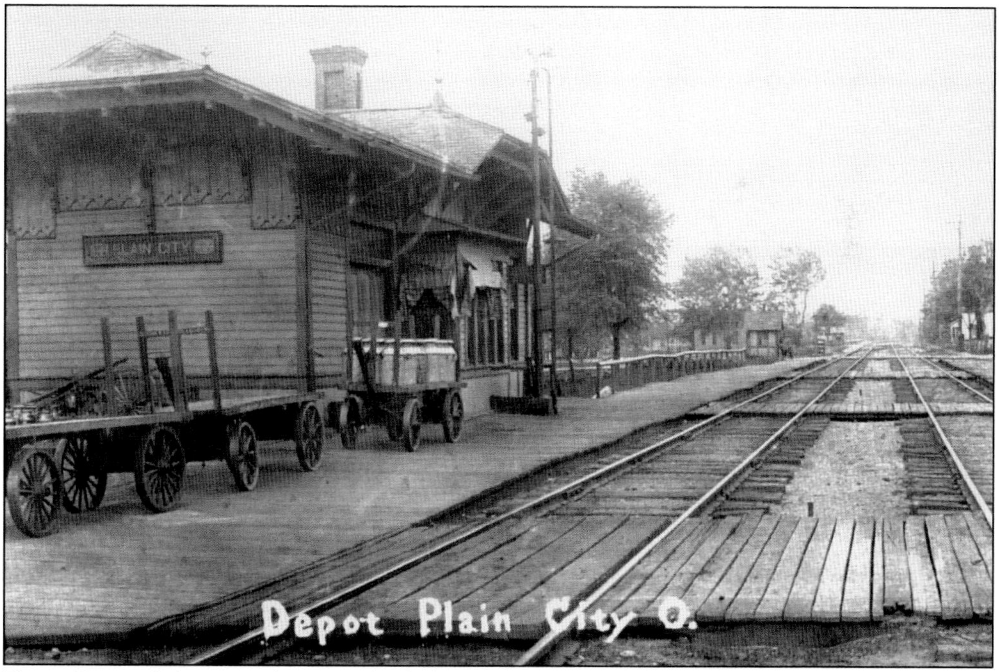


Plain City exhibits another standard design PCC&StL depot; this one for a little larger community. Note here and in the Hilliards view the ever-present crossing watchman and his shack. (Author's collection.)

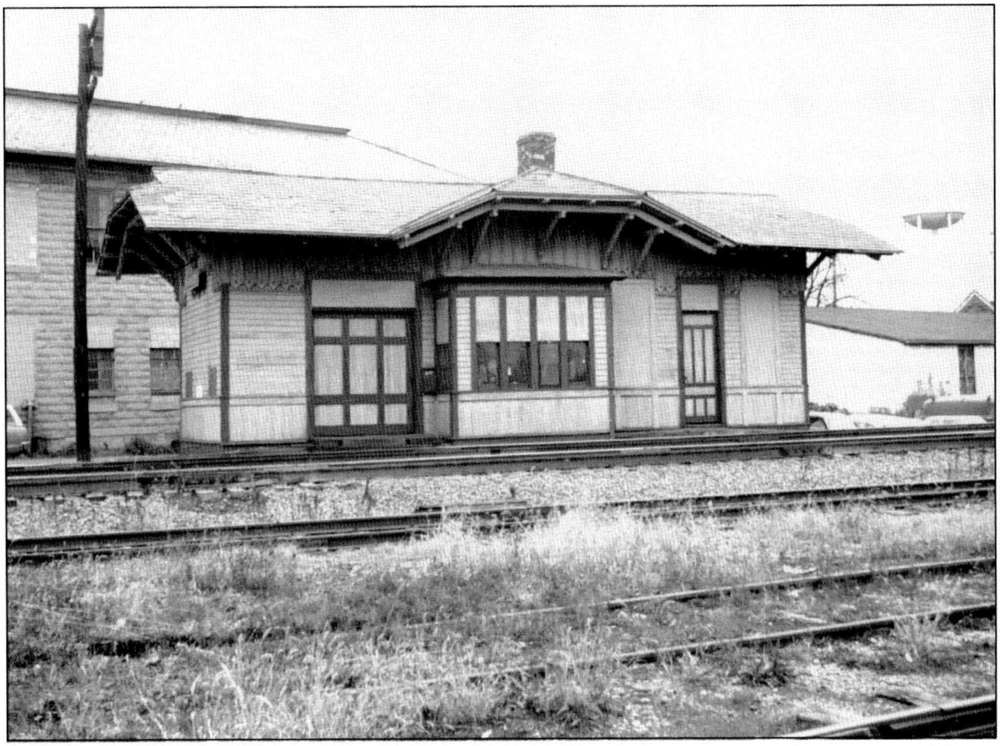

By 1968, the Plain City depot was still an attractive building, although the agent had been removed in 1963. Sometime after 1971 the depot was torn down. (Photograph by the author.)

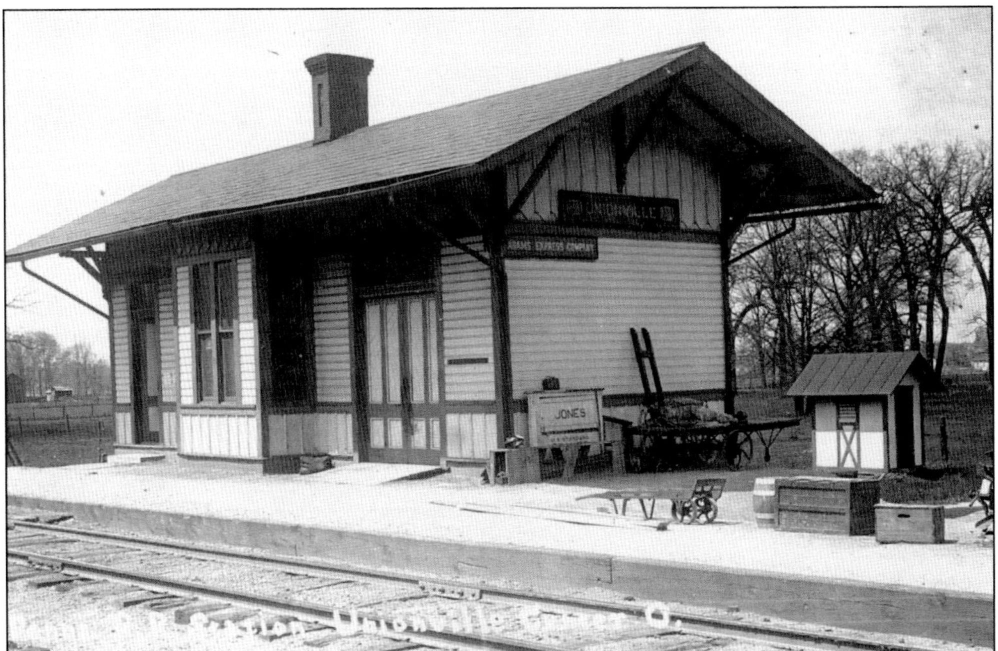


Compare the Unionville Center depot to Hilliards; they were quite similar. This 1912 view shows a well-kept depot grounds. (Author's collection.)

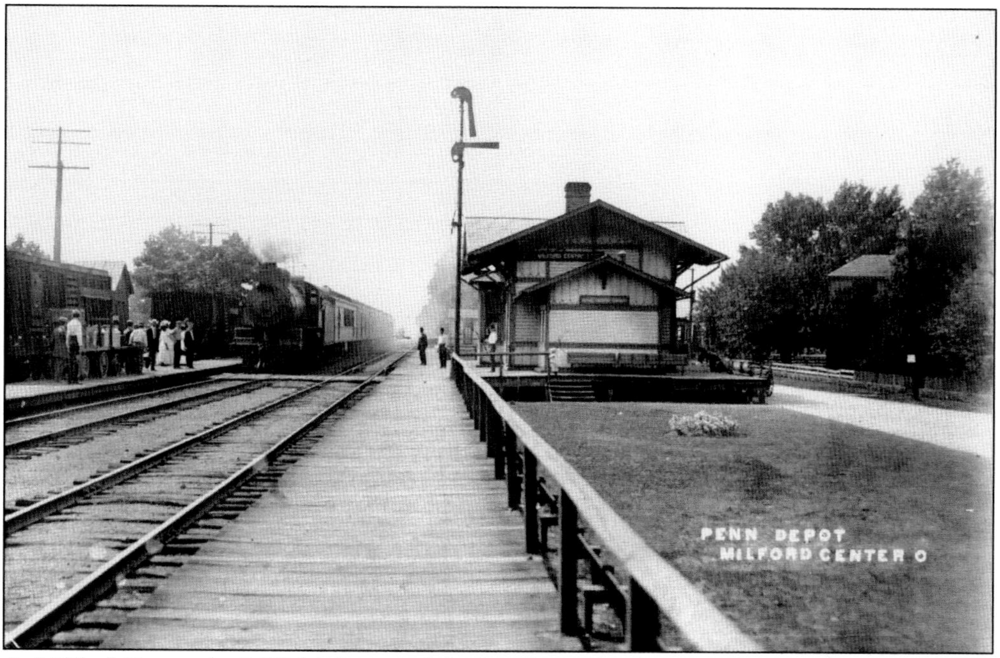


At Milford Center the PCC&StL crossed the Big Four. The depot is of the same design as Plain City. Note the raised plank platform. The signal tower in the background, below, is of an early design. Surprisingly it and the freight house outlived the depot and were still there in 1967. The freight house, which is to the far left in the view below, was previously the Milford Center combination depot. (Gary D. Rolih collection.)

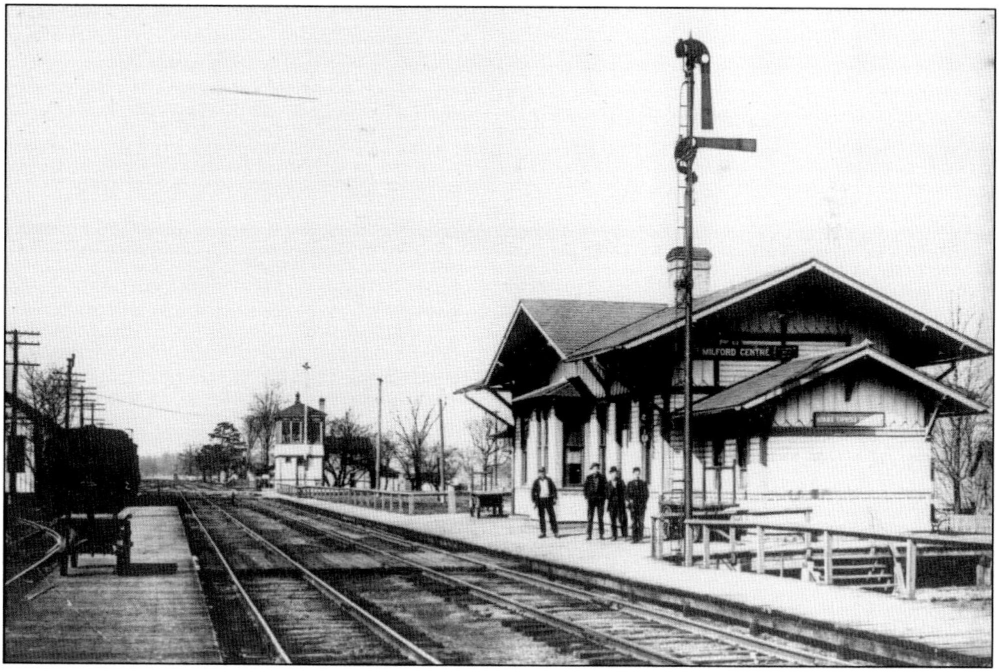

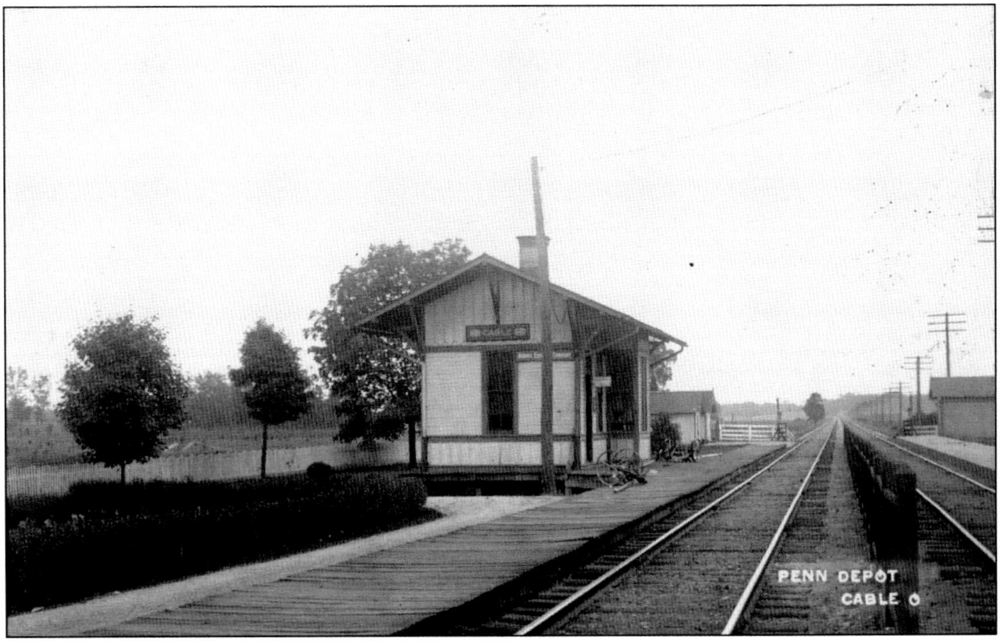


The PCC&StL combination depot at Cable has a similar plank platform for both eastbound and westbound trains. It also is built to the same plan as Hilliards and Unionville Center. The agency closed in 1930. (Author's collection.)

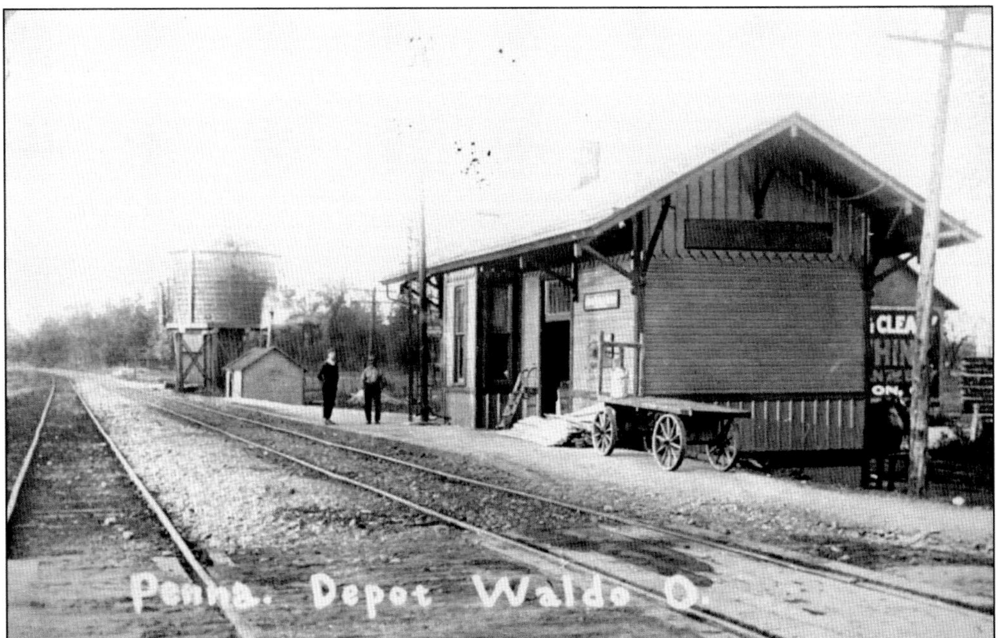


Waldo was on the PRR Sandusky branch. The depot was erected in 1895. Passenger service ended on this line in April 1931. This standard-design combination depot has been gone since the mid-1900s. In later years, the PRR maintained a small operators building at Troyton, also now gone. (Author's collection.)

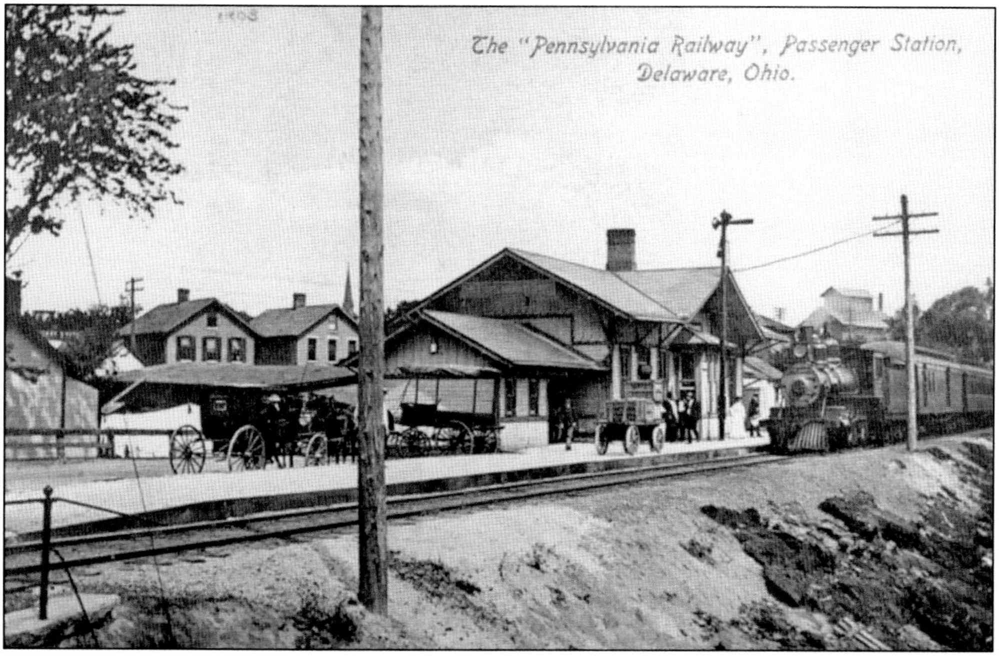


Here are two vintage views of the 1895 PRR depot at Delaware. The line originally followed the valley of the Olentangy River, but flooding problems led to a realignment further to the east. This depot was moved to the new alignment and a freight addition was added. A set of stairs led up to the elevated roadbed. The PRR closed the agency in 1962; the depot was still there into the 1970s. (David P. Oroszi collection.)

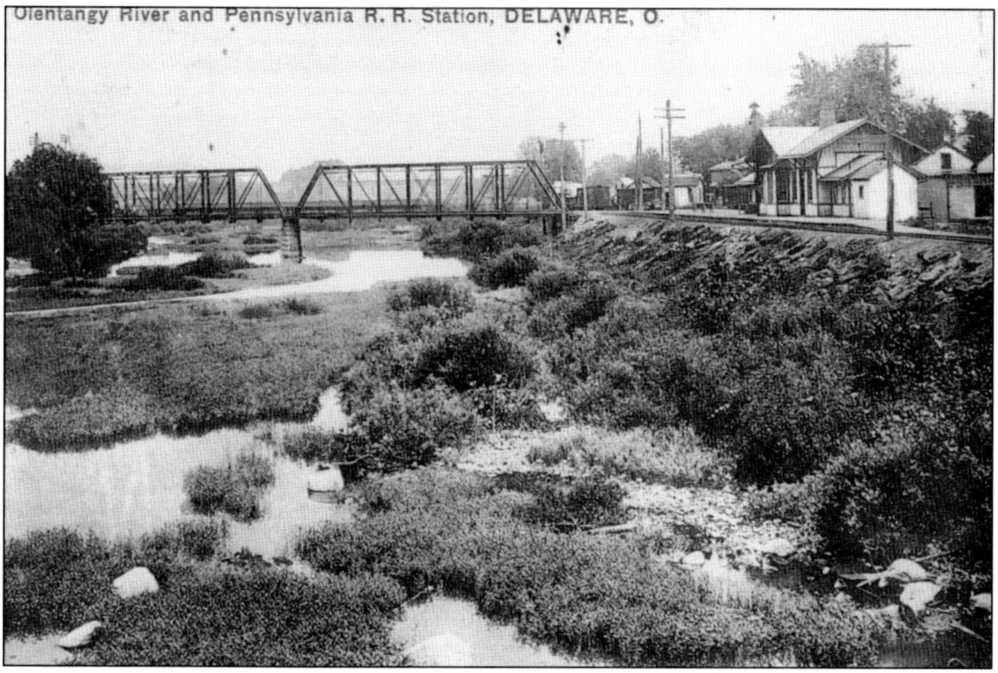

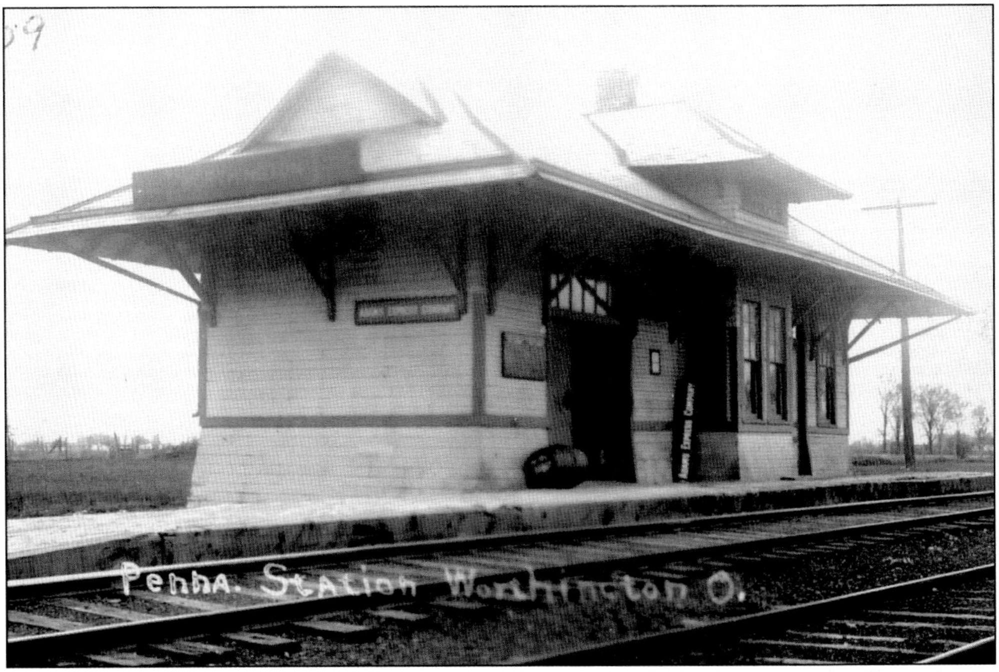


Above is a 1909 view of the 1895 PRR depot on the east side of Worthington. This depot design is related to the Columbus and Sandusky Short Line. A similar depot was located at Attica. Below is a *c.* 1950 view of the interlocking tower that guarded the crossing with the Big Four in Worthington. Both structures have been gone for some time. (Above, author's collection; below, photograph by Bernard Kern.)

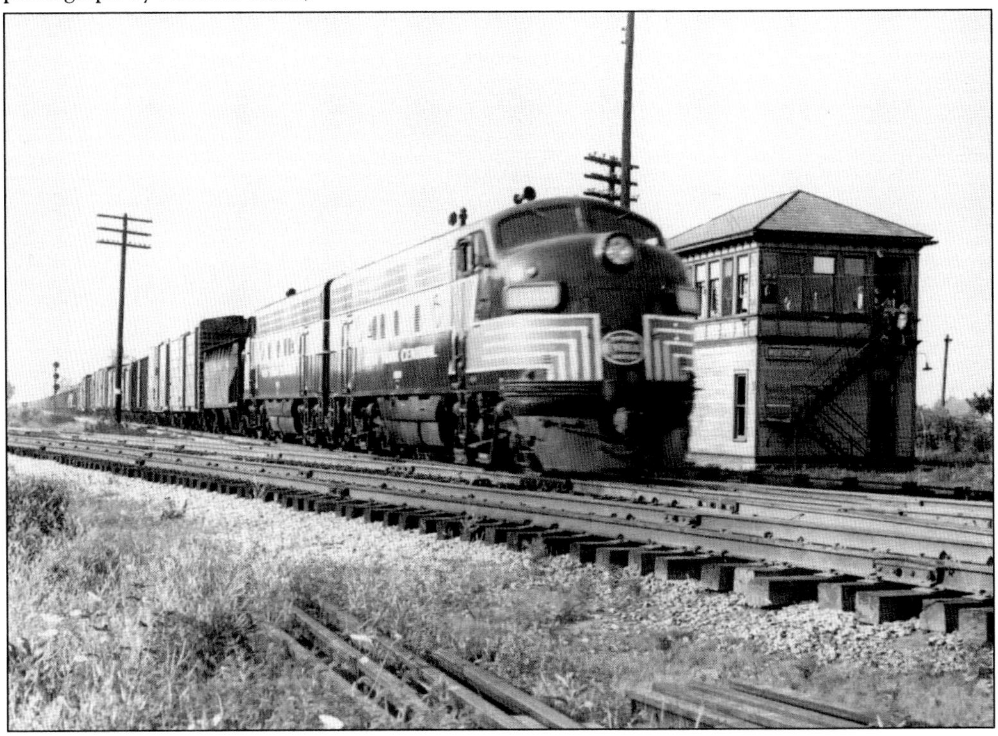

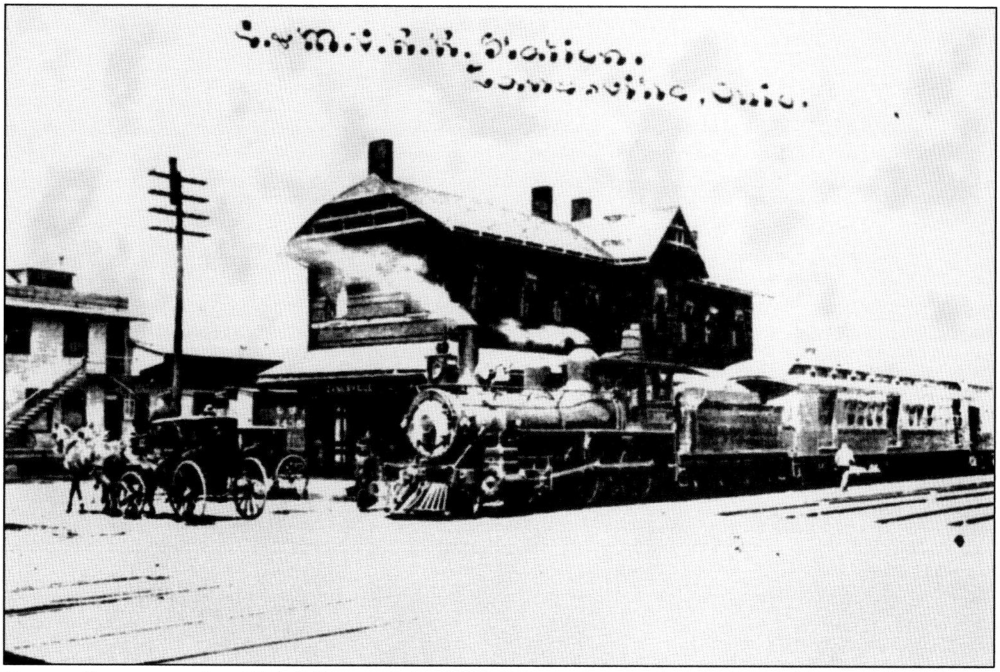

Zanesville was on the C&MV line of the PRR. The two-story brick depot dates to about 1870. Although tracks in this flood-prone downtown area have been removed, the depot and a NYC freight house remain, as seen below in 1969. (Above, author's collection; below, photograph by the author.)

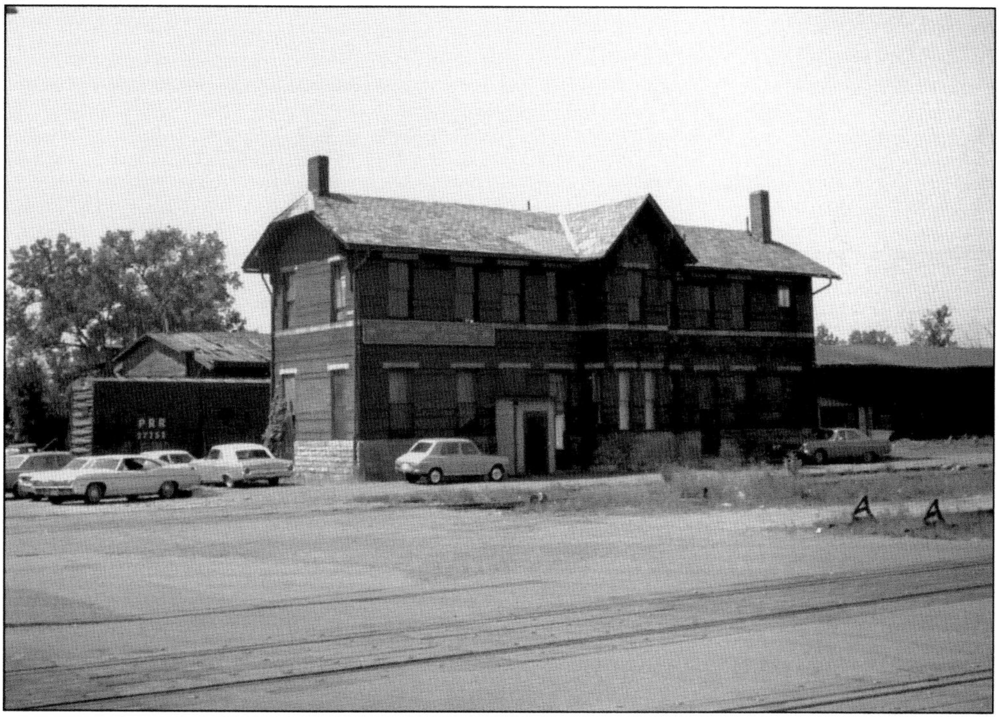

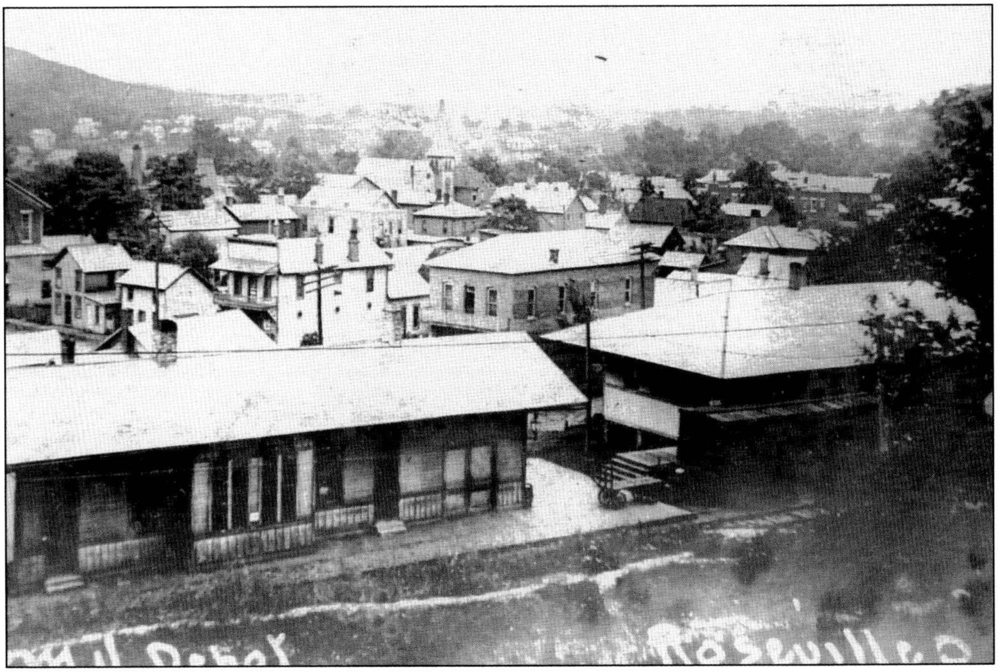

Roseville, above, and Crooksville, below, were important stations on the C&MV. Like Zanesville, they were major shipping points for pottery and other ceramic products. Each town had a separate freight house that was of similar size to the passenger depot. The freight house shows in the Roseville view. The Crooksville agency closed in the 1960s. Neither passenger depot was standing by 1970. (Author's collection.)

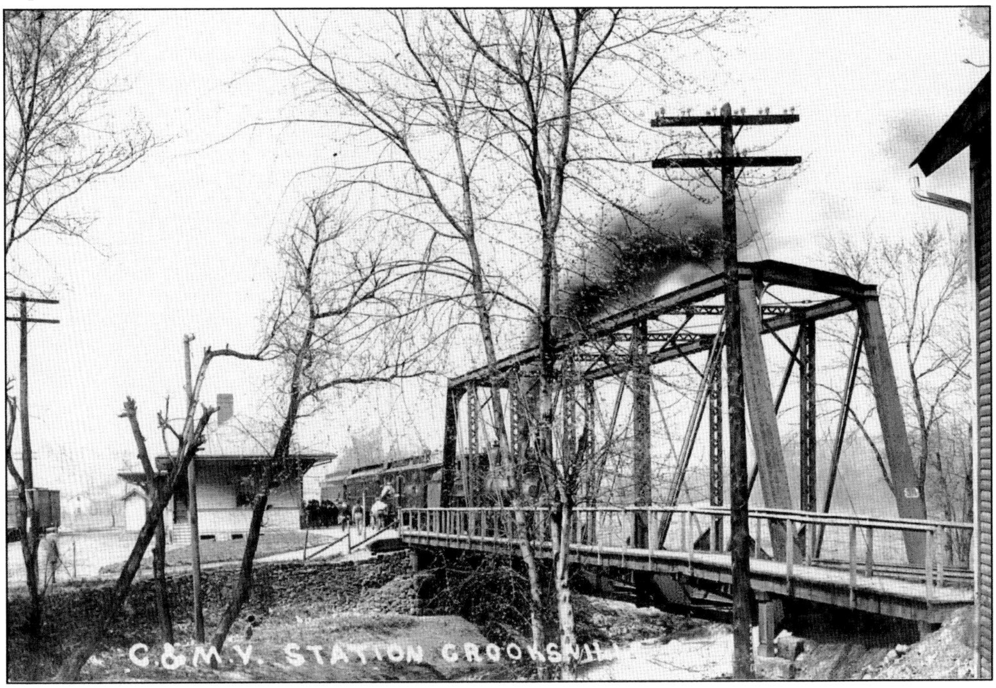

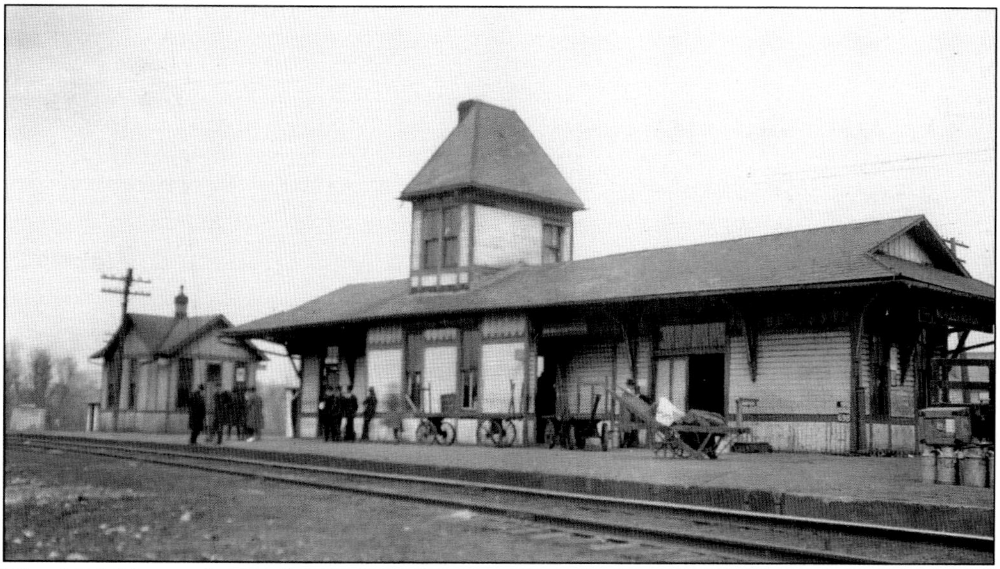

The C&MV met the T&OC and B&O at New Lexington. The C&MV depot was a union station. The above 1919 view shows the passenger depot and adjacent operators office. In later years, the tower on the depot was removed and the depot lost its distinctive appearance, as seen in the 1970 photograph below. A separate PRR freight house was nearby. (Above, T&OC photograph, Allen County [Ohio] Historical Society Collection; below, photograph by Charles Garvin.)

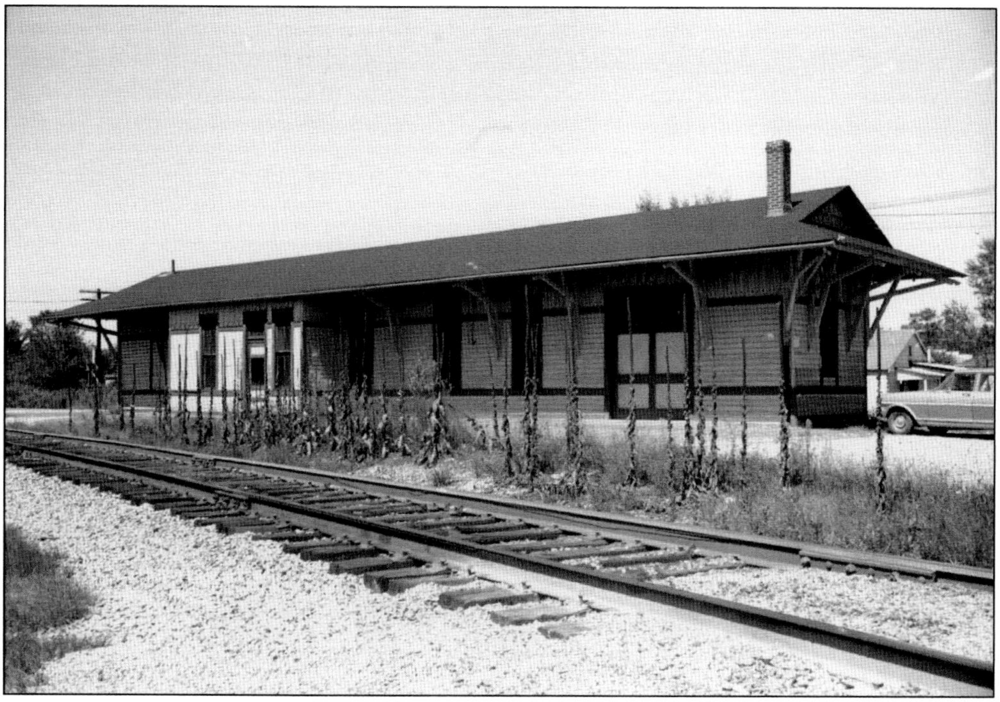

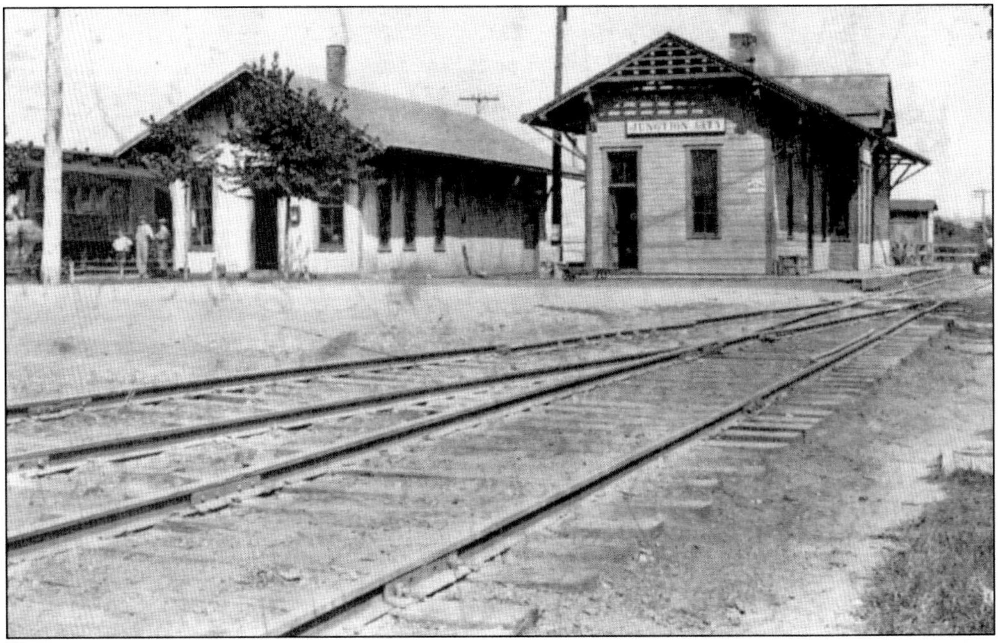


The C&MV apparently did not have a separate depot in Junction City, but instead used either the T&OC (on the left) or B&O (on the right). (Author's collection.)

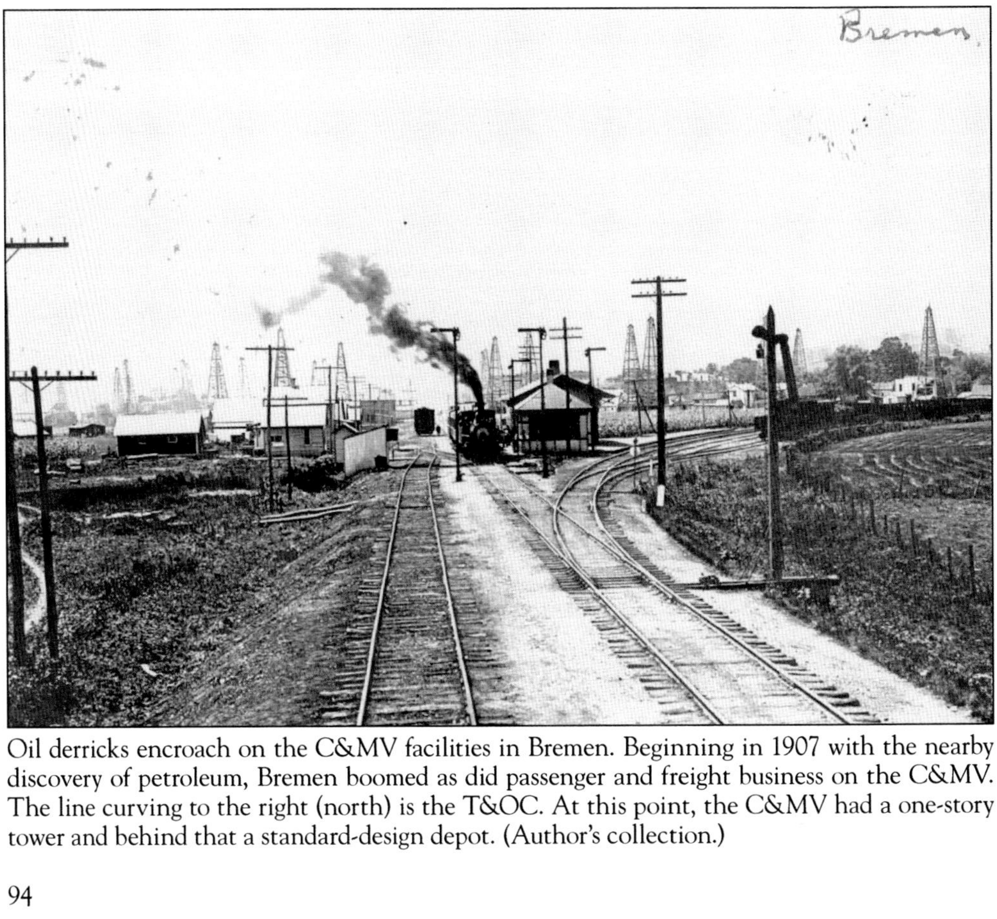


Oil derricks encroach on the C&MV facilities in Bremen. Beginning in 1907 with the nearby discovery of petroleum, Bremen boomed as did passenger and freight business on the C&MV. The line curving to the right (north) is the T&OC. At this point, the C&MV had a one-story tower and behind that a standard-design depot. (Author's collection.)

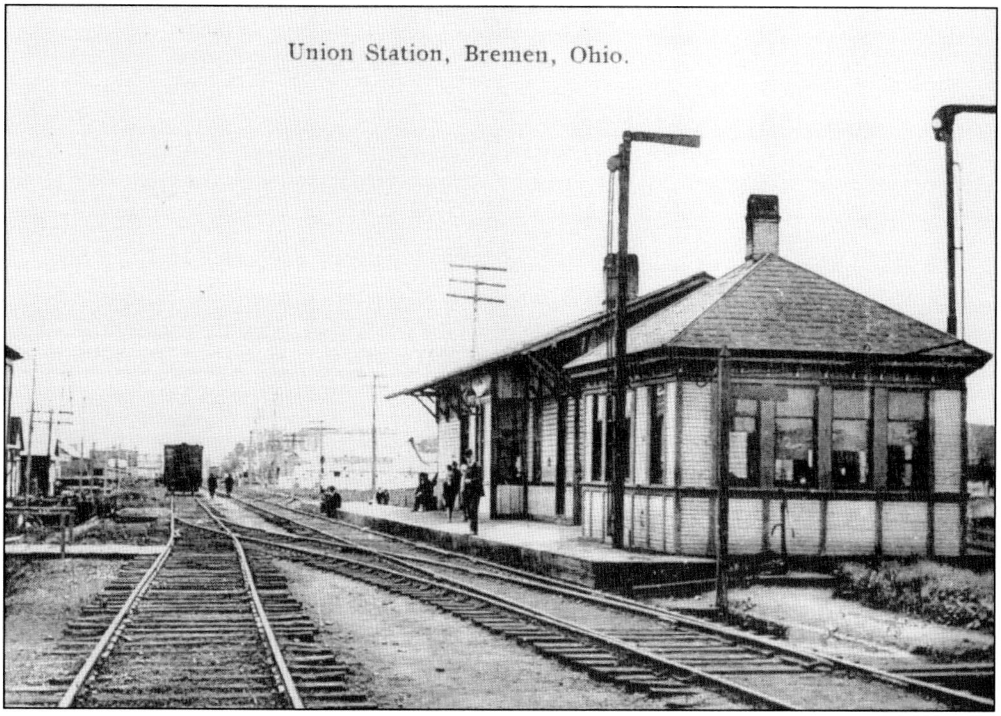


This early-1900s view of Bremen also looks west. The PRR closed their agency here in 1963. Only the tower remained in the early 1970s. (Author's collection.)

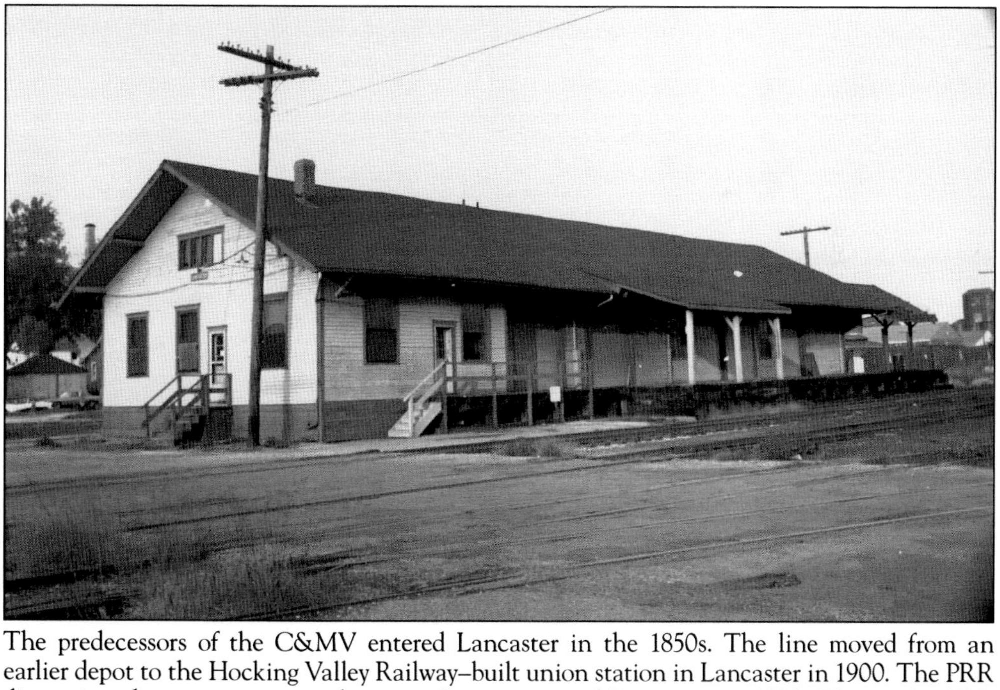

The predecessors of the C&MV entered Lancaster in the 1850s. The line moved from an earlier depot to the Hocking Valley Railway–built union station in Lancaster in 1900. The PRR discontinued passenger service between Cincinnati and Lancaster in 1930. This is the PRR freight station in 1967. Just south of this used to be the C&MV engine terminal. (Photograph by Charles Garvin.)

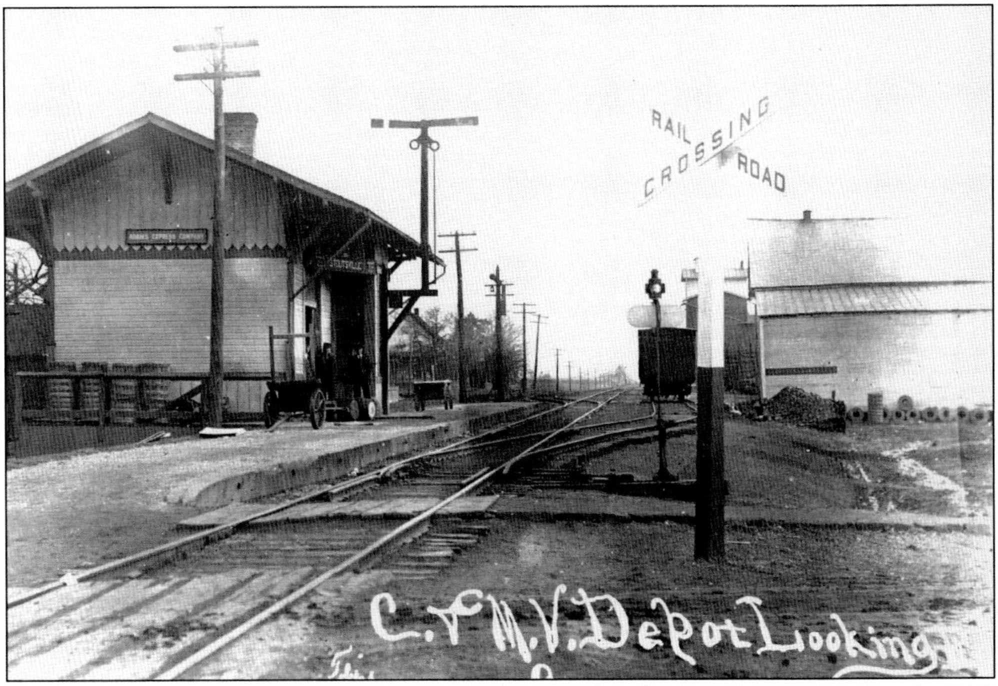


Amanda and Stoutsville had C&MV depots built to similar plans. Both were closed by the PRR in 1959 and have since disappeared. Around 1907, the Stoutsville station staff waits for the next train. (Author's collection.)

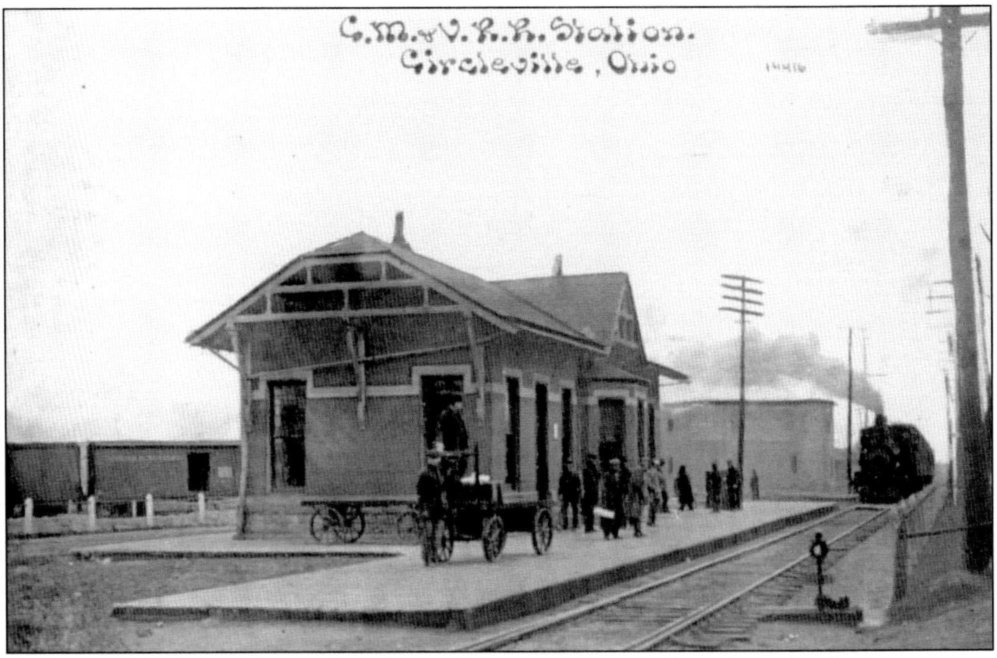


The C&MV built a substantial brick depot in Circleville to replace an earlier frame structure. The Scioto Valley Railroad (later N&W) also used this as its station stop in Circleville. Soon after this 1910 view was taken, the depot would be altered by the addition of long platform shelters along the N&W side. See page 109 for an additional view. (Author's collection.)

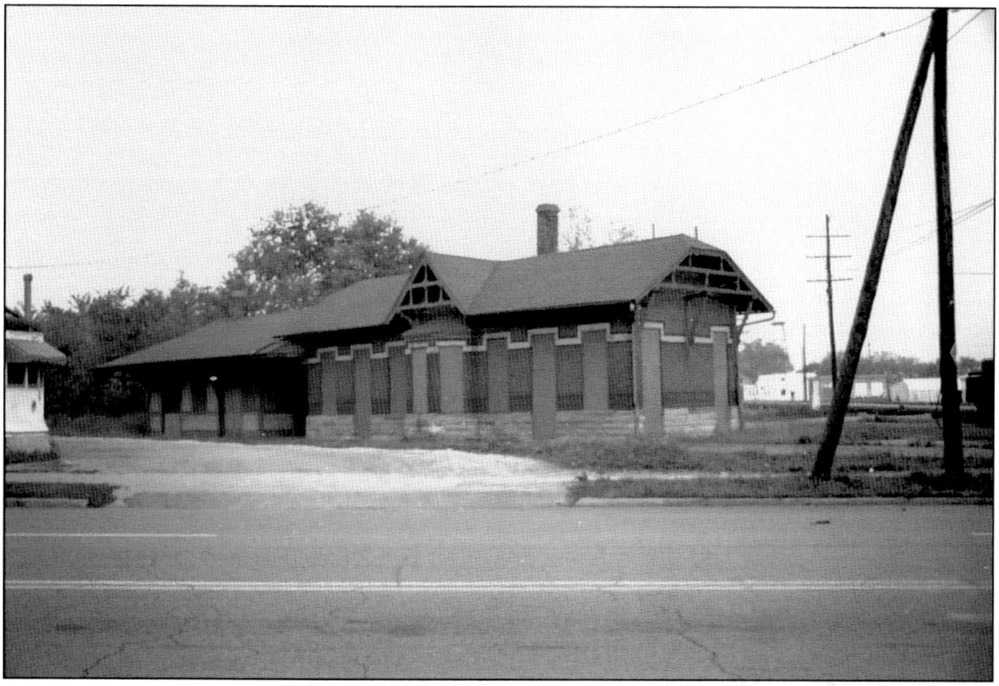

After passenger service was discontinued the platform shelters were removed. The C&MV maintained a separate nearby freight house and an interlocking tower once guarded the crossing of the N&W. The passenger depot remains in alternate use. (Photograph by Charles Garvin.)

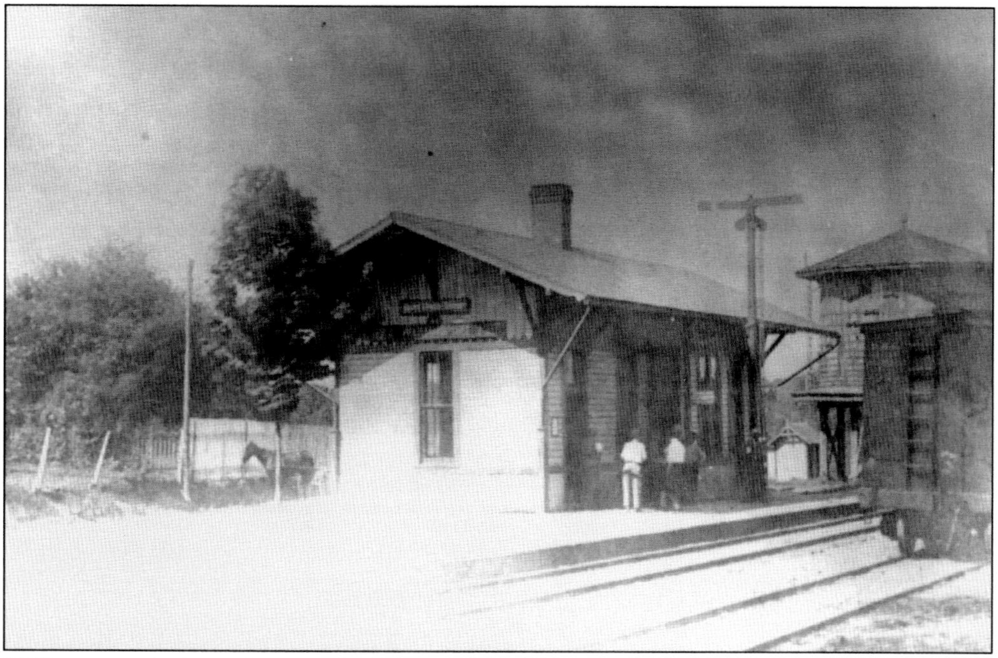

Williamsport had another standard design C&MV depot. It was also a water stop. Residents from nearby Woodlyn used this depot. The PRR closed the depot in either 1958 or 1963. It has since been razed. (Jim Henry collection.)

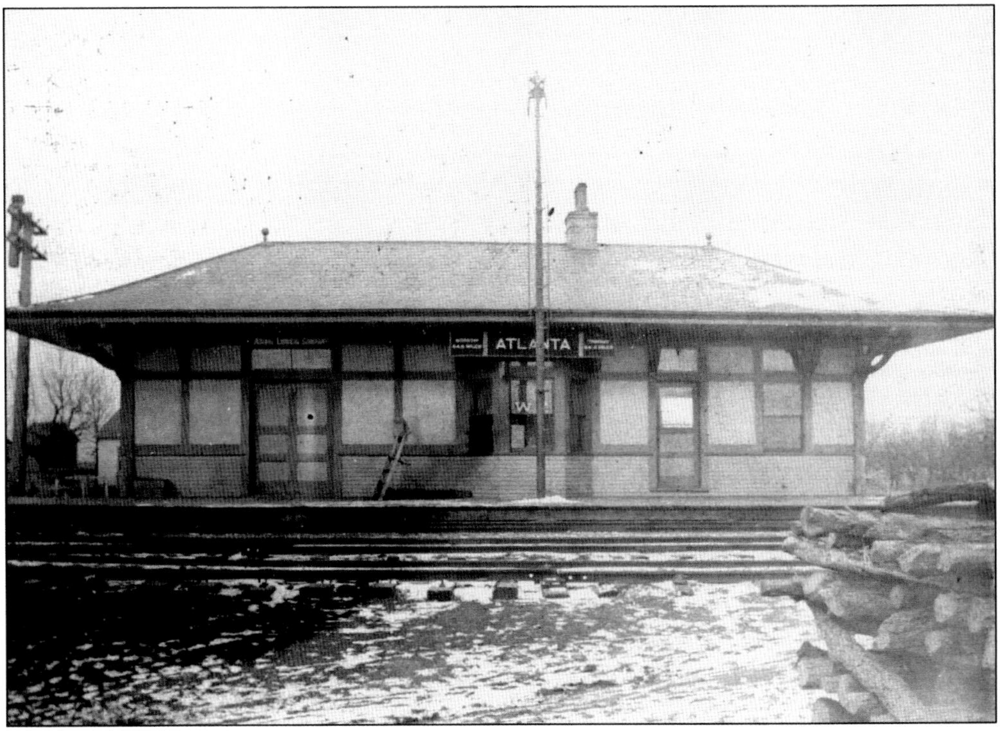


Atlanta's C&MV depot definitely showed the influence the PRR had on this line. Depots of similar hipped-roof architecture are found on other PRR lines throughout the state. There is also a question about closing dates—1959 or 1963. Unfortunately the building no longer exists. (Author's collection.)

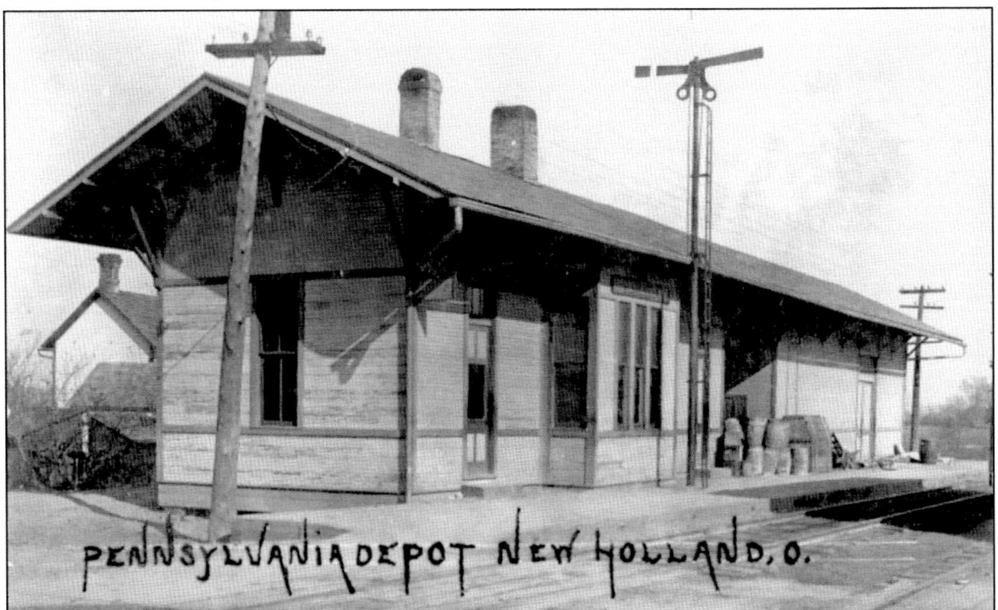


New Holland's depot has an extended freight room suggesting it was a busy shipping point. The PRR apparently closed this agency in 1962. Like Atlanta, it is gone. (Jim Henry collection.)

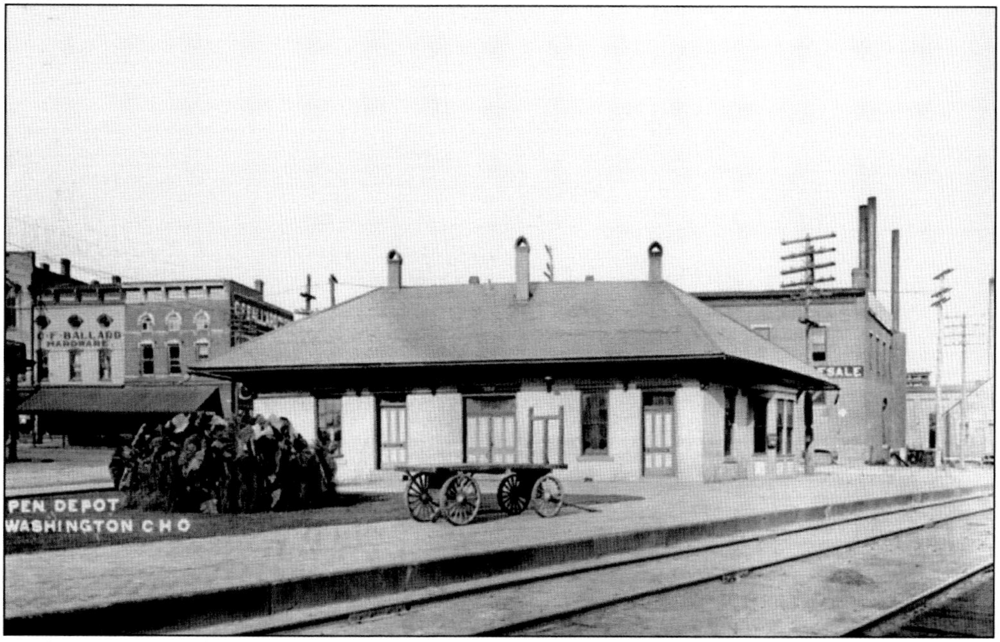


Washington Courthouse was a busy railroad town and the PRR's depot was indicative of the increased business at this point. These two views provide an interesting contrast between train time and quiet interludes. Note the flower garden. The C&MV had a brick freight house nearby. Both C&MV structures still stand in alternative use. (Gary D. Rolih collection.)

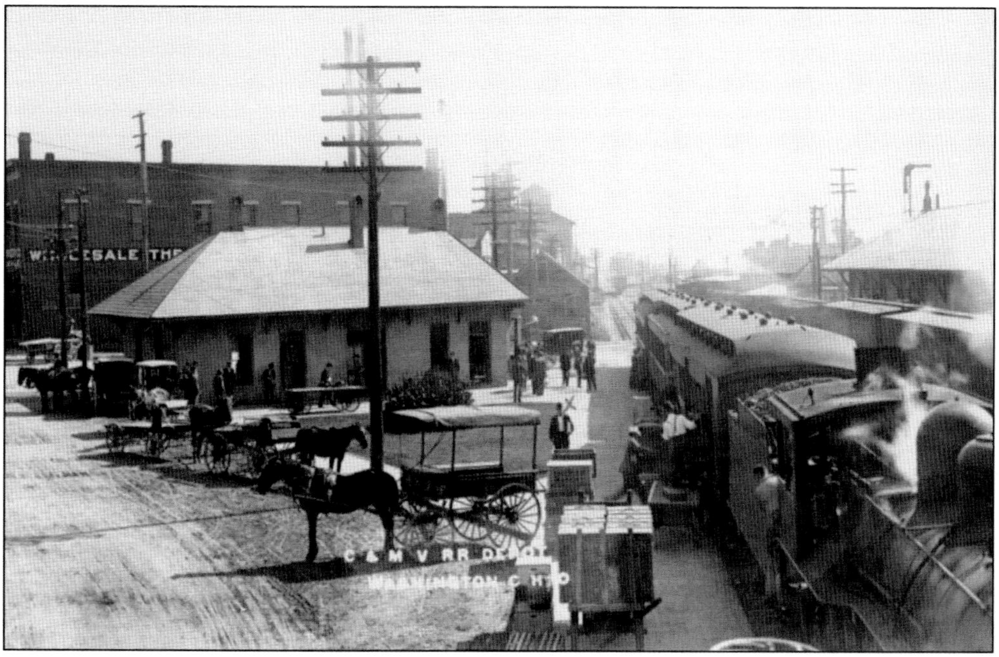

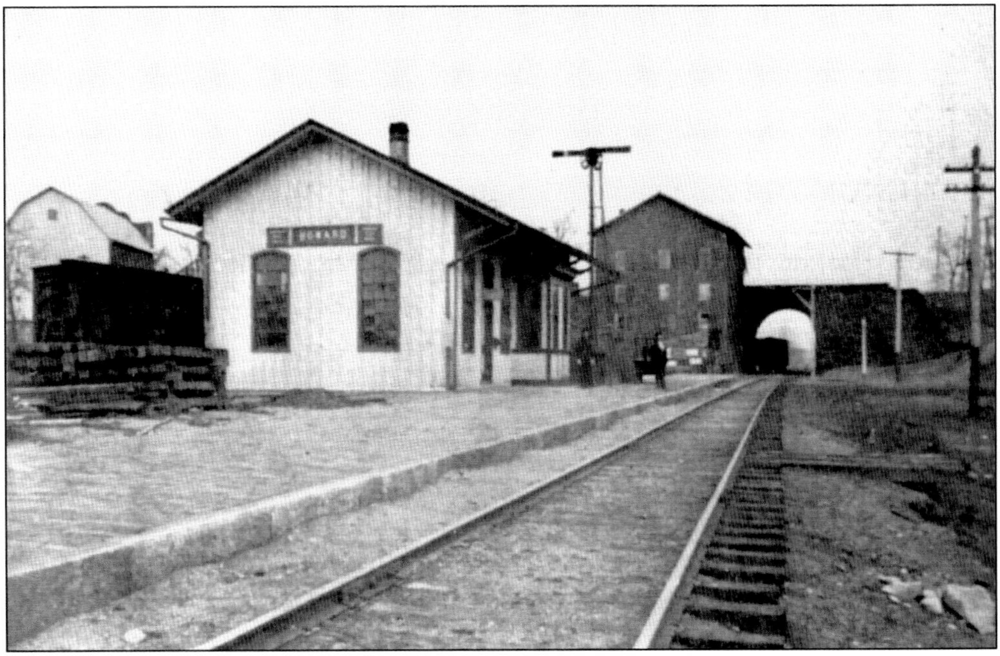

The Cleveland, Akron and Columbus (CA&C) also had some distinctive depot plans. Howard exhibits a typical small-town combination-depot plan. The gently arched lintels of the depot windows and raised freight platform are two characteristics often repeated. Howard's depot was closed by the PRR in 1963, and it was shortly torn down. (Author's collection.)

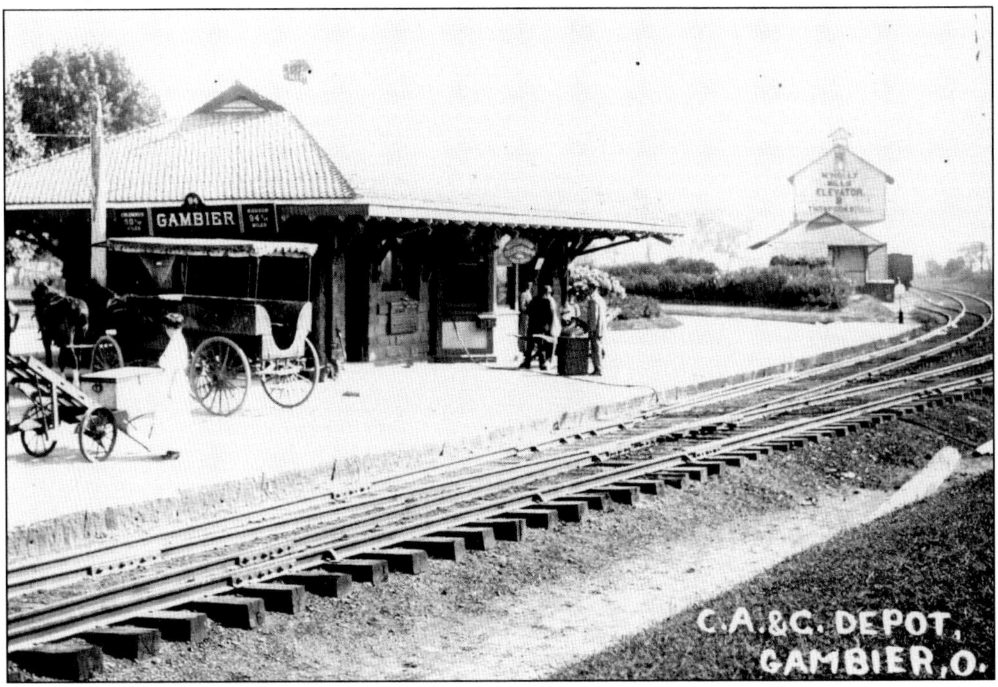


The CA&C realized the visibility of its depot in the college town of Gambier. Its only stone depot was built to serve as an impressive entrance for the many Kenyon College students, faculty, parents, and alumni. Note the separate frame freight house down the tracks. (Author's collection.)

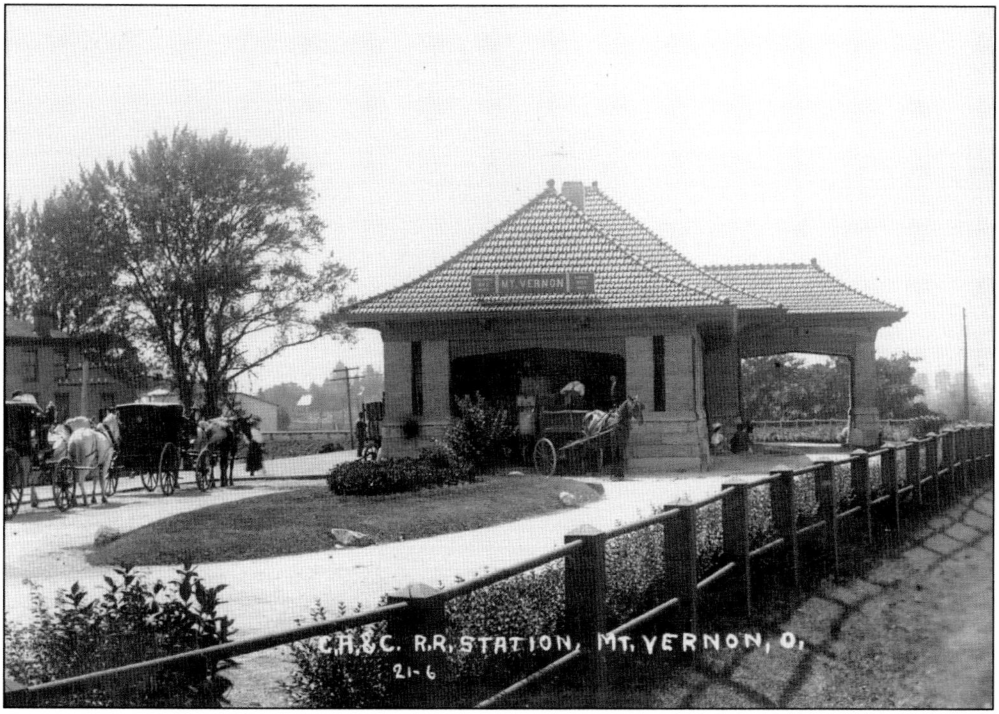


Another eye-catching depot was built at the Knox County seat of Mount Vernon. This depot plan also came out of the PRR engineering office. Nearby was a frame freight house. Both views show the depot at train time around 1908. Horse-drawn carriages and hacks are ready. It must have been a hot day in the above view. Note the ladies sitting in the shade of the eaves. Although the tracks are gone, the passenger and freight depots remain. The passenger depot has undergone some modifications and is now a senior center. (Author's collection.)

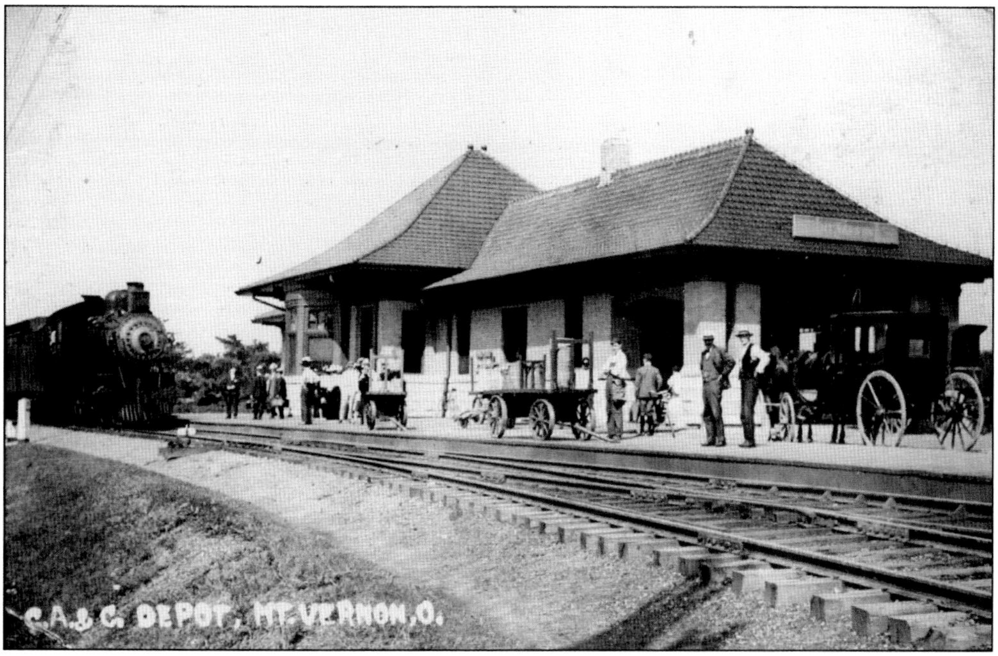

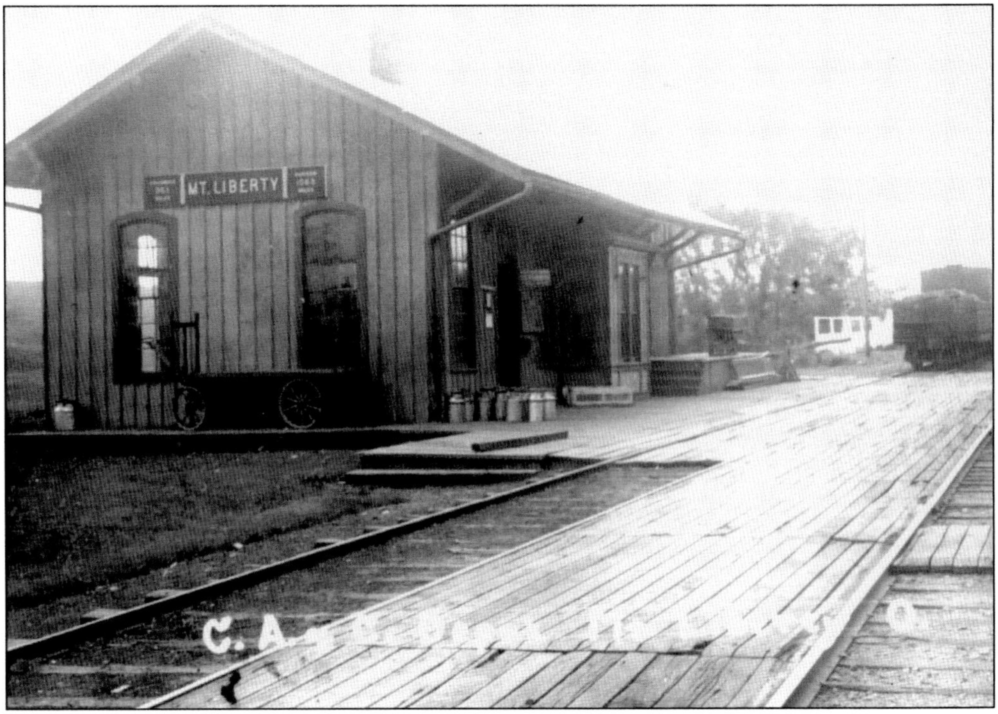


The CA&C had a standard frame depot at Bangs. Compare Mount Liberty's depot, shown here, to the one at Howard. The arched lintels are evident on the waiting room windows. The PRR noted the business at this depot had slowed down by the late 1920s and reclassified it as a non-agency station in late 1930. It has been gone for many years. (Author's collection.)

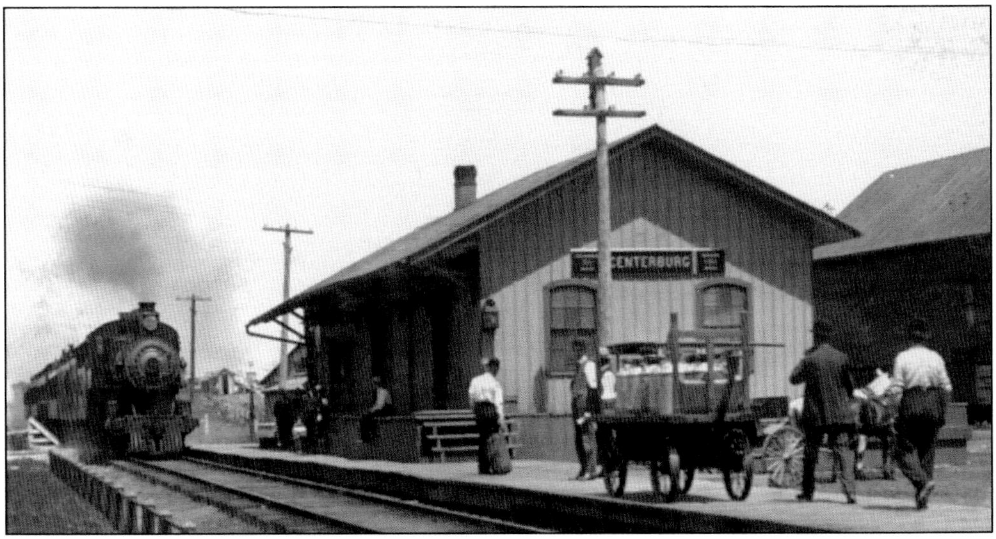


The CA&C erected another standard-design combination depot at Centerburg. Passenger service continued until 1949 on the CA&C. The Centerburg depot was greatly modified, including the removal of the bay window, around 1950, into a freight office. The depot was closed in 1961. Further down the line was a small depot and water tank at Condit. (Gary D. Rolih collection.)

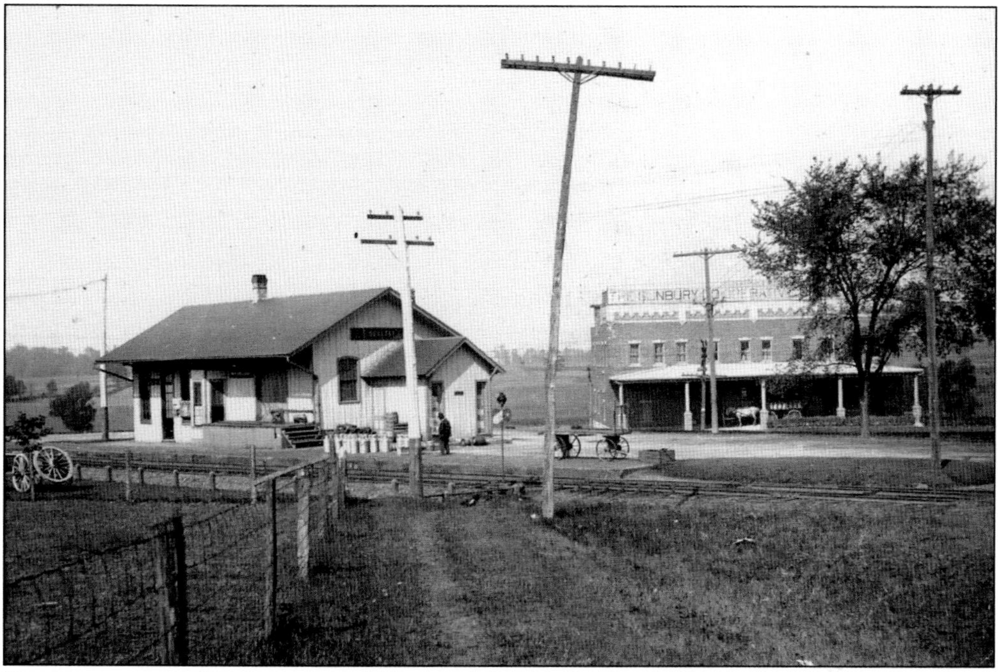

Here is an example of extreme depot modification by the PRR, similar to the changes at Centerburg. Above is a *c.* 1907 view of the CA&C combination depot at Sunbury. It is of typical CA&C design with a small attachment for the new restrooms, originally the depot had outhouses. To the right is the store of the local cooperative. Below is a 1969 view of the same depot. After passenger service was discontinued in 1949 the PRR removed the bay window, shortened the roof overhang, redid windows and doors, and sided the building with insul-brick. The building remains in alternative use, although it was closed by the railroad in 1963. (Above, author's collection; below, photograph by the author.)

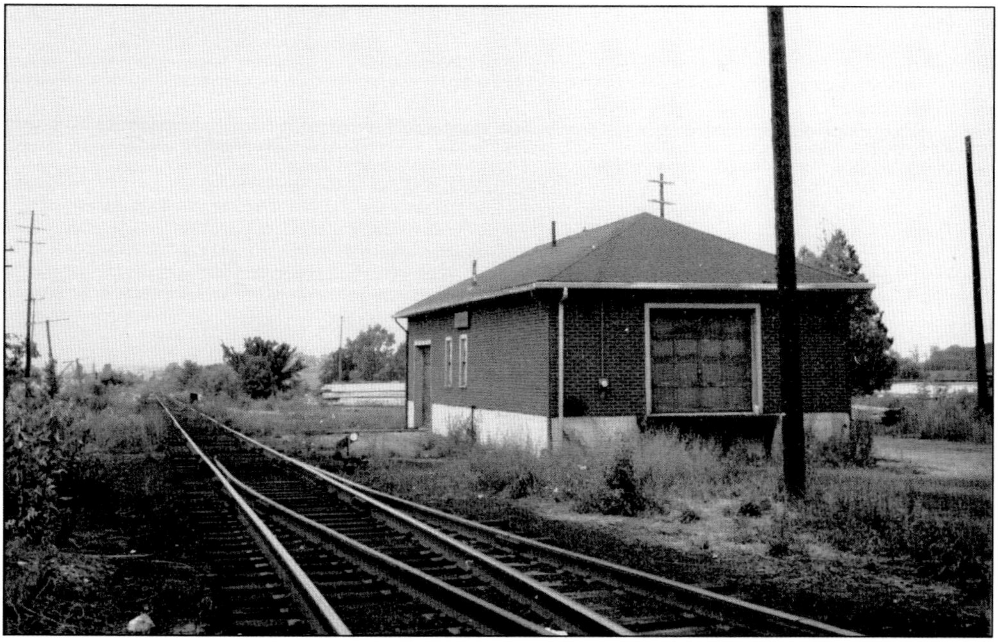

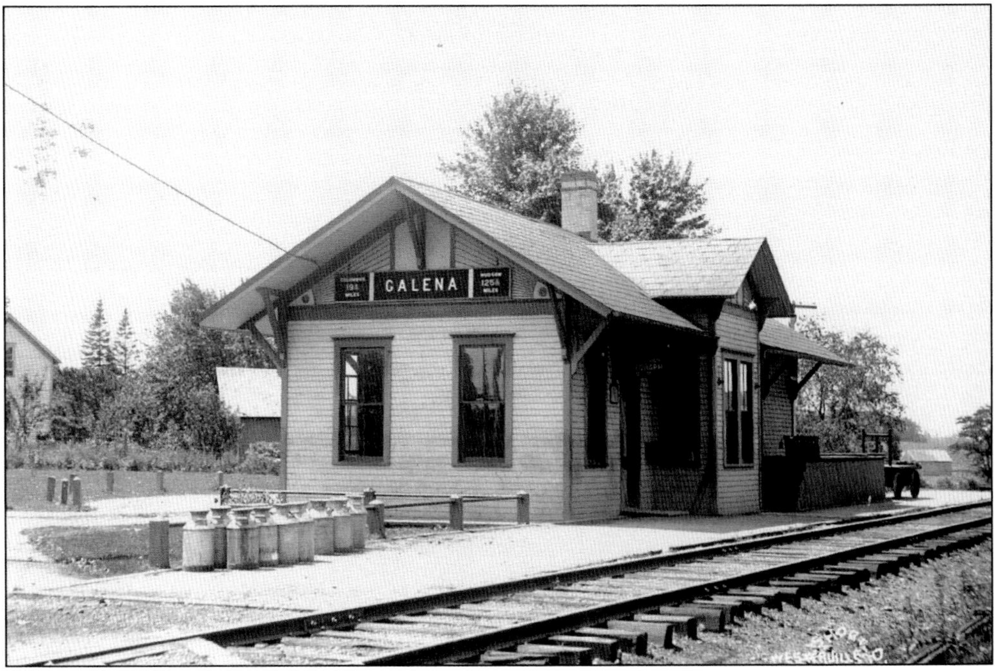


A different plan was used for the CA&C depot in Galena. A unique feature of this building was the design in the gable. Galena became an important stop on the CA&C when a brick plant opened. It was relegated to non-agency status before 1949 and is long gone. (Author's collection.)

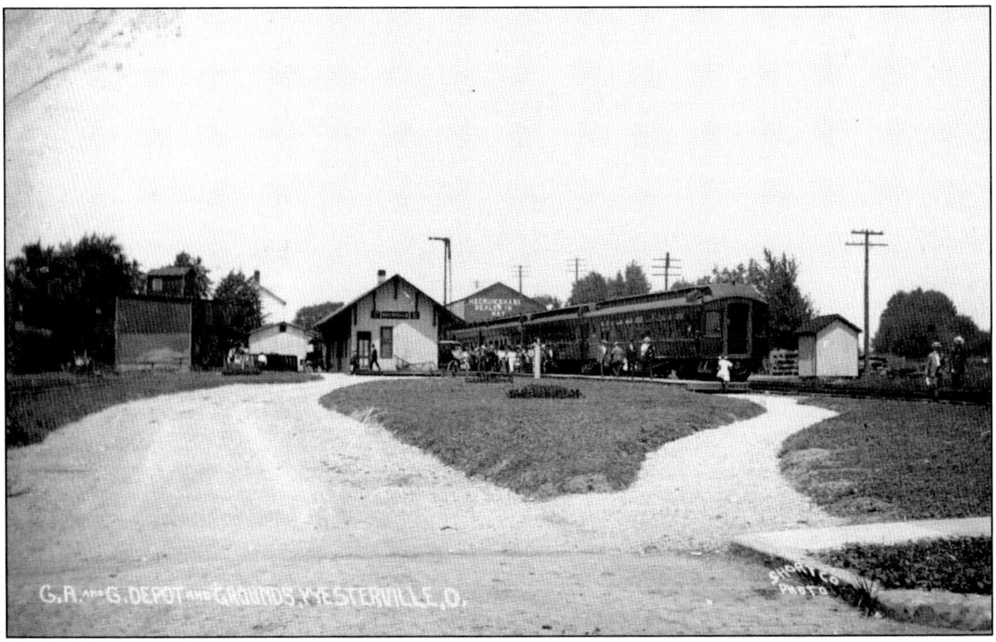


The train has arrived at Westerville on a nice summer day in the early 1900s. This CA&C combination depot was also modified around 1950 in a similar manner to Centerburg and Sunbury. Although closed in 1963, it still stood in 1972. Today even the track is gone. (Author's collection.)

# *Five*

# Other Lines

Additional railroads in central Ohio included the Akron, Canton and Youngstown Railroad (AC&Y), the Detroit, Toledo and Ironton Railway (DT&I), the Norfolk and Western Railway (N&W), and the Wheeling and Lake Erie Railway.

By 1886, the Pittsburg, Akron and Western Railroad served Plymouth on its way west to Delphos and east to Akron. This short line eventually became property of the AC&Y in 1920. The AC&Y merged with the N&W in 1964, but was operated separately until 1982. The new Wheeling and Lake Erie operates the remaining trackage.

The beginnings of the DT&I included the Springfield, Jackson and Pomeroy Railroad, which completed a narrow-gauge line from the Jackson-Wellston region to Springfield in 1878. The line was converted to standard gauge beginning two years later and eventually named the Ohio Southern Railroad in 1881. At Jeffersonville, branches were built toward Columbus and Cincinnati, but funds were depleted long before the cities were reached. After financial problems and reorganizations, the line became the DT&I in 1914. The year 1984 marked the end of the corporate history of the DT&I. The Indiana and Ohio Railroad operates the remaining DT&I tracks in central Ohio south of Springfield.

The year 1877 marked the opening of the Scioto Valley Railroad stretching from Columbus to Chillicothe by the way of Circleville. Two years later, the line reached Portsmouth on the Ohio River. The Scioto Valley was successful at first, but slowly began to lose money until bankruptcy came. The N&W purchased the Scioto Valley in 1890, and it rapidly became a major coal-hauling route, connecting the West Virginia coalfields with Lake Erie. The line was double-tracked in 1908. By the 1950s, only one passenger train made a daily stop at Columbus Union Station. The N&W inherited the Scioto Valley depots and undertook a depot modification in the mid-1920s that significantly changed their appearance. The N&W also acquired the old Columbus, Sandusky and Hocking line between Columbus and Sandusky, but by this time the route was for freight only. Norfolk Southern now operates the route.

The Cleveland, Canton and Southern Railroad, reached Zanesville in 1892; from Coshocton to Zanesville it used the route of the old Coshocton and Southern Railroad. This came under Wheeling and Lake Erie Railway control in 1900.

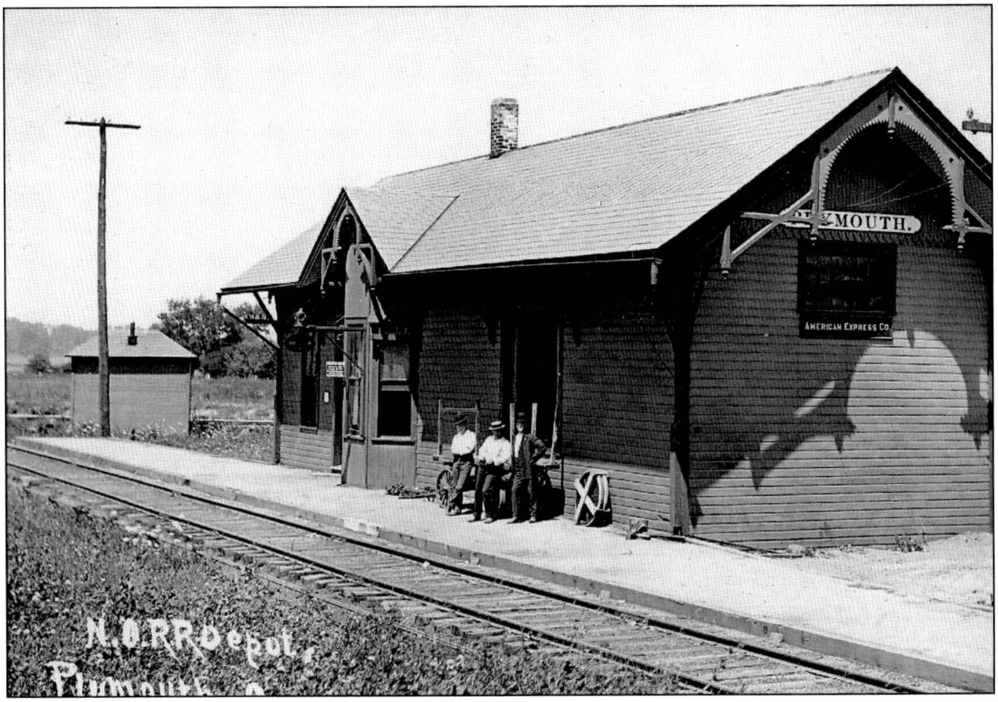


The Pittsburg, Akron and Western Railroad built this depot at the junction with the Sandusky, Milan and Newark (later B&O) in Plymouth in 1890. At the time this photograph was printed the line was known as the Northern Ohio Railroad. An interlocking tower was nearby. The last passengers used the depot in 1951. It has been relocated west of its original location since the below 1968 photograph. (Above, author's collection; below, photograph by Charles Garvin.)

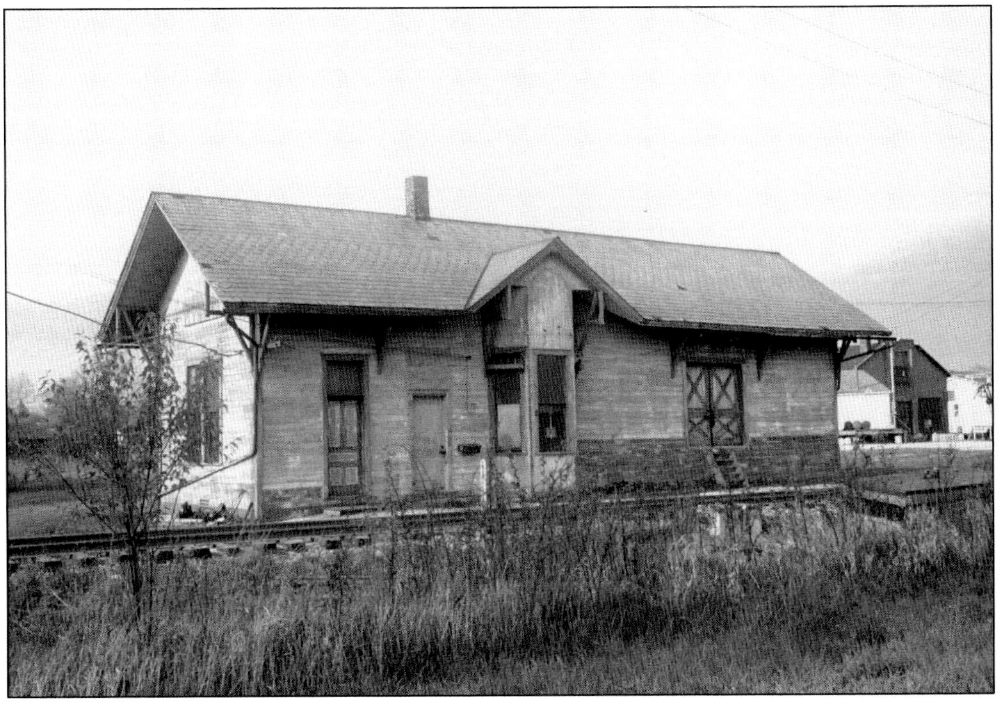

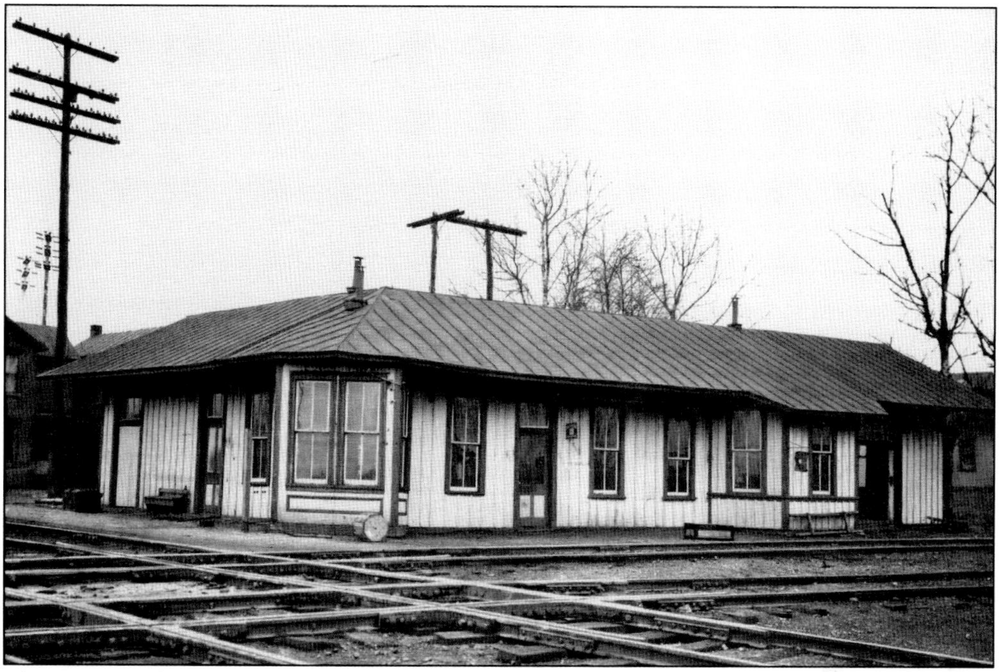

The N&W and Hocking Valley Railway cross at Valley Crossing, south of Columbus. This view shows the joint depot around 1915. Passenger trains no longer regularly stopped at this *c.* 1876 building by even this early date. The depot has been gone from trackside for many years. (N&W Historical Photograph Collection, Norfolk Southern Corporation.)

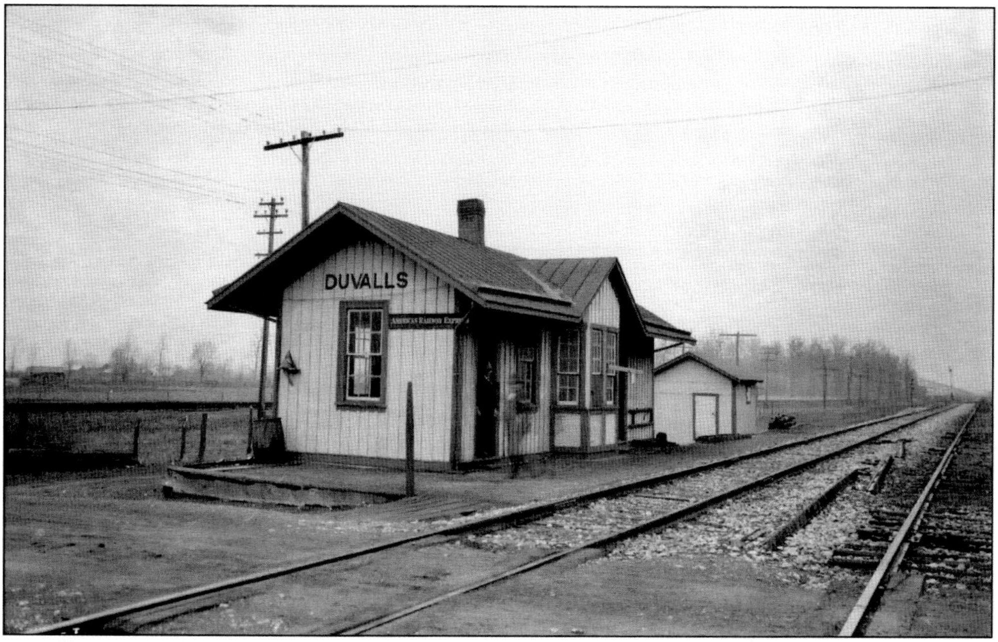


Duvalls was served by this standard-plan Scioto Valley Railroad combination depot with later N&W modifications. This rural scene dates to about 1915. The ghostly image is what happens when a person walks into the scene during the exposure. (N&W Historical Photograph Collection, Norfolk Southern Corporation.)

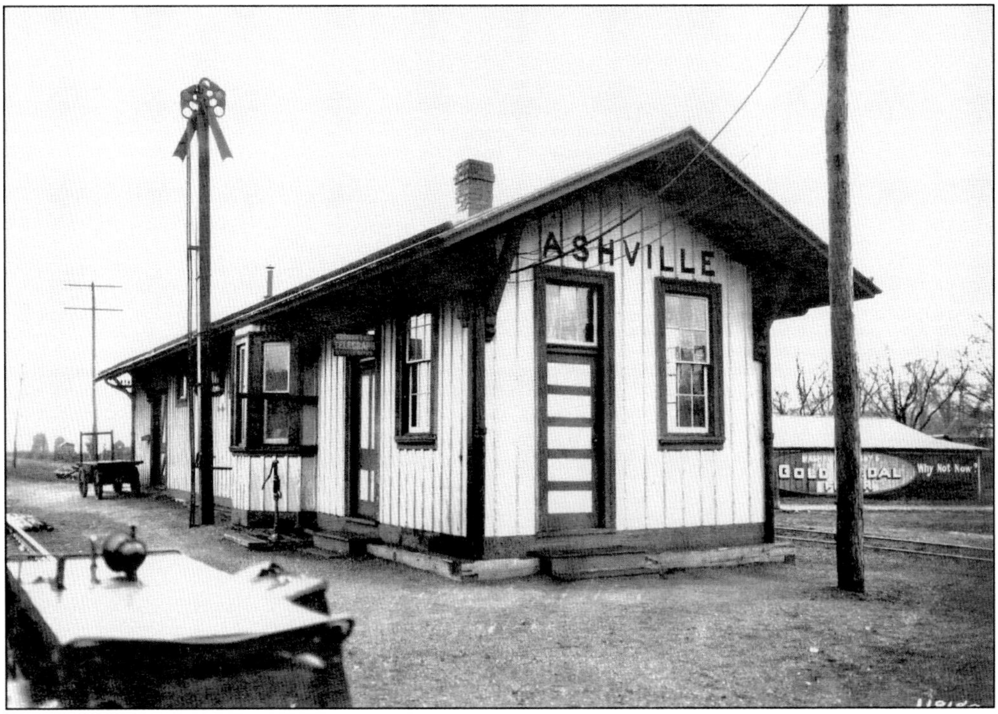


The N&W combination depot in Ashville is shown, above, around 1915 and, below, in 1972. Little has changed over some 50 years. The Scioto Valley Railroad opened this depot in 1876. The community managed to save the depot as a bicentennial project. It has been relocated to a lot at Madison and Cromley Streets and now serves as a community center and museum. (Above, N&W Historical Photograph Collection, Norfolk Southern Corporation; below, photograph by the author.)

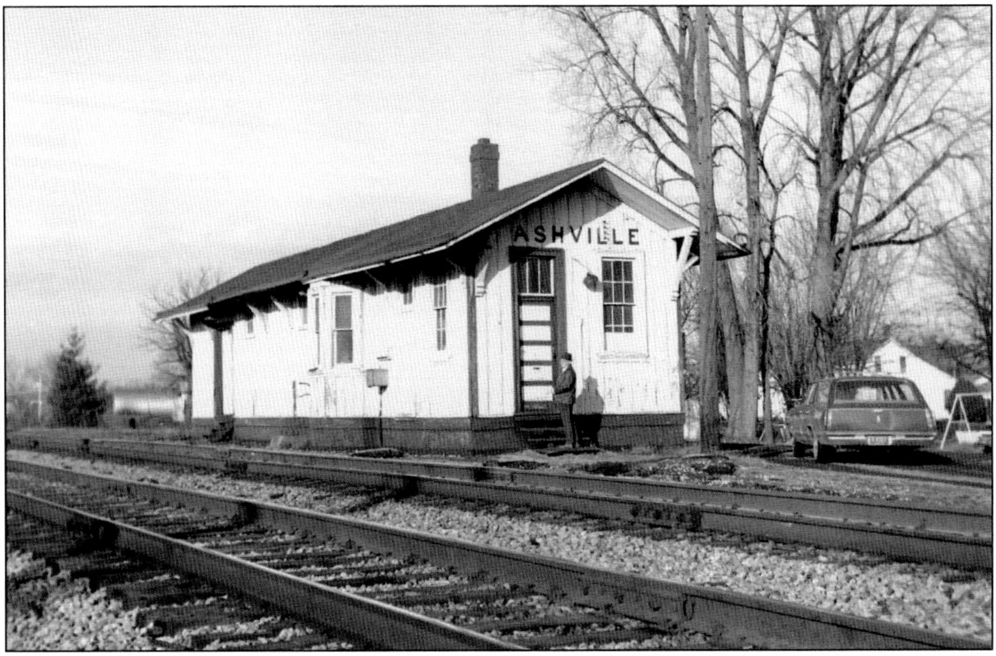

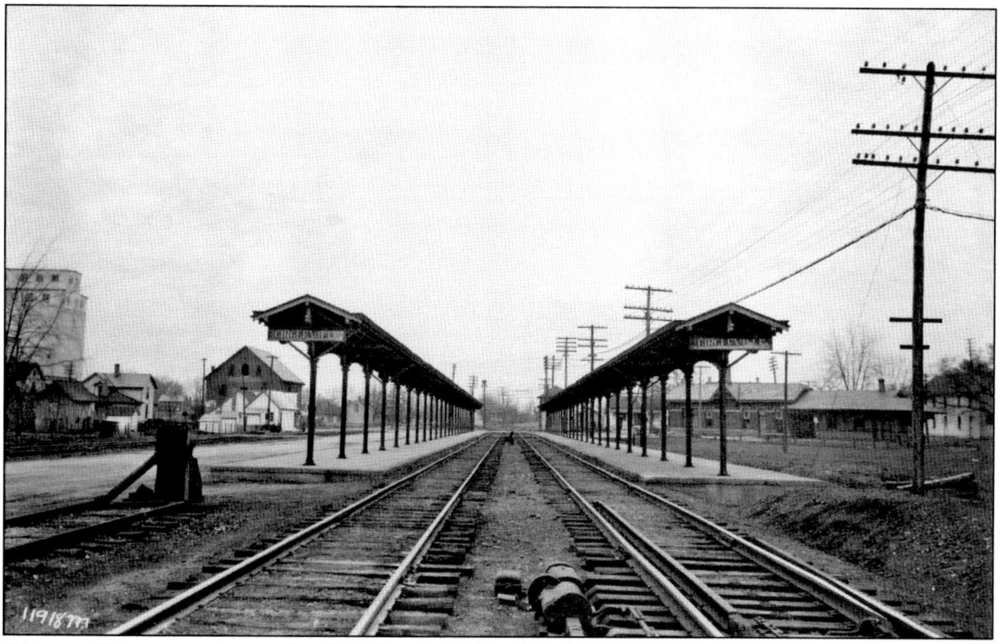

This *c*. 1915 scene shows the N&W side of Circleville's C&MV passenger depot. The N&W erected umbrella sheds for both north- and south-bound trains. Just beyond the depot is an N&W interlocking tower to control the crossing with the C&MV. The interior of this tower is depicted below; note the track plan and controls for switches. Further north was the N&W freight house, which stood until 1999. The Scioto Valley had its own Circleville depot in the late 1800s along Houston Street, but was using the C&MV depot by 1900. The Scioto Valley had its own Circleville depot along Houston Street in the late 1800s before switching to the C&MV depot. (N&W Historical Photograph Collection, Norfolk Southern Corporation.)

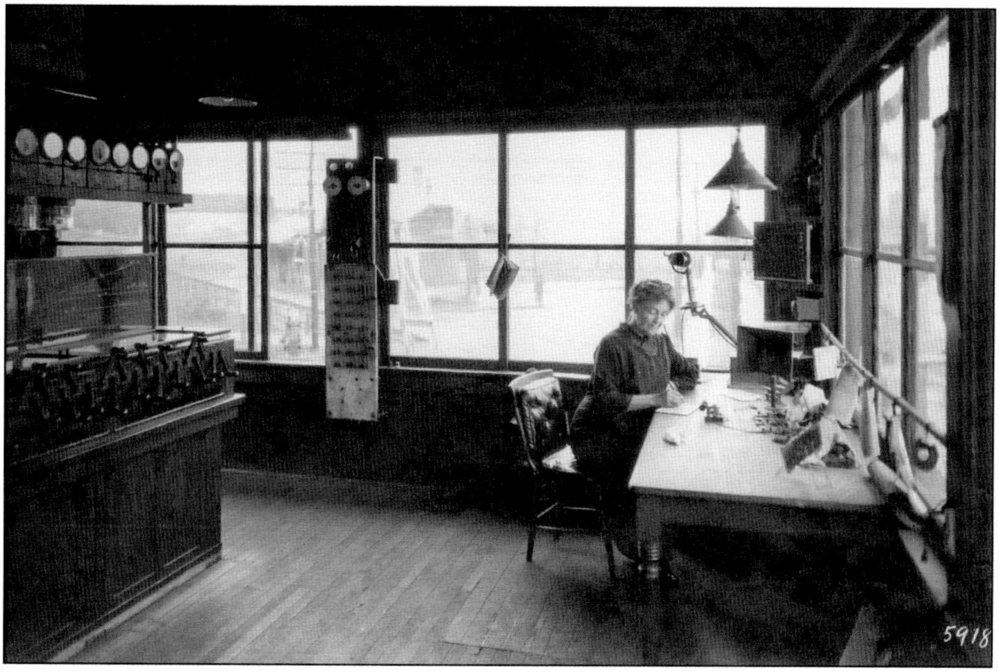

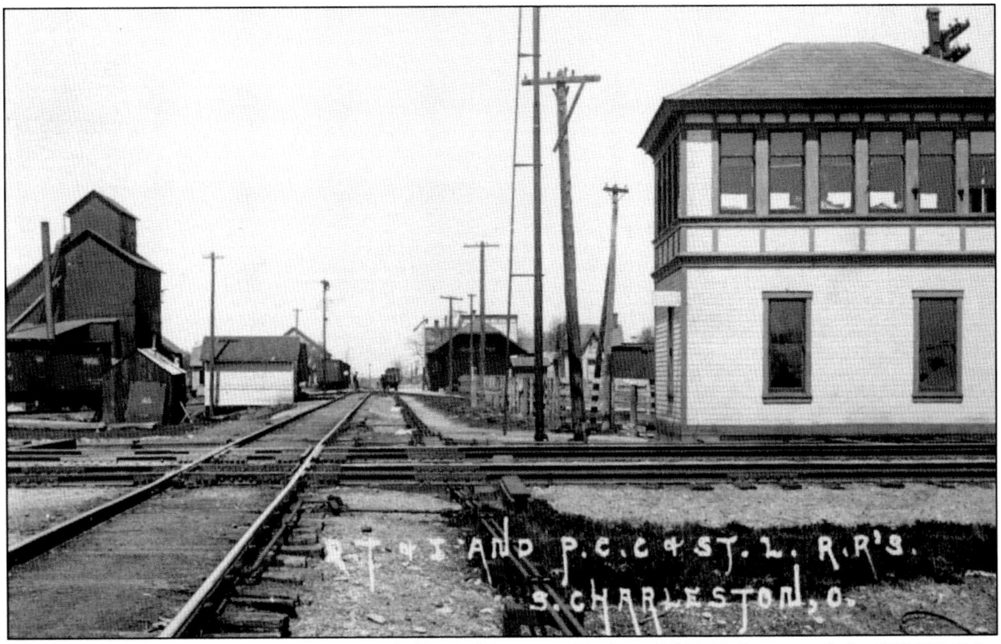


At South Charleston, the Detroit, Toledo and Ironton Railroad (DT&I) crossed the PCC&StL. The view above shows the PCC&StL interlocking tower guarding this crossing. To the right down the tracks were the PCC&StL depots; in the distance is the DT&I depot. The depot below was built by predecessor Springfield, Jackson and Pomeroy Railroad in the late 1870s. The trackside eaves were cut back by the DT&I resulting in this strange appearance. The depot was restored in the 1990s. (Above, author's collection; below, photograph by the author.)

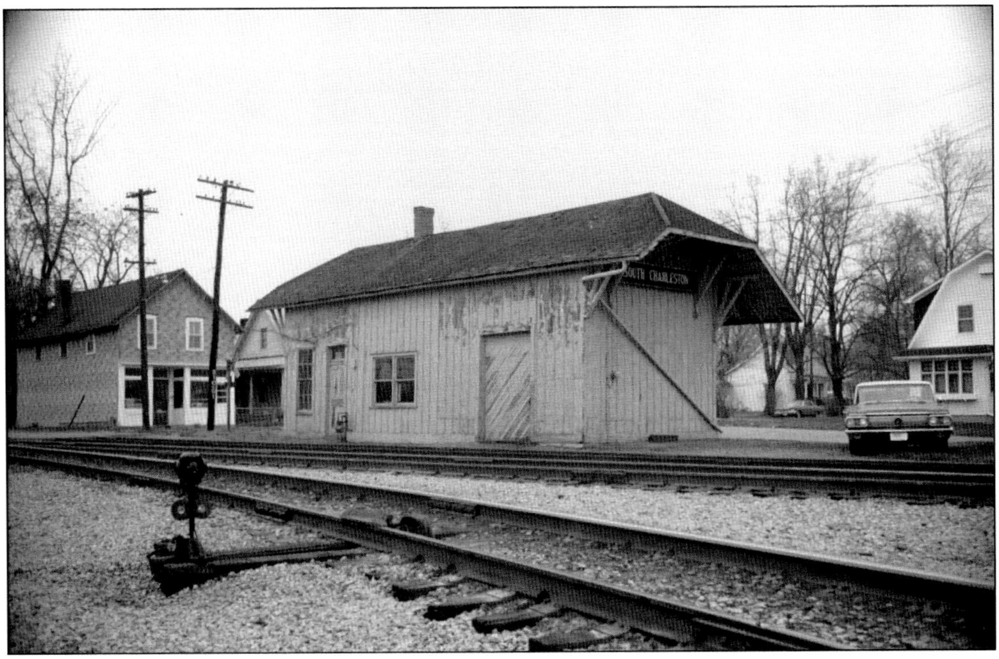

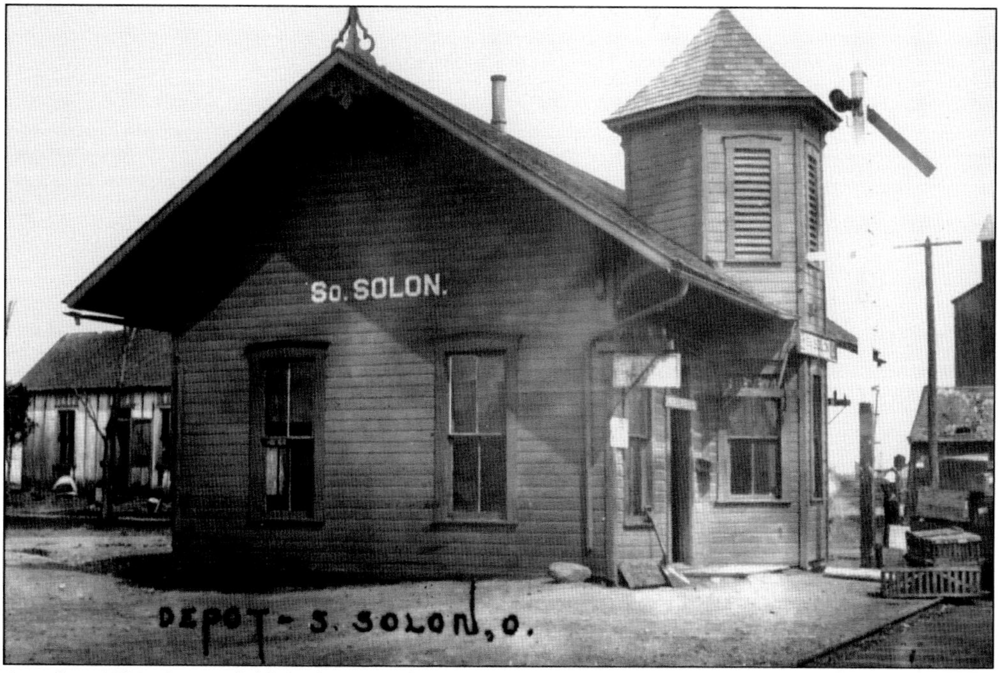

Another 1870s Springfield, Jackson and Pomeroy depot was this one at South Solon. The DT&I removed the tower portion in the mid-1900s. Beginning in 1931, the DT&I instituted mixed trains south of Springfield. All passenger service ended in 1954. The depot was still there in the early 1970s but has since disappeared. (David P. Oroszi collection.)

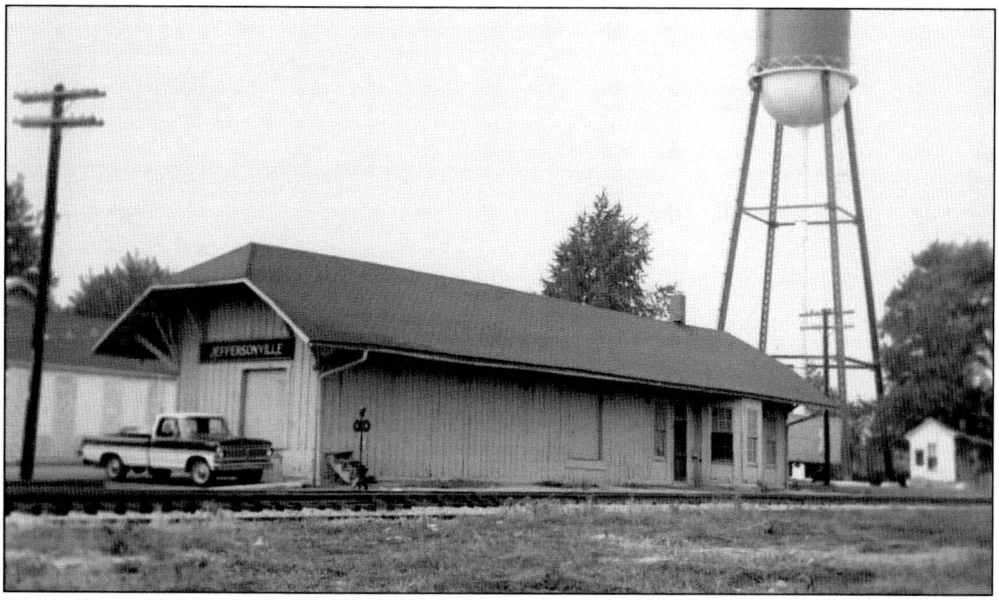

The Jeffersonville DT&I depot handled considerable amounts of freight necessitating additions to the freight end. By the time of this 1971 photograph, the DT&I had removed most of the ornamental features. This one has also been torn down. (Photograph by the author.)

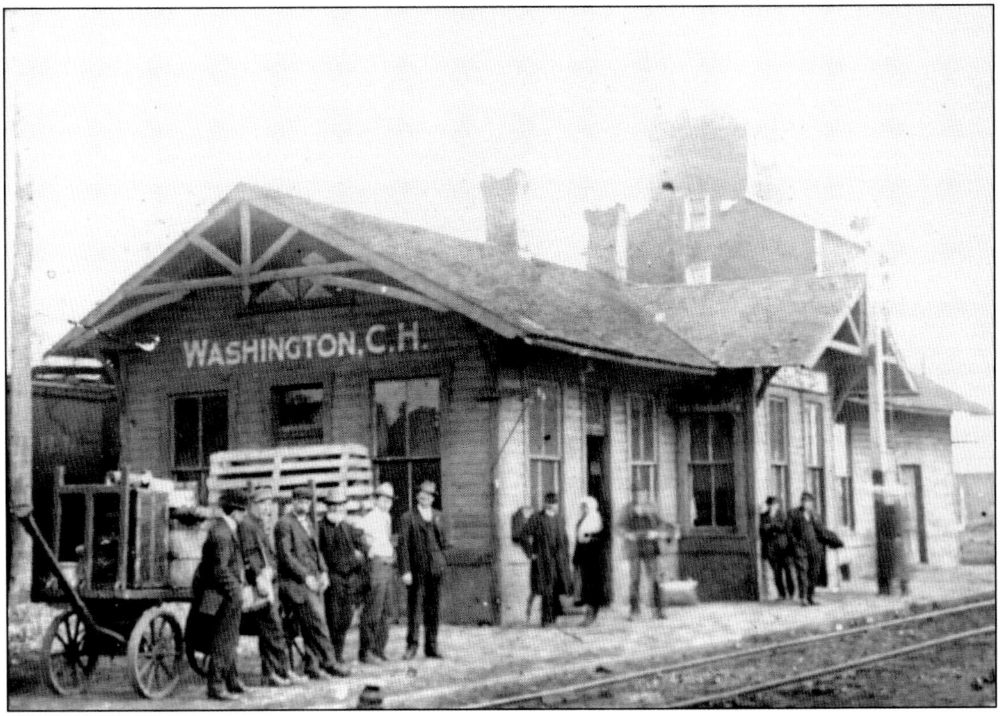


Here are the old and new DT&I facilities in Washington Courthouse. Above, travelers pose on the platform of the 1870s passenger depot. A tornado caused considerable damage in the town in 1885, including demolishing the original Springfield, Jackson and Pomeroy Railroad depot. Above, travelers pose on the platform of the rebuilt passenger depot. In the 1972 photograph below is the metal prefabricated replacement. (Above, Jim Henry collection; below, photograph by the author.)

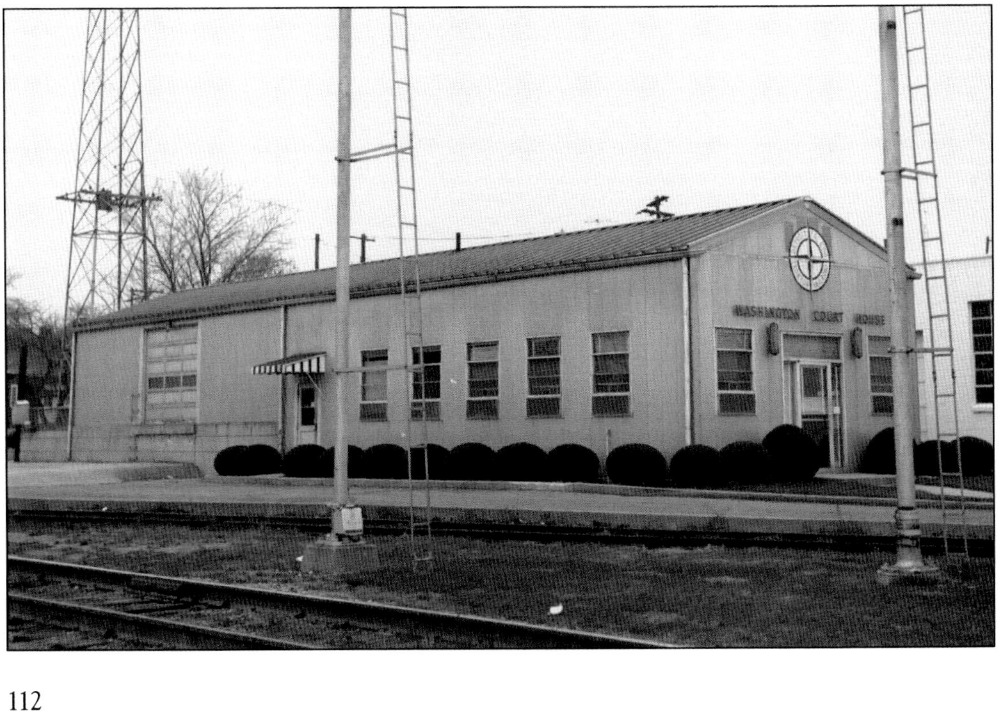

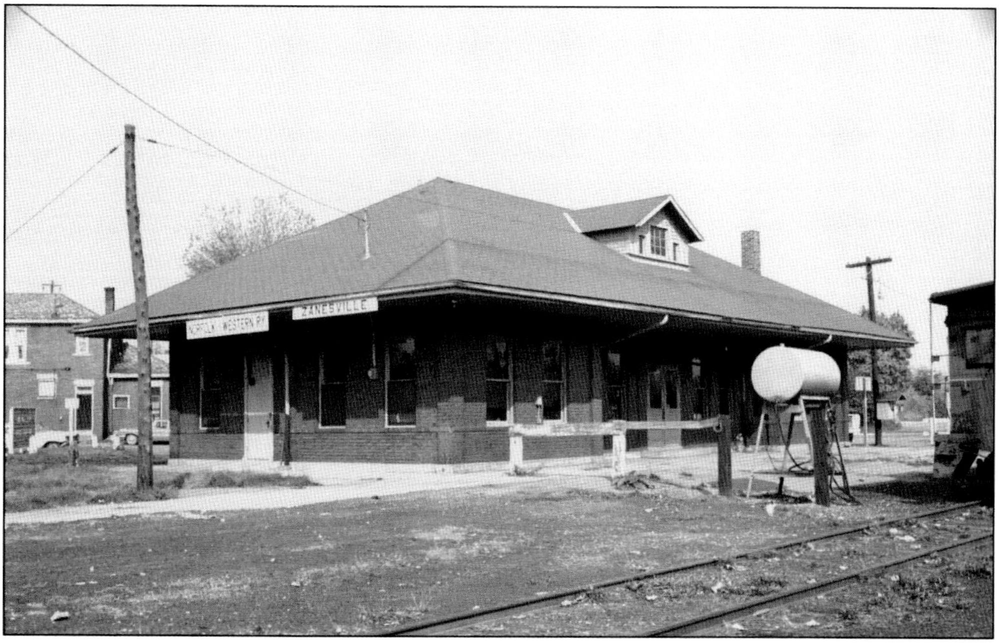


These views show the Wheeling and Lake Erie Railway depot in Zanesville as it looked in 1967. The line came into downtown Zanesville on the west side of the river with the depot on Linden Avenue. The last passenger service was in 1932. (Photographs by Charles Garvin.)

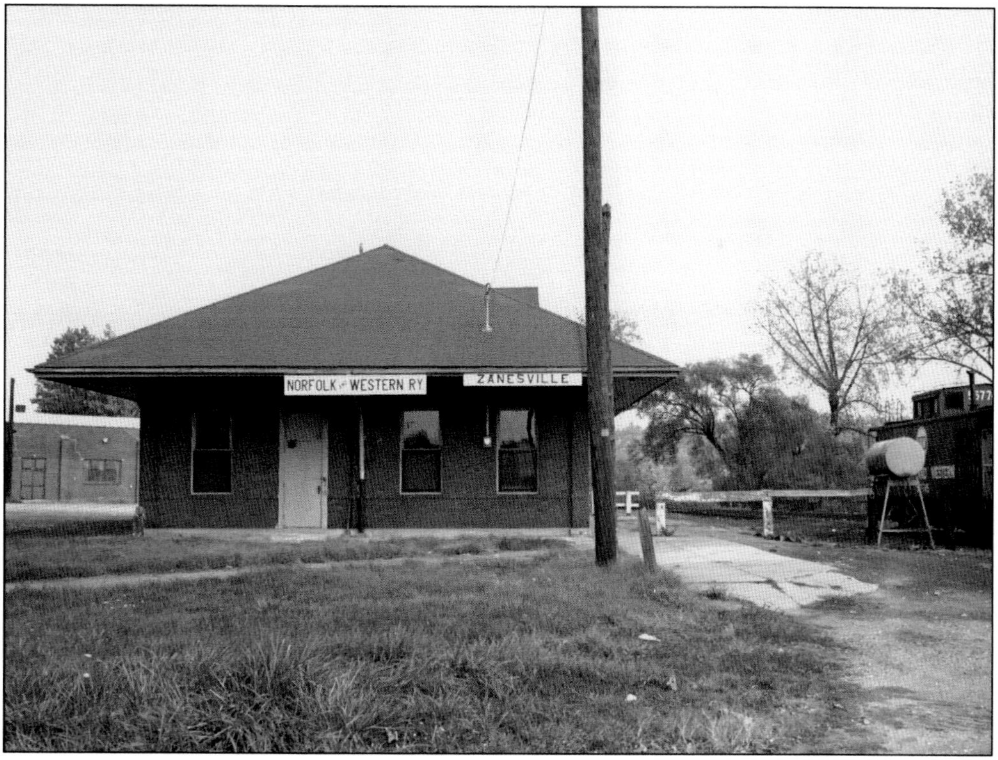

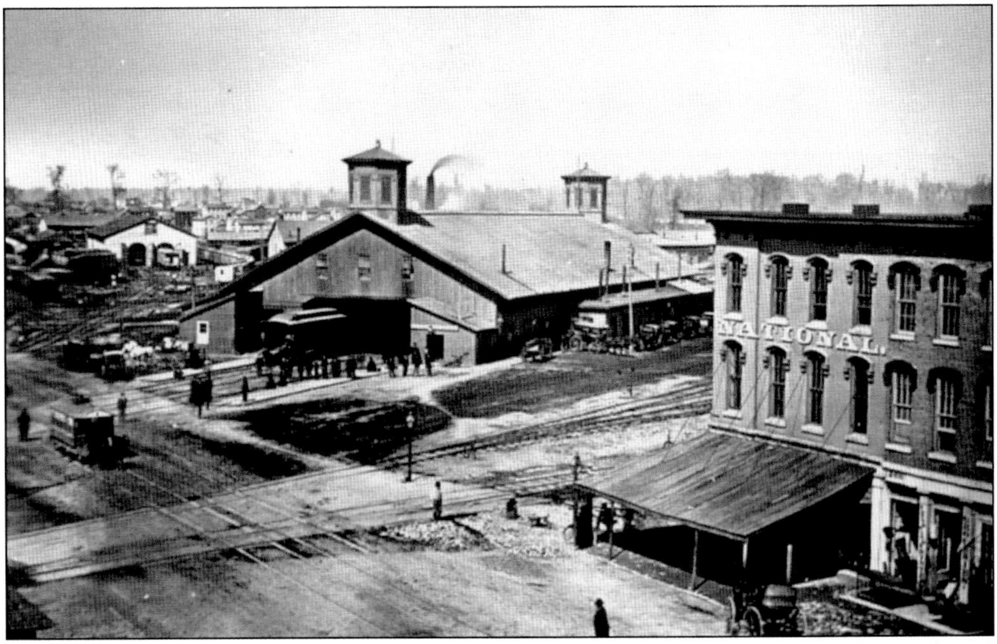


Above is the first Columbus Union Station. When built, the structure was on the north end of downtown, but soon the city encroached on the depot grounds. As more railroads entered the city, the facility became overtaxed, and the second union station, below, was completed. (Author's collection.)

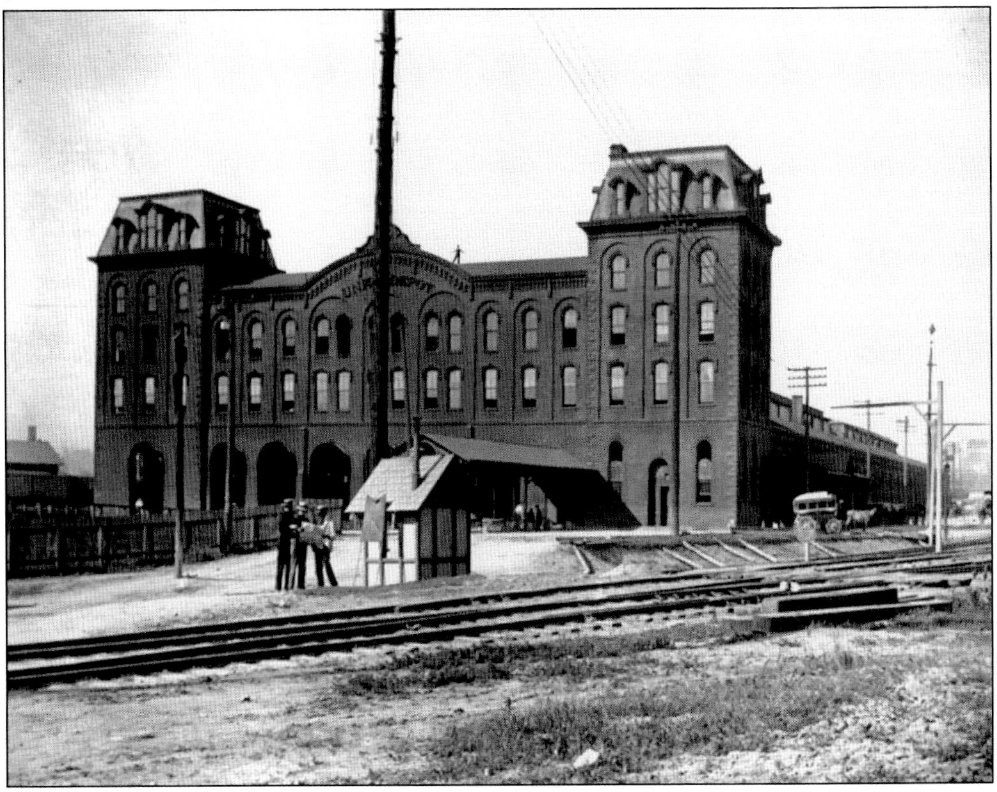

# *Six*

# COLUMBUS

The Columbus and Xenia and the CC&C Railroads located Columbus's first union station on the north side at High and Naghten Streets in 1851. This was a large barnlike structure covering three tracks at grade level. The Columbus, Piqua and Indiana Railroad and the Steubenville and Indiana Railroad entered the depot in 1854 and 1864, respectively. Additions were built on the union station in the early 1860s. With the onset of the Civil War and the addition of troop trains, the growth of Columbus, the increase of traffic on High Street, and the lack of passenger tracks, the union station fast became woefully inadequate.

Columbus's second union station was erected north of the 1851 depot; it opened in 1875. This depot was of brick construction and sheltered seven passenger tracks. A tunnel was excavated under the tracks to allow High Street streetcars and horsecars to pass by unimpeded. The growth of Columbus far exceeded the planners of this depot as well, and within less than 20 years, there was talk of replacement.

The third union station was planned to eliminate the grade crossing problem by building a High Street viaduct complete with storefronts on each side. The union station was reached by a driveway from the viaduct. The depot opened in 1897. In 1931, the original train shed was replaced by an enclosed concourse and umbrella sheds along the eight passenger tracks. The decline of rail passenger travel, beginning in the 1950s, spelled doom for the union station. A new convention center was planned for the site. Demolition began in 1976, first with the buildings on the High Street viaduct.

The T&OC used the Ohio Central Railroad depot on West Broad Street. This 1895 structure originally served trains at ground level, but traffic problems on city streets led to the elevation of the tracks in 1910. The depot ended its days as a passenger depot in 1929–1930 when the NYC moved all its trains to the union station. The depot then served the Volunteers of America until 2002. It is now the home of International Association of Firefighters, Local 67. Other Columbus depots included CHV&T combination depots at its West Mound Avenue terminal and across from a T&OC South Columbus depot, a suburban PRR depot in East Linden (gone by 1937), and a PRR passenger shelter at Port Columbus Airport.

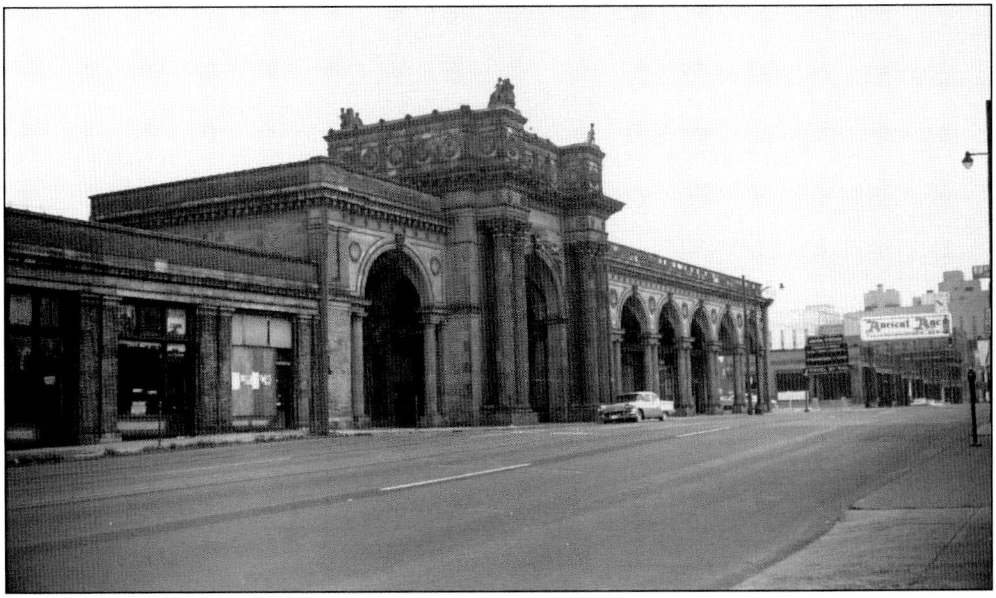

The third and final union station was completed in 1897. Above is the row of commercial buildings constructed on the High Street viaduct over the station tracks. By this 1965 view, most of the stores were vacant. The sign beyond the facade is where the driveway enters union station. Below is the actual union station in 1965, seen from track level on the north side. The High Street viaduct is out of view to the right; a couple of miles to the east are the former Twentieth Street shops of the PRR. (Photographs by Charles Garvin.)

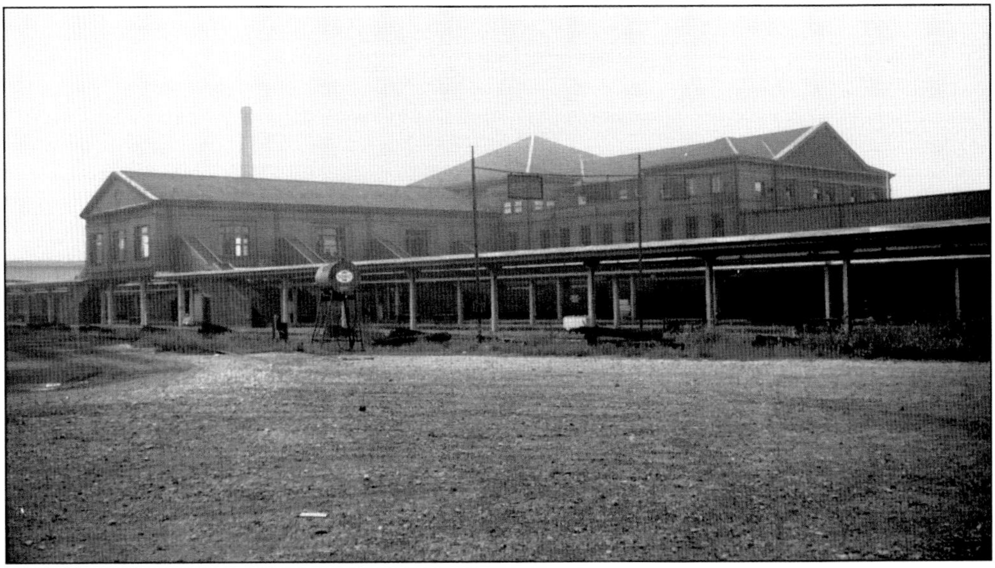

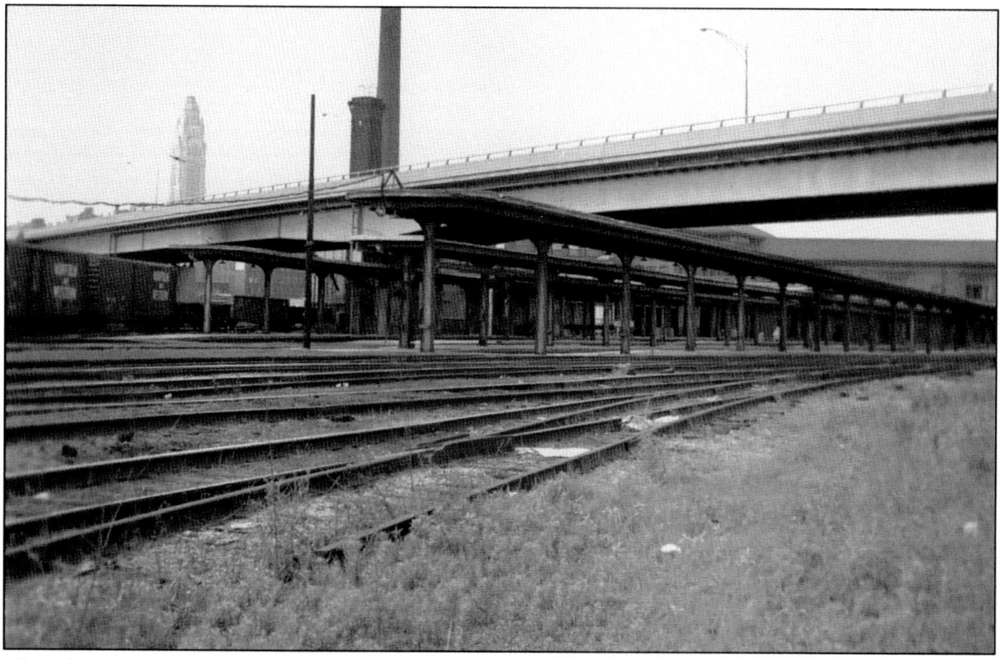

The above 1972 photograph was taken looking toward High Street, showing the track-level umbrella sheds. Passengers descended to these platforms from the overhead concourse seen beyond the highway bridge. Below, the High Street viaduct storefronts are coming down in the first phase of union station demolition in November 1976. In just a few years, the union station, seen through the arch, would be just a memory. (Photographs by the author.)

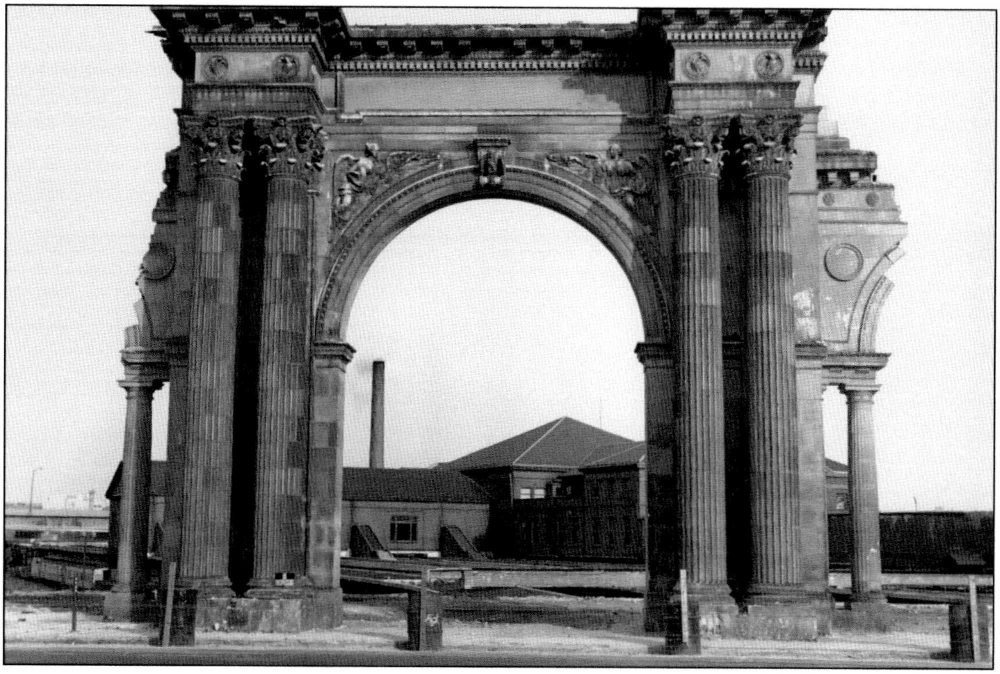

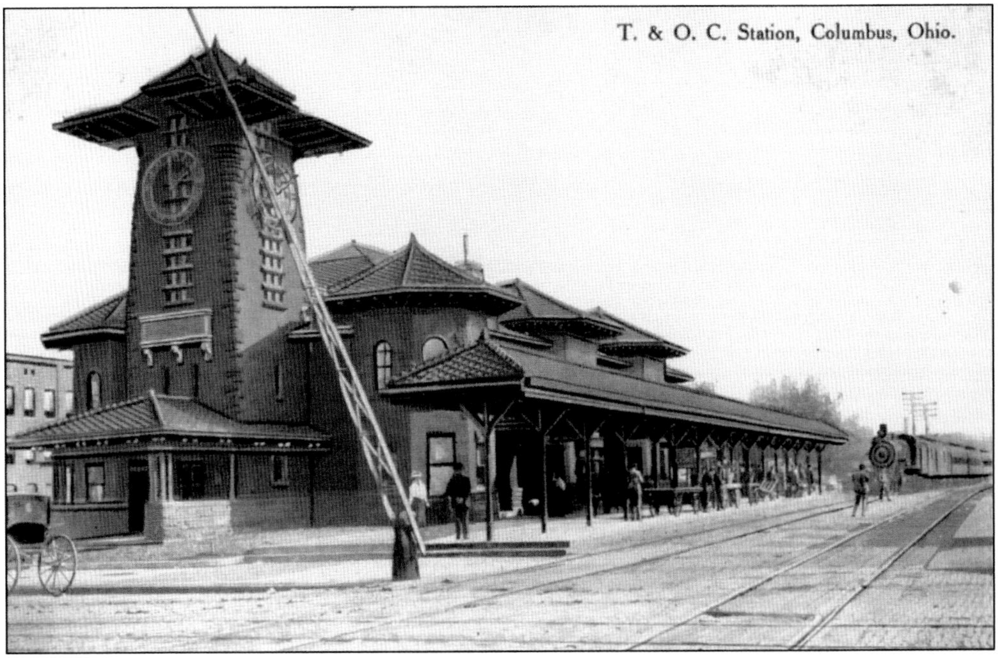


The T&OC hired local architects to design plans for its main Columbus depot at 379 West Broad Street. Note the large clocks on the tower; many a Broad Street traveler referred to them. These views were taken before the tracks were elevated in 1910. The T&OC had experienced the same problems with traffic congestion due to trains blocking Broad Street as had the union station on High Street. (Author's collection.)

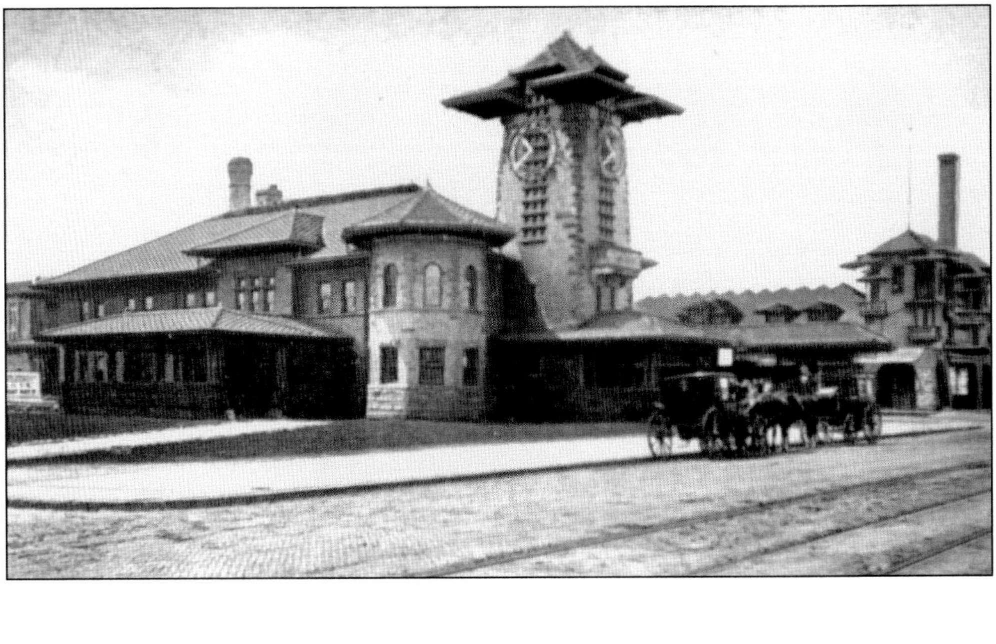

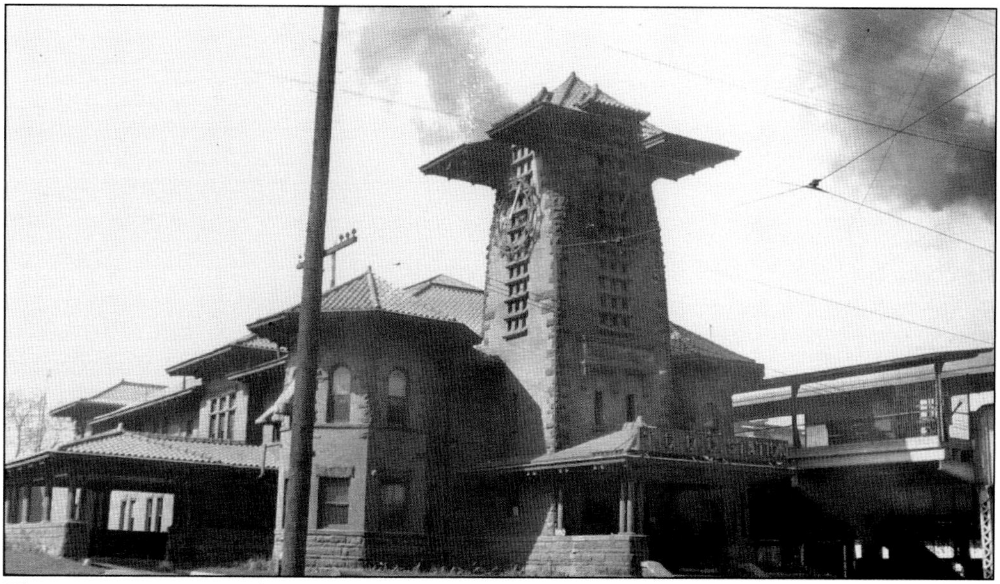

These two 1919 views show the T&OC depot in its last few years of service as a passenger station. After the NYC takeover, the depot was abandoned for the union station. In 1930, the depot was sold to the Volunteers of America. After over 70 years of service to the charitable organization, the depot is now undergoing another adaptive reuse by the firefighters union. (T&OC photographs, Allen County [Ohio] Historical Society Collection.)

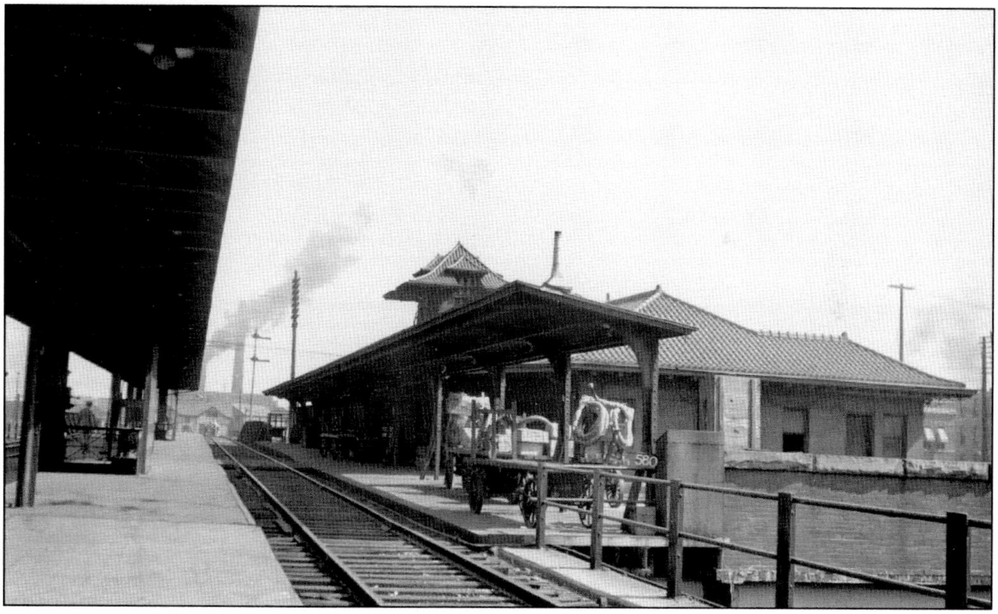

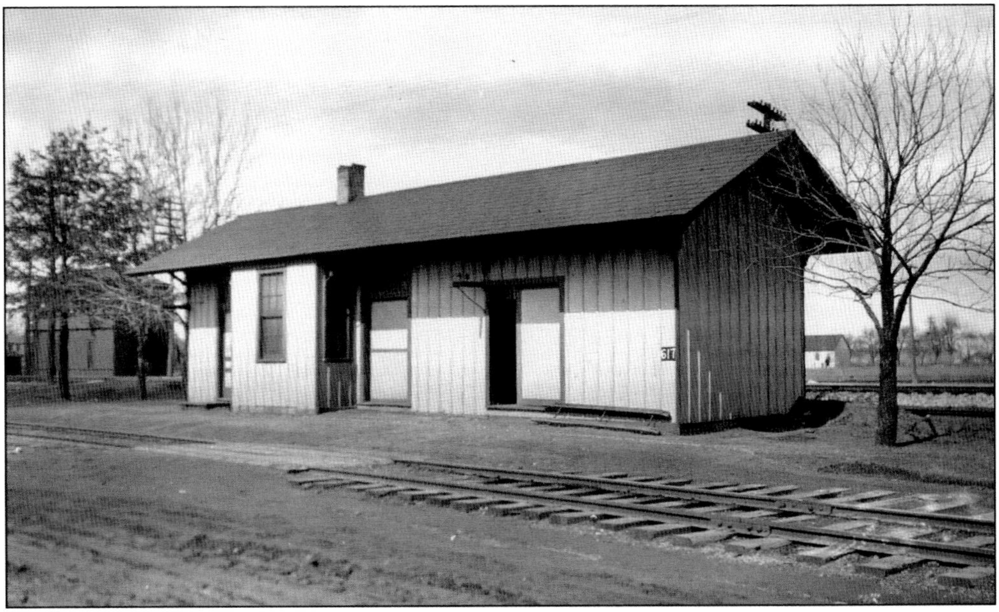

The T&OC used the PRR's East Linden depot on the east side of Columbus, shown above in 1919. Note the interlocking tower to the left. Below is the South Columbus passenger depot of the T&OC. Nearby was a freight house, which was still there in the early 1970s. (T&OC photographs, Allen County [Ohio] Historical Society Collection.)

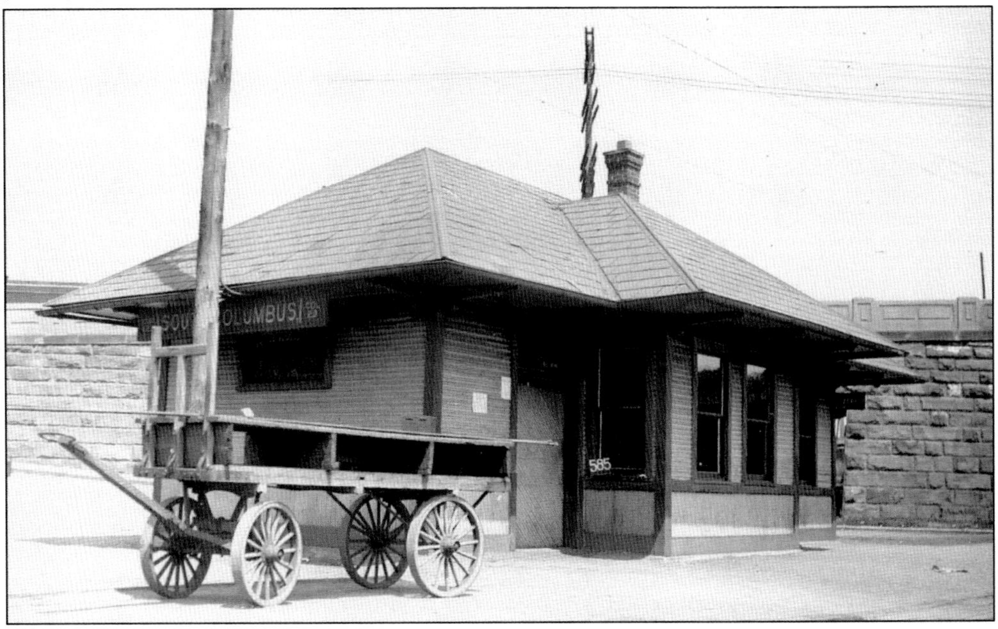

# *Seven*

# Reuse of Depots

Only a small percentage of the passenger, freight, and combination depots that served central Ohio communities remain today. Most were removed shortly after their closing by the railroads. Some were moved to other sites as storage facilities but not properly kept up and allowed to decay away. Citizens have since realized that in many cases they have lost important ties to the early history of their towns. More widespread historical preservation has led to the renovation and restoration of many of the depots that have survived. The small-town depot, although designed for a particular function, has proved to be quite adaptable to alternative uses. A few examples follow. An early example of reuse was when the T&OC depot from Croton was moved to the country and renovated into a house in the 1940s. The B&O depot from Fredericktown has been moved the farthest. It now is a store on U.S. 36 in West Lafayette in Coshocton County. Broad Street station in Columbus, after serving many years as a Volunteers of America facility, is property of the local firefighters union. Delaware's Big Four depot has been a florist shop since 1981. The Mount Gilead Short Line Railroad depot in Mount Gilead is a municipal building. Some depots have become museums of local history including those at Ashville, Canal Winchester, and Grove City. Florence's small frame PCC&StL depot is restored and has been relocated to the Madison County Historical Museum in London. The Hocking Valley Railway depot from Carroll now resides at the Fairfield County Fairgrounds in Lancaster; the PRR Hilliards depot has been relocated to the Franklin County Fairgrounds in Hilliard, formerly Hillards. The T&OC depot at Pickerington has been beautifully restored as has the adjacent section house. Brice's T&OC depot has been moved twice and now serves as a conference center in Columbus. The PRR and B&O depots in Mount Vernon, both architectural gems, have been preserved and put to good alternative uses. Another architectural beauty—the PRR depot in Newark—is on the National Register of Historic Places and well kept. Centerburg, Granville, Johnstown, London (PRR), National Road, Prospect (a restaurant), Thornville (B&O), Utica, and Washington Courthouse (DT&I and PRR) are in civic or business use. Millersport, New Dover, New Salem, and Sayre are relocated and used for storage. Mount Sterling's B&O depot still serves the railroad, now CSX, as a maintenance facility.

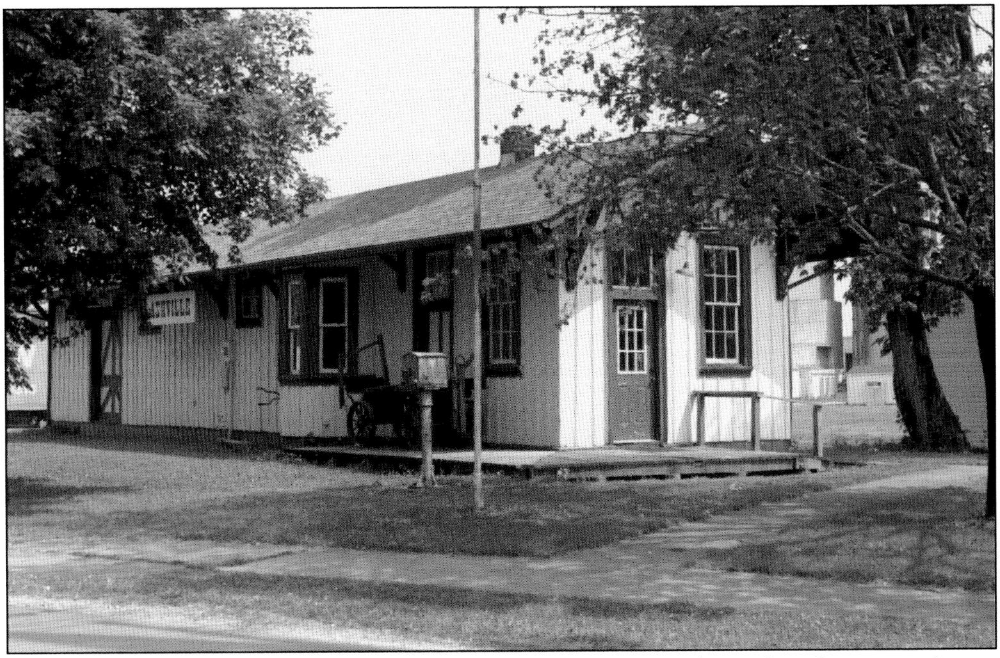


Ashville's former Scioto Valley Railroad (N&W) depot was relocated and renovated as a bicentennial project by the Ashville community. The depot now exhibits the early history of this Pickaway County town. The restored depot, photographed in 2002, and a caboose are within view of the current Norfolk Southern main. (Photograph by the author.)

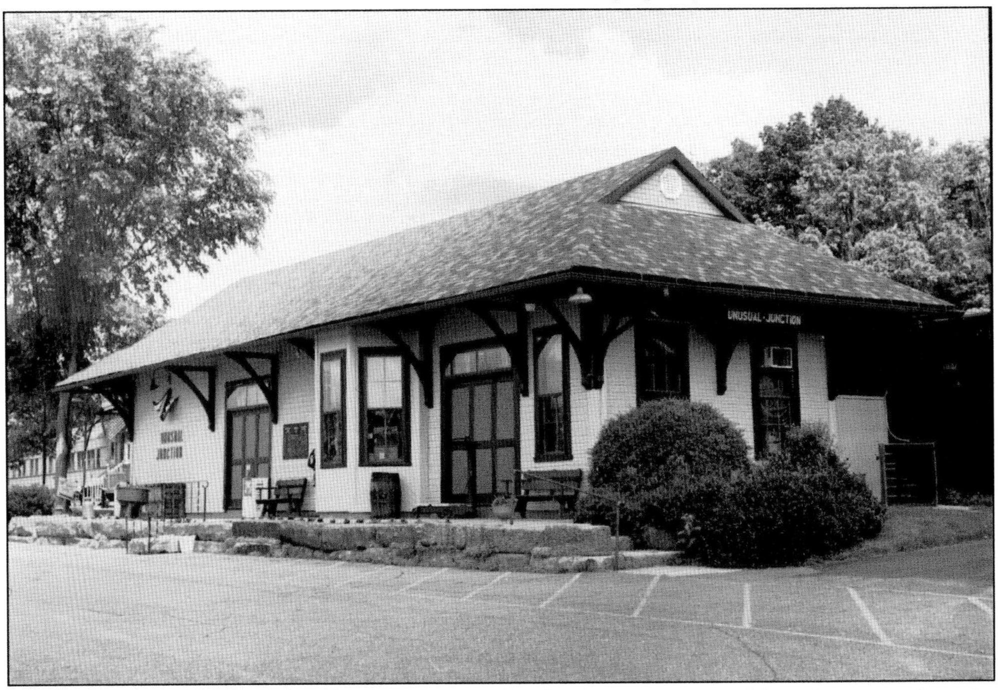


The B&O depot from Fredericktown now resides far from its original location, seen here in 2001. It is part of Unusual Junction, a specialty foods, candy, and cheese store, in West Lafayette. Other railroad artifacts are also on the property. (Photograph by the author.)

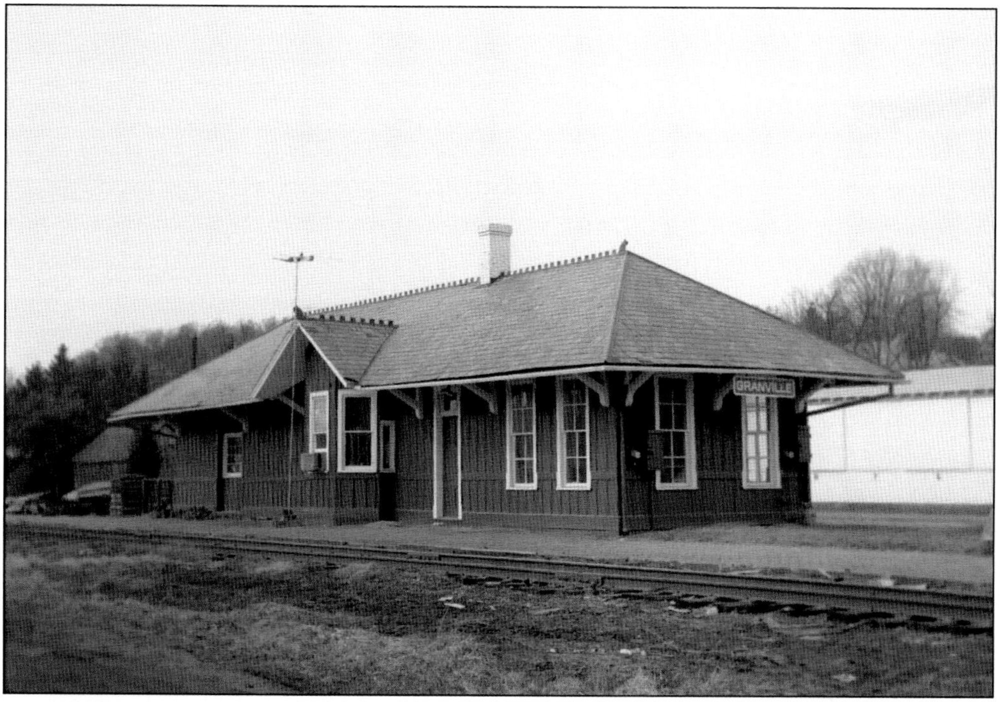


The T&OC depot in Granville has been well kept throughout its many years of nonrailroad use. The track was still there in this 1973 view. (Photograph by the author.)

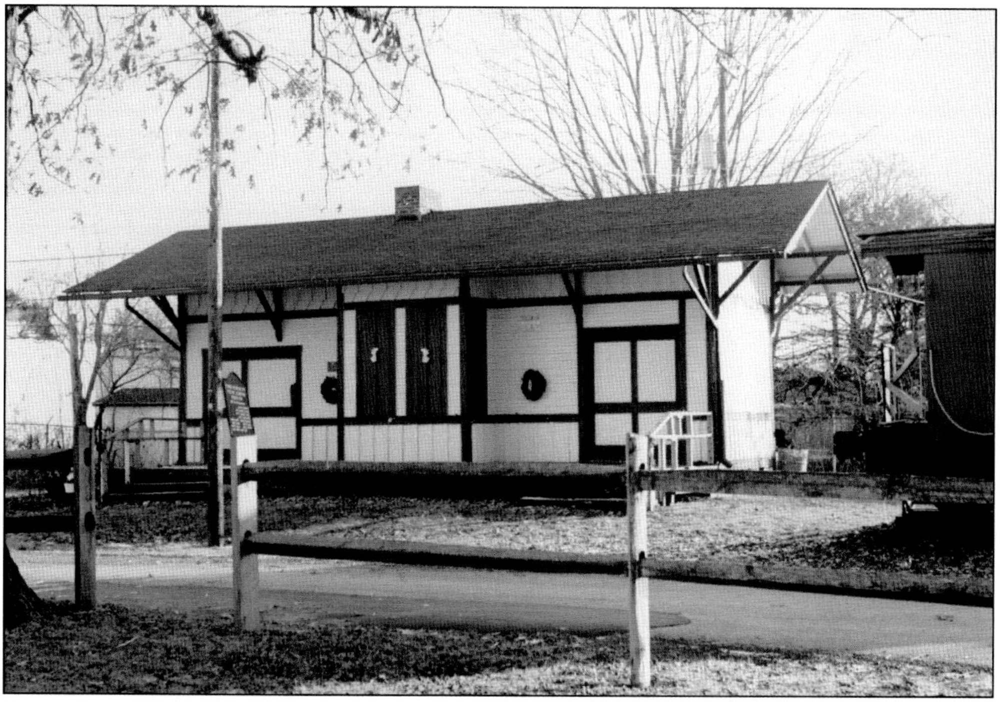

A number of depots have been relocated to fairgrounds to become parts of historic villages. The PRR depot in Hilliards, photographed here in 2000, now houses historical displays on the Franklin County Fairgrounds, not very far from its original site. (Photograph by the author.)

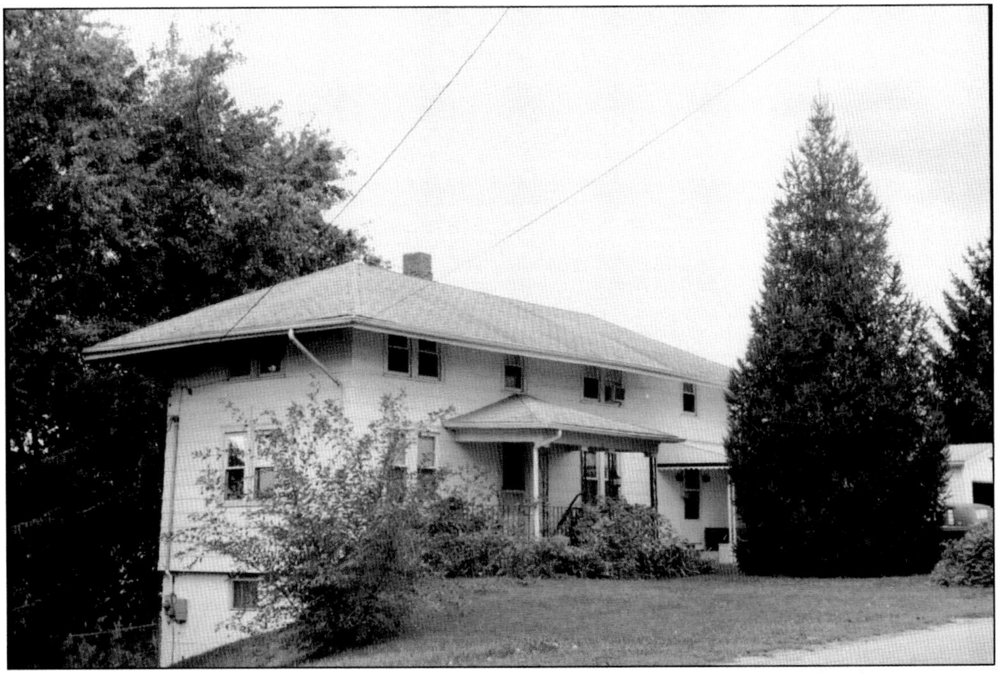

Some depots continue to exist but have been greatly modified, losing many of the characteristics that identify them as former railroad depots. This house, seen in 2000, is the former Hocking Valley Railway depot from Hookers. (Photograph by the author.)

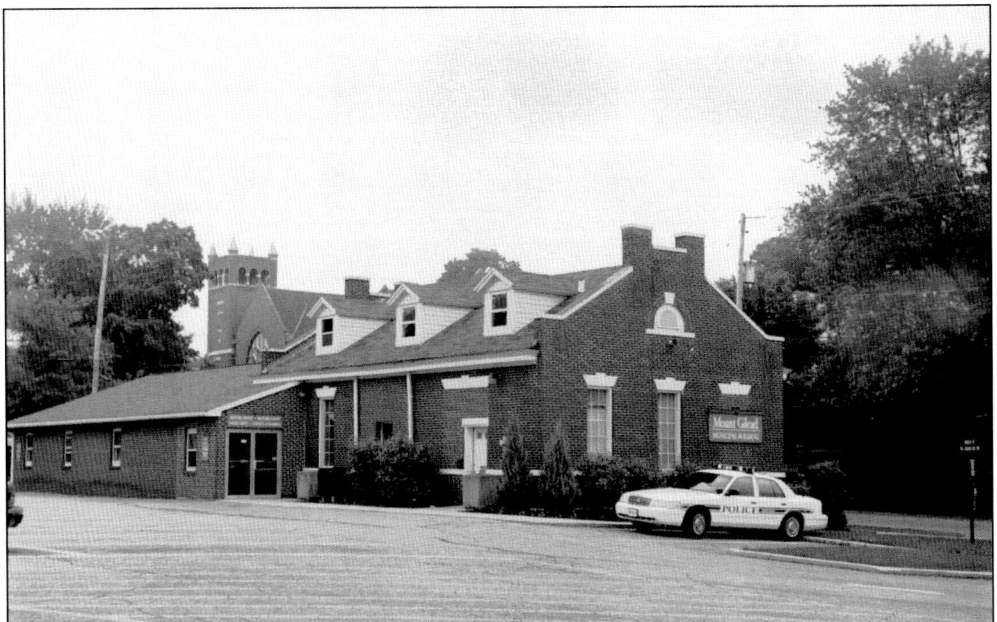


Seen here in 2001, the depot built by the Mount Gilead Short Line Railroad in Mount Gilead has been remodeled into city offices. (Photograph by the author.)

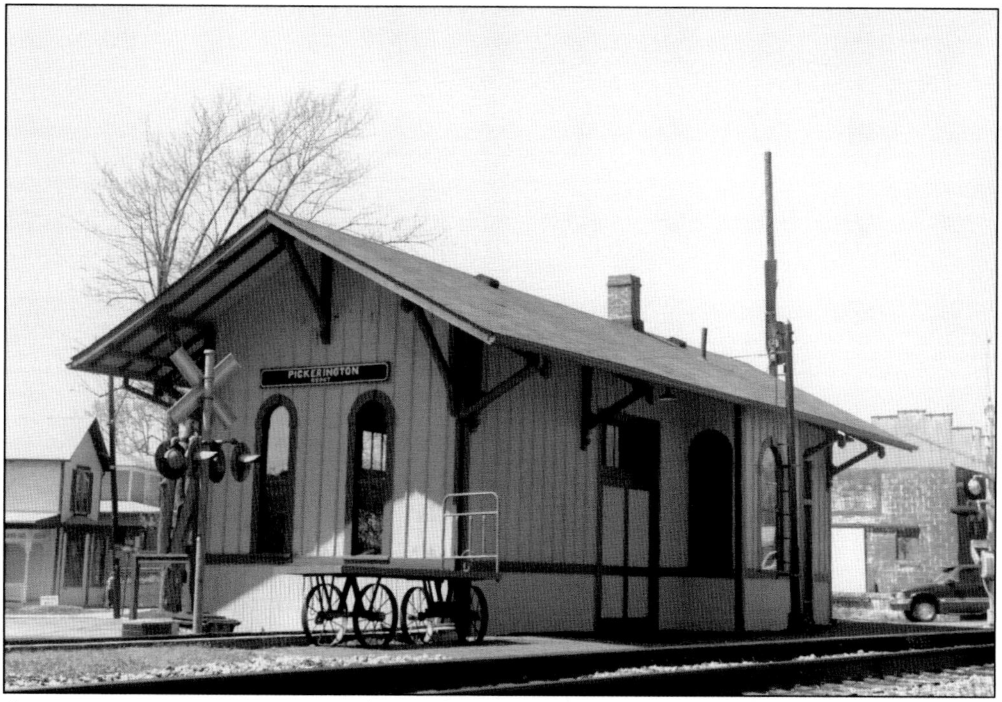


An insurance company now uses the nicely restored T&OC depot in Pickerington. The depot is on the original site. (Photograph by the author, 2001.)

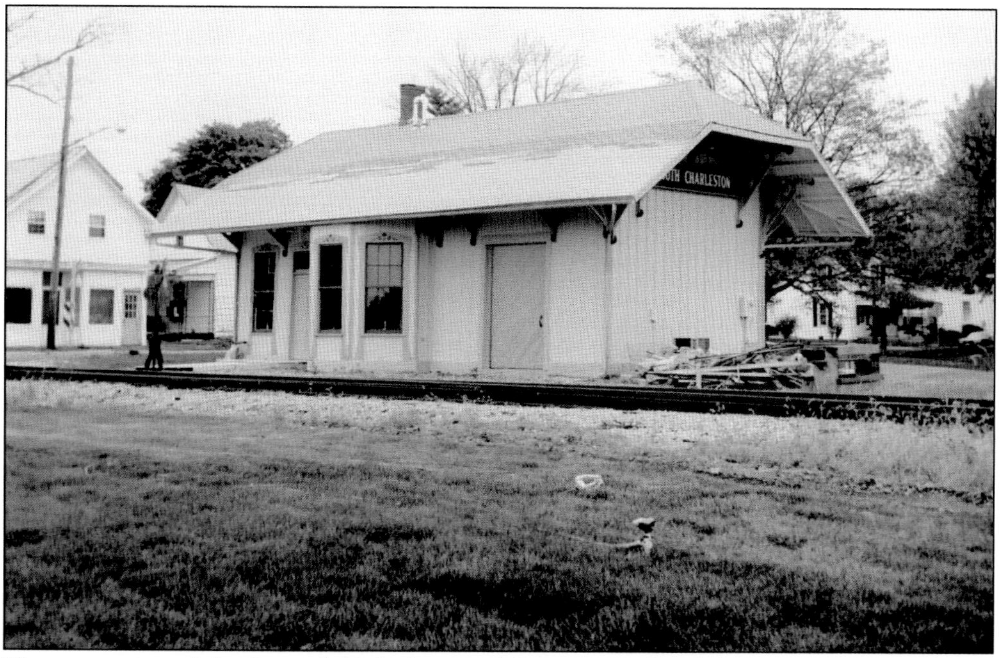

The restoration of the Springfield, Jackson and Pomeroy Railroad depot in South Charleston involved a rebuilding of the original roof. It is seen here in 2000. (Photograph by the author.)

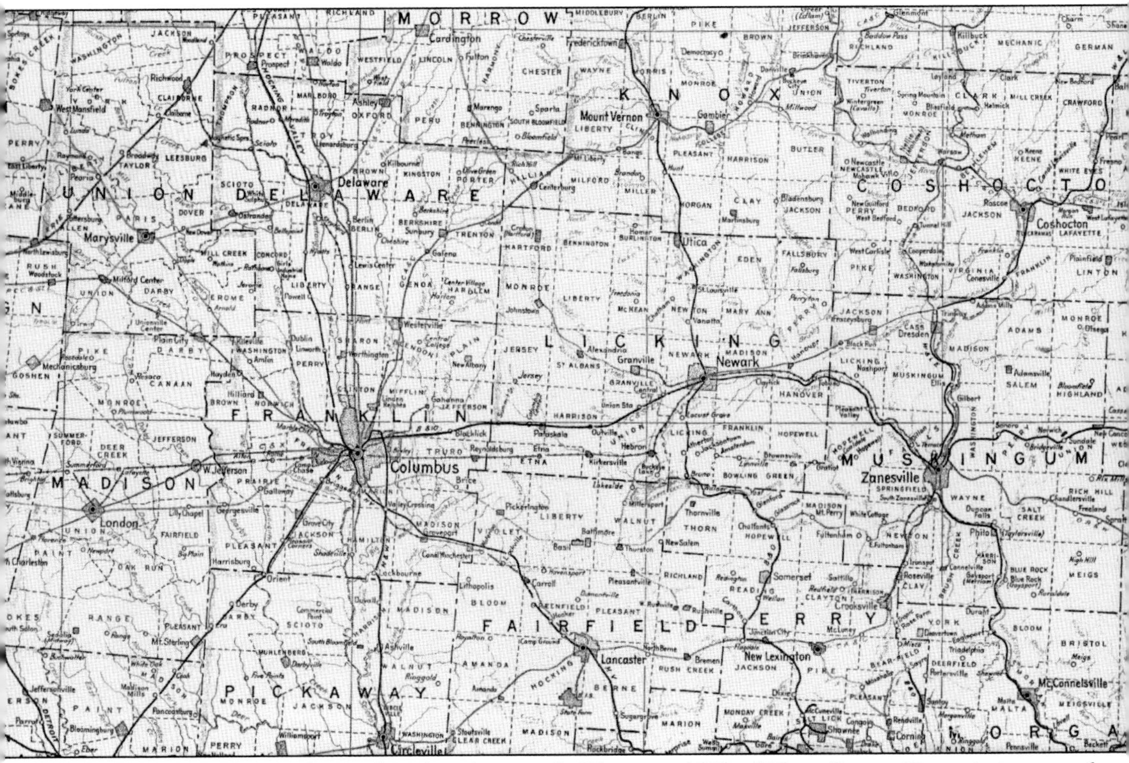


This map shows the railroads of central Ohio in 1918. (Ohio State Commissioners of Public Printing.)

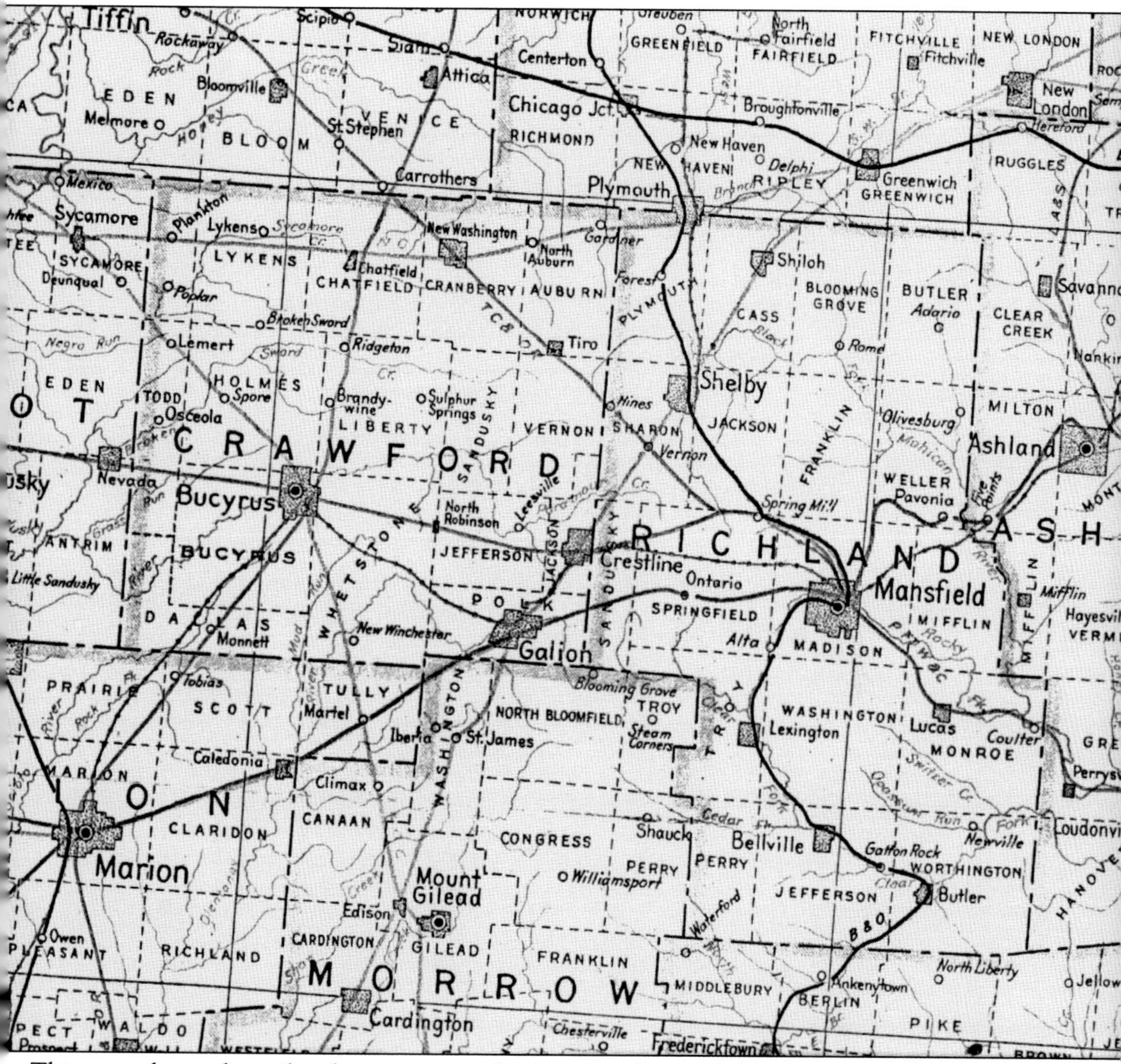

This map shows the railroad routes in northern parts of central Ohio in 1918. (Ohio State Commissioners of Public Printing.)